NORTHAMPTONSHIRE TOWNS AND VILLAGES

Achurch J5
Althorp House D7
Apethorpe J3
Ashby Saint Legers B7
Aynho B12

Barnwell J5
Barton Seagrave H6
Blatherwycke I3
Brackley B11
Brigstock H4
Brixworth E7
Broughton G6
Bugbrooke D9
Burton Latimer H6

Castle Ashby G8
Catesby B8
Charlton B12
Clipston E5
Courteenhall E9
Cranfords H5
Crick C6
Culworth B10

Deene H3
Desborough F5

Dingley E4

East Carlton G4
East Haddon D7
Easton Maudit G8
Easton Neston E10
Ecton G7
Evenley B12

Fawsley B9
Finedon H6
Fotheringhay J3

Gayton E9
Grafton Underwood H5
Great Addington I6
Great Billing F8
Great Brington D8
Great Oakley G4
Great Oxenden E4
Gretton H3
Guilsborough D6

Hardingstone F8
Hardwick G7
Hazelbech E6
Higham Ferrers I7

Horton G9

Islip I5

Kettering G5
King's Cliffe I2

Lamport E6
Long Buckby C7
Lowick I5

Marston Saint Lawrence B11
Moreton Pinckney B10

Northampton E8
(Abington, Dallington, Weston Favell)
Norton C8

Oundle J4

Paulerspury E10
Pipewell F4
Quinton F9

Rockingham G3

Rushton G4

Sibbertoft D5
Southwick I3
Stanford C5
Steane B11
Stoke Albany F4
Stoke Doyle [illegible]
Sulgrave [illegible]
Sywell [illegible]

Thenford [illegible]
Thrapston [illegible]
Titchmarsh [illegible]
Towcester [illegible]

Warkton H[illegible]
Weedon Lois [illegible]
Weekley G5
Weldon H4
Wellingborough [illegible]
Whittlebury E11
Wicken E11
Woodford I6
Woodnewton J3

Yardley Hastings G9

The Grid References are to the map overleaf

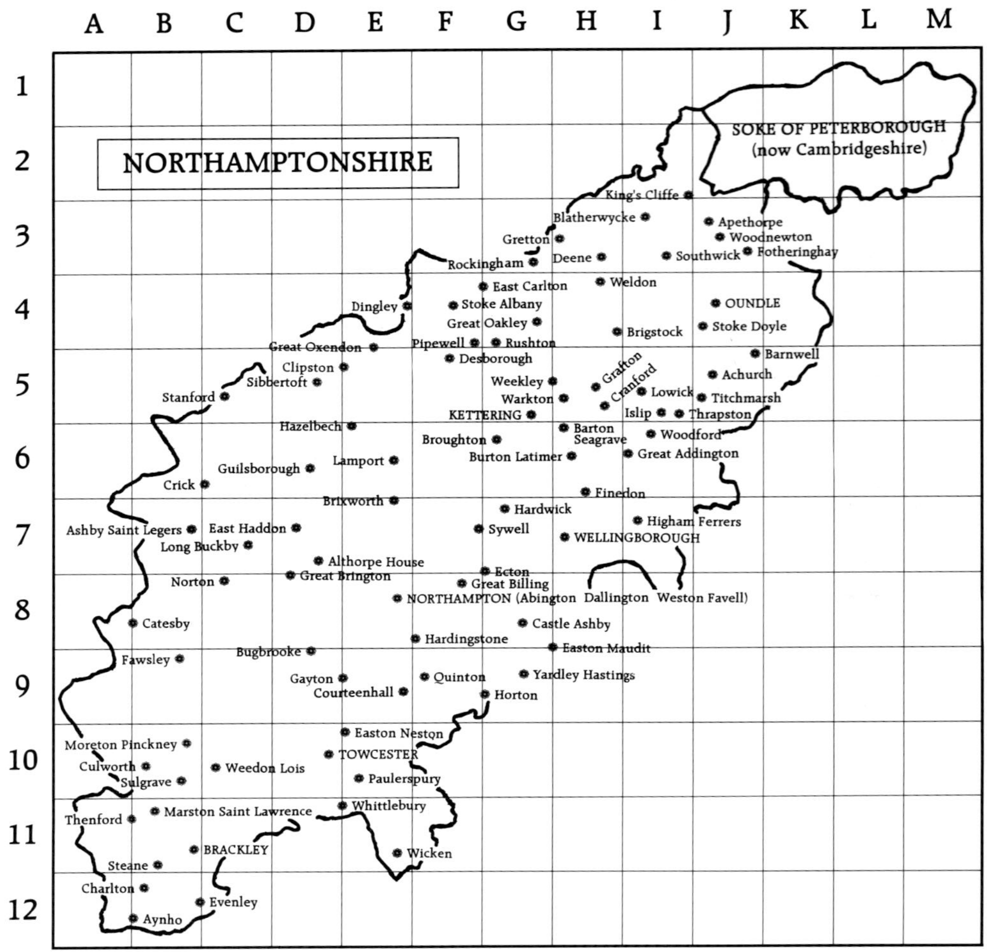
NORTHAMPTONSHIRE
SOKE OF PETERBOROUGH (now Cambridgeshire)
A B C D E F G H I J K L M
1 2 3 4 5 6 7 8 9 10 11 12
King's Cliffe
Blatherwycke
Apethorpe
Woodnewton
Fotheringhay
Gretton
Deene
Southwick
Rockingham
East Carlton
Weldon
OUNDLE
Dingley
Stoke Albany
Great Oakley
Brigstock
Stoke Doyle
Great Oxendon
Pipewell
Rushton
Desborough
Barnwell
Clipston
Sibbertoft
Weekley
Grafton
Cranford
Lowick
Achurch
Stanford
Warkton
Titchmarsh
KETTERING
Islip
Thrapston
Hazelbech
Barton Seagrave
Woodford
Broughton
Burton Latimer
Great Addington
Guilsborough
Lamport
Crick
Finedon
Brixworth
Hardwick
Higham Ferrers
Ashby Saint Legers
East Haddon
Sywell
WELLINGBOROUGH
Long Buckby
Althorpe House
Ecton
Norton
Great Brington
Great Billing
NORTHAMPTON (Abington Dallington Weston Favell)
Catesby
Castle Ashby
Hardingstone
Easton Maudit
Bugbrooke
Fawsley
Gayton
Quinton
Yardley Hastings
Courteenhall
Horton
Easton Neston
Moreton Pinckney
TOWCESTER
Culworth
Weedon Lois
Sulgrave
Paulerspury
Whittlebury
Thenford
Marston Saint Lawrence
BRACKLEY
Wicken
Steane
Charlton
Evenley
Aynho

WHO'S BURIED WHERE IN NORTHAMPTONSHIRE

RICHARD COWLEY

Illustrated by Rosslyn Nisbet-Smith

HOODED LION BOOKS
KETTERING
NORTHAMPTONSHIRE
2000

First published 2000

ISBN 0 9537037 1 1

Published by
Hooded Lion Books
147 Russell Street
KETTERING
Northamptonshire NN16 0EW

Printed and Bound in Great Britain by Woolnough Bookbinding,
Irthlingborough, Northamptonshire NN9 5SE

Set in Raleigh and Times New Roman

To
VALERIE

ACKNOWLEDGEMENTS

Many people have helped with this book:

I am especially grateful to His Grace the Duke of Buccleuch and Queensberry, KT for his kind permission to reproduce photographs of the monuments and graves in Warkton and Weekley; also to Mr Francis Sitwell, of Weston Hall, Towcester for permission to reproduce the photograph of the monument to Dame Edith Sitwell; and also to Mrs Pat Nimmo for permission to photograph the grave of Mr Derek Nimmo.

I wish to thank the following Incumbents who gave permission to reproduce photographs of monuments from churches within their care:

Reverend Doctor Judith Rose, Achurch and Stoke Doyle. Reverend Ann Slater, Ashby Saint Legers. Reverend Peter Gompertz, Aynho, Evenley and Steane. Reverend Peter Trenchard, Barnwell. and Titchmarsh. Reverend Martin Perris, Barton Seagrave. Reverend Bob Giles, Broughton. Reverend Michael Ryall, Castle Ashby and Yardley Hastings. Reverend S. Carter. Clipston Baptist Church. Reverend Richard Ormston, Courteenhall. Reverend Robert Barlow, Crick. Reverend Brian Eaves, Culworth and Sulgrave. Reverend Neil Clarke, Dingley. Reverend Miles Falla, Gretton, Rockingham and East Carlton. Reverend Michael Baker, Towcester and Easton Neston. Reverend Stephen Evans, Ecton. Reverend Michael Pettitt, Fawsley. Reverend Brian Rogers, Fotheringhay. Reverend Paul Broadbent, Gayton. Reverend Daniel Foot, Grafton Underwood. Reverend Gillian Jessop, Great Addington and Woodford. Reverend Kevin Ashby, Great Billing. Father Damian Walne, Great Billing Roman Catholic Church. Reverend David MacPherson, Great Brington and Norton. Reverend Michael Craggs, Great Oakley. Reverend Brian Stephens, Hardingstone. Reverend Roderick Lee, Hardwick. Reverend Daniel Faulks, Hazelbech. Reverend Grant Brockhouse, Higham Ferrers. Reverend Doctor Frank Coleman, Islip. Reverend Graeme Stockdale, Kettering Fuller Baptist Church. Reverend Philip Davies, King's Cliffe. Reverend Graeme Bell, Thrapston. Reverend Brian Lee, Lamport. Reverend Clive Evans, Long Buckby. Reverend Albert Turner, Marston Saint Lawrence and Thenford. Reverend David Bird, Northampton Saint Giles. Reverend Simon Godfrey, Northampton Saint Peter. Reverend Stephen Adams, Abington. Reverend Colin Wake, Weston Favell. Reverend Edward Houston, Paulerspury and Wicken. Reverend David Scholes, Quinton. Reverend George Burdon, Rushton. Reverend Kenneth Baker, Sibbertoft. Reverend Robert Stapleton, Stoke Albany. Reverend Michael Asquith, Weldon. Reverend Robert Loveless, Woodnewton.

And, because of their interregna, my thanks to the Churchwardens and Parochial Church Councils of Apethorpe, Brigstock, Easton Maudit, Great Oxenden, Lowick and Southwick.

I acknowledge permission from the Chief Executives of the Daventry District Council, East Northamptonshire District Council, Kettering Borough Council, Northampton Borough Council, South Northamptonshire District Council, and the Borough of Wellingborough Council, for permission to photograph graves in the cemeteries kept within their care.

My thanks also to Mrs Thompson and Mrs Longrigg of the Northampton Borough Council Cemeteries Department; and to Mrs Richardson of the Borough of Wellingborough Council Cemeteries Department, for their courteous and charming manner when I was researching through registers held in their keeping.

INTRODUCTION

Celebrity status has a strong attraction to others, and lots of people boast about knowing 'famous' people. This, I feel, applies equally in death as well as in life, and to visit the grave of a famous person can provide a *frisson* that is hard to match.

To stand just a few feet away from Napoleon's daughter-in-law; or a man who fought at Trafalgar or at Waterloo; or the man who invented the sandwich; gives a fascination that is almost inexplicable. And in Northamptonshire, we can experience just that, for the graves of Caroline Walewska, John Clarke, William Cartwright and John, Earl of Sandwich, are within this county.

You will meet many internationally famous people in this book, some who witnessed the great axis points of British and world history, and some whose contribution to life is far more humble. But all have one thing in common, all are buried within Northamptonshire, and we can visit their graves and remember their life stories, bad as well as good.

And surely, isn't this interest and remembrance the greatest luxury of all – in death as well as in life?

CATEGORIES OF ACHIEVEMENTS OR INTEREST

AMBASSADORS, STATESMEN

Birkenhead, Frederick, 1st Earl of *Charlton*
Cartwright, Frederick *Aynho*
Lyveden, Robert, 1st Baron *Brigstock*
Mildmay, Anthony *Apethorpe*
Montagu, Ralph, 1st Duke of *Warkton*
Morton, Thomas *Easton Maudit*
Sandwich, John, 4th Earl of *Barnwell*
Spencer family, The *Great Brington*
Westmorland, The Earls of *Apethorpe*
Wimbourne, Ivor, 1st Viscount *Ashby Saint Legers*
York, Richard, 1st Duke of *Fotheringhay*

AMERICAN HISTORY

Beatty, Ethel, Countess *Dingley*
Franklin, Thomas and Eleanor *Ecton*
Godkin, Edwin *Hazelbech*
Washington family, The *Great Brington, Islip, Sulgrave and Thrapston*

ARCHITECT

Gotch, John *Kettering*

ARTISTS

Bellamy, Frank *Kettering*
East, Alfred *Kettering*
Harrison, George *Kettering*
Smith, John *Northampton*
Westmorland, Priscilla, Countess of *Apethorpe*

AUTHORS, POETS, PLAYWRIGHTS

Archer, Ferdinando *Northampton*
Bagshaw, Edward *Moreton Pinckney*
Bell, Thomas *Barnwell*
Bostock, Susan *Northampton*
De Capell-Brooke, Arthur *Great Oakley*
Gotch, John *Weekley*
Harrison, George *Kettering*
Hervey, James *Weston Favell*
Jeffreys, George *Weldon*
Keene, Talbot *Brigstock*
Law, William *King's Cliffe*
Leapor, Mary *Brackley*
Mackworth-Dolben, Digby *Finedon*
Montagu-Douglas-Scott, Charles *Weekley*
Morton, Thomas *Easton Maudit*
Northampton, Marquis and Marchioness of *Castle Ashby*
Randolph, Thomas *Blatherwycke*
Sitwell, Edith *Weedon Lois*
Wastell, Simon *Northampton*
Westmorland, Mildmay, Earl of *Apethorpe*
Whiting, Nathaniel *Cranford*
Wild, Robert *Oundle*

BIBLIOPHILES, LEXICOGRAPHERS, SCHOLARS

Lye, Edward *Yardley Hastings*
Wodhull, Michael *Thenford*

CAUSE CELEBRE

The Germaines *Lowick*

CHURCHMEN, BISHOPS, THEOLOGIANS

Bagshaw, Edward *Moreton Pinckney*
Bolton, Robert *Broughton*
Browne, Robert *Northampton*
Butler, George *Gayton*
Cary-Elwes, Dudley *Great Billing*
Crewe, Nathaniel, 3rd Baron *Steane*
Dod, John *Fawsley*
Fuller, Andrew *Kettering*
Hervey, James *Weston Favell*
Law, William *King's Cliffe*

Montagu, John *Barnwell*
Morton, Thomas *Easton Maudit*
Paul, Samuel and George *Finedon*
Thomas, Francis *Great Billing*
Tresham, Thomas *Rushton*
Tresham, William *Bugbrooke*
Wild, Robert *Oundle*

DECORATED FOR BRAVERY

Copperwheat, Dennis *Weekley*
Lewin, Roger *Kettering*
Wake, Sir Hereward *Courteenhall*

EPONYMOUS

Cardigan, James, 7th Earl of *Deene*
Sandwich, John, 4th Earl of *Barnwell*

EXPLORER

Abbott, George *Northampton*

FARMERS

Pell, Albert *Hazelbech*
Spencer, Robert, 1st Baron *Great Brington*

FOUNDERS OF SOCIETIES

De Capell-Brooke, Arthur *Great Oakley* (Royal Geographical Society)
Fuller, Andrew *Kettering* (Baptist Missionary Society)
Graves, John *Lamport* (National Union of Teachers)
Lilford, Lord *Achurch* (British Ornithologists Union, etc)
Wake, Joan *Courteenhall* (Northamptonshire Record Society, etc)
Westmorland, John 11th Earl of *Apethorpe* (Royal Academy of Music)

HISTORIANS

Bell, Thomas *Barnwell*
Bridges, John *Barton Seagrave*
Cole, John *Woodford*
Isham, Gyles *Lamport*
Poulton, Ferdinando *Desborough*
Harrison, George *Kettering*
Wake, Joan *Courteenhall*

INDUSTRIALISTS

Fermor, Richard *Easton Neston*
Penrhyn, George, 1st Baron *Wicken*
Spencer, Robert, 1st Baron *Great Brington*

JUDGES, BARRISTERS, LEGAL

Alexander, John *Wellingborough*
Birkenhead, Frederick, 1st Earl of *Charlton*
Blencowe, John *Marston Saint Lawrence*
Brudenell, Robert *Deene*
Catesby, John *Northampton*
Denman, Thomas, 1st Baron *Stoke Albany*
Dilhorne, Reginald, 1st Viscount *Deene*
Dolben, Gilbert *Finedon*
Knyvet, John *Southwick*
Levinz, Cresswell *Evenley*
Montagu, Edward and William *Weekley*
Palmer, Geoffrey *East Carlton*
Poulton, Ferdinando *Desborough*
Powys, Thomas *Achurch*
Rainsford, Richard *Northampton*
Simon of Pattishall *Pipewell*
Tresham, William *Sywell*
Ward, Edward *Stoke Doyle*
Westmorland, Earls of *Apethorpe*
Yelverton, Christopher and Henry *Easton Maudit*

MILITARY, NAVAL, AIRIAL

Buckingham, Humphrey, 1st Duke of *Northampton*
Cardigan, James, 7th Earl of *Deene*
Cartwright, Fairfax and William *Aynho*
Catesby, William *Ashby Saint Legers*
Clarke, John *Weldon*
Copperwheat, Dennis *Weekley*
Culme-Seymours, The *Rockingham*

Gowran, Richard, 1st Baron *Grafton Underwood*
Lewin, Roger *Kettering*
Montagu, William *Barnwell*
Pomfret, Thomas, 4th Earl of *Easton Neston*
Spencer, Frederick, 4th Earl *Great Brington*
Sunderland, Henry, 1st Earl of *Great Brington*
Vere, Henry *Great Addington*
Wake, Sir Hereward *Courteenhall*
Westmorland, Earls of *Apethorpe*
York, Dukes of *Fotheringhay*

MURDER VICTIMS

Gardner, Eliza *Long Buckby*
Johnson, Louisa *Burton Latimer*
Kemp, James *Northampton*
Linnell, George *Whittlebury*
Pritchard, Annie *East Haddon*
Tresham, William *Sywell*
Unknown man *Hardingstone*

MURDERERS

Byrne, Claydon, Eayrs, MacRae, Parker, Rowledge, Sabey, *Northampton*

MUSICIANS

Jarman, Thomas *Clipston*
Jeffreys, George *Weldon*
Westmorland, John, 11th Earl of *Apethorpe*

NATURALISTS

Berkeley, Miles *Sibbertoft*
Lilford, Thomas, 4th Baron *Achurch*
Morton, John *Great Oxenden*

ORDER OF SAINT JOHN

Cave, Ambrose *Stanford*
Tresham, Thomas *Rushton*

PHILANTHROPISTS, BENEFACTORS

Chisholm, Caroline *Northampton*
Pembroke, Mary, Countess of *Fotheringhay*
Pomfret, Henrietta, Countess of *Easton Neston*
Smith, George *Crick*
Wicksteed, Charles *Kettering*

POLICE

Alexander, John *Wellingborough*
Ball, Joseph *Northampton*
Cartwright, Fairfax and William *Aynho*
Keenan, Henry *Northampton*
Kellie-MacCallum, James *Quinton*
Kemp, James *Northampton*
Knight, Luke *Wellingborough*
Lees, Thomas *Guilsborough*
Linnell, George *Whittlebury*
MacLeod, Hector *Wellingborough*

POLITICIANS

Bagshaw, Edward *Moreton Pinckney*
Birkenhead, Frederick, 1st Earl of *Charlton*
Blencowe, John *Marston Saint Lawrence*
Brudenell, Robert *Deene*
Cartwright family, The *Aynho*
Catesby, William *Ashby Saint Legers*
Cave, Ambrose *Stanford*
Crewe, Barons *Steane*
Dilhorne, Reginald, 1st Viscount *Deene*
Dolben family, The *Finedon*
Fermor, William *Easton Neston*
Gowran, Richard, 1st Baron *Grafton Underwood*
Knightley family, The *Fawsley and Norton*
Leominster, William, 1st Baron *Easton Neston*
Lyveden, Robert, 1st Baron *Brigstock*
Montagu family, The *Barnwell, Warkton and Weekley*

Northampton, Spencer, 2nd Marquis of *Castle Ashby*
Palmer, Geoffrey *East Carlton*
Penrhyn, George, Lord *Wicken*
Powys, Thomas *Achurch*
Rainsford, Richard *Northampton*
Sandwich, Earls of *Barnwell*
Spencer, Earls *Great Brington*
Sunderland, Earls of *Great Brington*
Tresham, Thomas and William *Rushton and Sywell*
Westmorland, Earls of *Apethorpe*
Wimbourne, Ivor, 1st Viscount *Ashby Saint Legers*
Yelverton, Christopher and Henry *Easton Maudit*

PRACTICAL JOKER

Montagu, John, 2nd Duke of *Warkton*

RELATIVES OF, FRIENDS OF, THE FAMOUS/INFAMOUS/ ROYALTY ETC

Barnard, Elizabeth, Lady *Northampton*
Beatty, Ethel, Countess *Dingley*
Buckingham, Humphrey, 1st Duke of *Northampton*
Carey, Edmund *Paulerspury*
Catesby, John *Northampton*
Cave, Ambrose *Stanford*
Chicheley, Thomas and Agnes *Higham Ferrers*
Creed family, The *Titchmarsh*
Crewe, The Barons *Steane*
Denman, Thomas, 1st Baron *Stoke Albany*
Dod, John *Fawsley*
Dolben family, The *Finedon*
Dryden, Erasmus and Mary *Titchmarsh*
Elwes, Gervase *Great Billing*
Fermor, Richard *Easton Neston*
Franklin, Thomas and Eleanor *Ecton*
Hervey, James *Weston Favell*
Knightley family, The *Fawsley and Norton*
Lees, Thomas *Guilsborough*
Margaret of Catesby *Catesby*
Mildmay, Anthony *Apethorpe*
Montagu family, The *Barnwell, Warkton and Weekley*
Northampton, Spencer, 2nd Marquis of *Castle Ashby*
Parr, William, 1st Baron *Horton*
Pomfret, Henrietta, Countess of *Easton Neston*
Randolphe, Thomas *Blatherwycke*
Richmond, Anne, Duchess of *Deene*
Simon of Pattishall *Pipewell*
Smith, George *Crick*
Smith, John *Northampton*
Smith, (Vernon) Robert *Brigstock*
Spencer family, The *Great Brington*
Sunderland, Dorothy, Countess of *Great Brington*
Thomond, Henry, 7th Earl of *Great Billing*
Tresham, Thomas *Rushton*
Vere, Henry *Great Addington*
Walewska, Caroline, Countess *Barnwell*
Walewska, Louisa *Barnwell*
Washington family, The *Great Brington, Islip, Sulgrave and Thrapston*
Westmorland, Earls of *Apethorpe*
Wiltshire, Edward, 2nd Earl of *Lowick*
Wimbourne, Ivor, 1st Viscount *Ashby Saint Legers*
Yelverton, Christopher *Easton Maudit*

ROYALTY

Boudicca, Queen of the Iceni *Whittlebury*
Lancaster, Thomas, Earl of *Higham Ferrers*
Rutland, Edmund, 1st Earl of *Fotheringhay*
Wales, Diana, Princess of *Althorp*
York, Dukes and Duchesses of *Fotheringhay*

SAINTS

Boniface *Brixworth*
Margaret *Catesby*

SCIENTISTS, GEOLOGISTS, ASTRONOMERS

Cottingham, Edwin *Thrapston*
Northampton, Spencer, 2nd Marquis of *Castle Ashby*
Smith, William *Northampton*

SHOWMEN, ENTERTAINERS, ACTORS

Coco the Clown *Woodnewton*
Elwes, Gervase *Great Billing*
Fossett, Robert *Northampton*
Nimmo, Derek *Easton Maudit*
Thurston, Henry and Henry *Thrapston and Wellingborough*

SLAVES

Bacchus, Charles *Culworth*
Kitty, *Woodford*
Williams, Anthony *Blatherwycke*

SPIES, CODE BREAKERS

Blencowe, William *Marston Saint Lawrence*
Westmorland, Mildmay, Earl of *Apethorpe*

SPORTSMEN

Henfrey, Arthur *Finedon*
Penrhyn, George, 2nd Baron *Wicken*
Wimbourne, Ivor, 1st Viscount *Ashby Saint Legers*

TEACHERS, HEADMASTERS

Butler, George *Gayton*
Graves, John *Lamport*
Sanderson, Frederick *Oundle*
Shillibeer, John *Stoke Doyle*

UNKNOWNS

Hardingstone
Higham Ferrers

WITNESSES TO HISTORY

Abbott, George *Northampton*
Buckingham, Humphrey, 1st Duke of *Northampton*
Cardigan, James, 7th Earl of *Deene*
Cartwright, William *Aynho*
Clarke, John *Weldon*
Crewe, John, 1st Baron *Steane*
Denman, Thomas, 1st Baron *Stoke Albany*
Dolben, Gilbert *Finedon*
Dray, James *Kettering*
Fossbrook, Maude *Cranford Saint Andrew*
Knightley family, The *Fawsley and Norton*
Levinz, Cresswell *Evenley*
Montagu family, The *Warkton and Weekley*
Nicholls, Francis *Hardwick*
Palmer, Geoffrey *East Carlton*
Parr, William, 1st Baron *Horton*
Poulton, Ferdinando *Desborough*
Powys, Thomas *Achurch*
Rainsford, Richard *Northampton*
Rockingham, Lewis, 1st Baron *Rockingham*
Rutland, Edmund, 1st Earl of *Fotheringhay*
Simon of Pattishall *Pipewell*
Spencer, Frederick, 4th Earl *Great Brington*
Spencer, George, 2nd Earl *Great Brington*
Throckmorton, Arthur *Paulerspury*
Tresham, Thomas and William *Rushton and Sywell*
Vere, Henry *Great Addington*
Ward, Edward *Stoke Doyle*
Westmorland, Francis, 12th Earl of *Apethorpe*
Yelverton, Christopher *Easton Maudit*
York, Dukes of *Fotheringhay*

INDEX OF HISTORIC FIGURES ALSO MENTIONED

Bacon, Francis *Easton Maudit*
Boycott, Charles *Guilsborough*
Brahms, Johannes *Great Billing*
Brian Baru *Great Billing*
Bridges, Robert Poet Laureate *Finedon*
Burghley, Lord *Northampton*
Campion, Saint Edmund *Rushton*
Carey, William *Kettering, Paulerspury*
Catesby, William, 'The Cat' *Northampton*
Chamberlain, Joseph *Ashby Saint Legers*
Charles I *Easton Neston, Weekley, Weldon*
Charles II *Deene, Easton Neston, Steane, Weekley*
Charnock, Robert *Stoke Doyle*
Chicheley, Henry, Archbishop of Canterbury *Higham Ferrers*
Churchill, Winston *Ashby Saint Legers*
Clarence, Duke of *Fotheringhay*
Cromwell, Oliver *Fawsley*
Cromwell, Richard *Steane*
'Dan Dare' *Kettering*
Darwin, Charles *Sibbertoft*
Dickens, Charles *Stoke Albany*
'Doctor Who' *Kettering*
Dolben, John, Archbishop of York *Finedon*
Dryden, John *Titchmarsh*
Edmund, Saint *Catesby*
Edward III *Fotheringhay, Southwick*
Edward IV *Fotheringhay, Northampton*
Edward VI *Norton, Weekley*
Elgar, Sir Edward *Great Billing*
Elizabeth I *Apethorpe, Hardwick, Stanford*
Field, Marshall *Dingley*
Fox, Charles James *Great Brington*
Franklin, Benjamin *Ecton*
French, Lord *Ashby Saint Legers, Dingley*
Garrick, David *Brackley*
'Garth' *Kettering*
George V *Courteenhall*
Gibbon, Edward *King's Cliffe*
Granger, Percy *Great Billing*
Grey, Lady Jane *Weekley*
Hampton, John *Fawsley*
Henry IV of France *Apethorpe*
Henry VI *Cranford*
Henry V *Sywell*
Henry VII *Ashby Saint Legers, Great Addington, Lowick, Northampton*
Henry VIII *Deene, Fotheringhay, Rushton*
Herrick, Robert *Apethorpe*
Hesilrigge, Arthur *Fawsley*
James I *Apethorpe, Steane, Weekley*
James II *Finedon, Steane, Warkton*
Jeffreys, Judge *Easton Neston, Evenley, Weekley*
Joan of Arc *Cranford, Northampton*
John, King *Pipewell*
Johnson, Samuel *Yardley Hastings*
Jonson, Ben *Blatherwycke*
Kidd, Captain, pirate *Stoke Doyle*
Kneller, Sir Godfrey *Northampton*
Leicester, Earl of *Norton*
Lely, Sir Peter *Northampton*
Louis XIV *Deene, Warkton*
Lovell, Lord *Ashby Saint Legers*
Marlborough, Duke of *Warkton*
Mary I *Rushton*
Monck, George, General *Oundle*
Napoleon Bonaparte *Aynho, Barnwell*
Nelson, Horatio *Great Brington, Weldon*
North, Lord *Barnwell*
Oates, Titus *Evenley, Weekley*
Parker, 'Nosey' *Bugbrooke*
Parr, Queen Catherine *Horton*
Pepys, Samuel *Barnwell, Steane, Titchmarsh*
Perceval, Spencer *Castle Ashby*
Pitt, William the Younger *Apethorpe, Barnwell*
Princes in the Tower, The *Northampton*
Pym, John *Fawsley*
Raglan, Lord *Apethorpe*
Raleigh, Sir Walter *Paulerspury*
Ratcliffe, Sir Richard *Ashby Saint Legers*

Richard II *Fotheringhay*
Richard III *Ashby Saint Legers, Fotheringhay*
Roberts, Lord, VC *Courteenhall, Dingley*
Sancroft, William, Archbishop of Canterbury *Achurch*
Seymour, Queen Jane *Norton*
Shakespeare, William *Easton Maudit, Great Brington, Northampton*
Shaftesbury, Lord *Crick*
Sheldon, Gilbert, Archbishop of Canterbury *Finedon*
Sitwell brothers *Weedon Lois*
Smith, Sydney *Brigstock*
Strauss, Johann *Apethorpe*
Tait, Archibold, Archbishop of Canterbury *Courteenhall*
Van Dyck, Sir Anthony *Great Brington*
Vaughan-Williams, Ralph *Great Billing*
Victoria, Queen *Great Brington, Guilsborough, Northampton, Rockingham*
Walewski, Count *Barnwell*
Walton, Sir William *Weedon Lois*
Washington, George *Great Brington, Islip, Sulgrave, Thrapston*
Wellington, Duke of *Apethorpe*
Wesley, John and Charles *King's Cliffe, Northampton*
White, Thomas, Bishop of Peterborough *Achurch*
Wilberforce, William *Finedon, Castle Ashby*
Wilkes, John *Barnwell*
William III (of Orange) *Lowick*
Wolsey, Cardinal *Easton Neston, Rushton, Weekley*
Wood, Sir Henry *Great Billing*

INDEX OF HISTORIC EVENTS

Adams, Doctor John Bodkin, Trial of *Deene*
Agincourt, Battle of *Fotheringhay*
Aix-la-Chapelle, Treaty of *Barnwell*
American Civil War, The *Hazelbech*
Armada, The *Hardwick*
Ashantee War, The *Quinton*
Baltic campaign, The *Rockingham*
Blenheim, Battle of *Titchmarsh*
'Bloody Assizes', The *Easton Neston, Evenley, Weekley*
Boer War, The *Courteenhall, Dingley*
Bosworth, Battle of *Ashby Saint Legers, Fotheringhay, Great Addington*
Burma War, The *Rockingham*
Cadiz, storming of *Paulerspury*
Caroline, Queen, Divorce of *Stoke Albany*
Casement, Sir Roger, Trial of *Charlton*
'Charge of the Light Brigade' *Apethorpe, Deene, Kettering*
China War, The Second *Rockingham*
Civil War, Great English, The *Rockingham*
Conference of Vienna 1855 *Apethorpe*
Congress of Vienna 1815 *Apethorpe*
Coronation of James I *Apethorpe*
Coronation of Charles I *Apethorpe*
Coronation of Charles II *Easton Neston, Fawsley*
County Police Act 1839 and 1856 *Aynho*
'Covenant, The' *Apethorpe*
Crimean War *Apethorpe, Aynho, Brigstock, Hazelbech, Rockingham*
'Declaration of Indulgence' *Achurch*
Dissolution of the Monasteries *Apethorpe*
Easter Rising, Ireland 1916 *Ashby Saint Legers*
'Eleven Years Tyranny' *Apethorpe, Fawsley*
Essex and Southampton Case, The Earls of *Easton Maudit*
'Field of the Cloth of Gold', The *Horton*
Five Knights case *Northampton*
'Glorious Revolution' *Finedon*
Great War, The *Aynho, Courteenhall, Dingley, Rockingham*
Gunpowder Plot, The *Desborough,*

Rushton
Hanover, Sicilly and Egypt campaigns *Apethorpe*
'Holy War' 1848 *Aynho*
Howard, Queen Catherine, Trial of *Weekley*
India, British Army in *Barnwell*
Indian Mutiny *Brigstock*
Jutland, Battle of *Rockingham*
London, Great Fire of *Northampton*
Magna Carta, signing of *Pipewell*
Malplaquet, Battle of *Warkton*
Malta, Seige of *Kettering, Weekley*
'Marprelate Tracts', The *Norton*
Mary, Queen of Scots, execution of *Norton*
Monmouth Rebellion, The *Evenley*
Monasteries, Suppression of *Fawsley*
Mutinies, Naval *Great Brington*
National Strike 1926 *Ashby St Legers*
Newbury, Battle of *Great Brington*
Navarino, Battle of *Great Brington*
'Night of the Long Knives' *Deene*
Northampton, Battle of *Northampton*
Northampton, Great Fire of *Northampton*
Oudenarde, Battle of *Warkton*
Peninsular War *Apethorpe, Aynho, Easton Neston*
Parliaments, The 'Addled' *Easton Maudit* 'Long' *Barnwell, East Carlton, Fawsley, Moreton Pinckney, Steane, Weekley* 'Merciless' *Fotheringhay* 'Pensioners' *Easton Neston,* 'Oxford' *Moreton Pinckney* 'Short' *Fawsley, Steane, Weekley*
'Popish Plot', The *Evenley*
'Pride's Purge' *Fawsley, Steane*
Reform Act, 1832 *Stoke Albany*
Restoration of the Monarchy *Apethorpe, Fawsley, Oundle, Steane*
Rosetta, Seige of *Apethorpe*
Rouse Murder case *Hardingstone, Quinton*
Russian Revolution, The *Woodnewton*
'Rye House Plot' The *Evenley*
Sacheverell case, The *Finedon*
Saint Albans, Battle of *Fotheringhay*
Scott's Antarctic Expedition *Northampton*
Second World War *Kettering, Warkton*
Seven Bishops case, The *Achurch, Evenley*
Somme, First Day of battle of *Courteenhall*
'Sports, The Book of' *Easton Maudit*
Strafford Case, The Earl of *East Carlton*
Test Acts, The *Great Brington*
Trafalgar, Battle of *Weldon*
Vigo Bay, Battle of *Grafton Underwood*
Wakefield, Battle of *Fotheringhay*
Wars of the Roses *Fotheringhay*
Wars of the Spanish succession *Grafton Underwood, Warkton*
Waterloo, Battle of *Aynho*
Wellingborough Election Riot, 1852 *Wellingborough*
'Wilkes Affair, The *Barnwell*

ACHURCH

IN THE CHURCH OF SAINT JOHN THE BAPTIST

Sir Thomas Powys (1649-1719)

Attorney General
Member of Parliament
Judge of the Queen's Bench
Prosecutor of the Seven Bishops

Born in Shropshire, Thomas Powys was called to the bar by Lincoln's Inn in 1673. By 1686 he was the Solicitor General, and in 1687 the Attorney General. The Attorney General is the principal law officer of the crown, and it is the Attorney General who institutes law proceedings for the crown. Thus it was in 1688, that Sir Thomas Powys conducted the prosecution of the Seven Bishops.

The marble symphony of the tomb of Sir Thomas Powys.

In 1687, the Catholic James II had ordered that all clergy read to their congregations the 'Declaration of Indulgence' which amongst other things demanded that Catholics be allowed to worship in public. In those days religious affairs were far more widely debated and were far more relevant to the common man than they appear to be nowadays, and the 'Declaration of Indulgence' provoked a great storm.

Seven bishops (led by William Sancroft, the Archbishop of Canterbury, and including Thomas White, the Bishop of Peterborough) petitioned the king asking that they not be forced to make their diocesan clergy read the 'Declaration'. As a result, the seven were arrested for seditious libel and clapped into The Tower.

It was Powys' job to prosecute, although he apparently disapproved of the prosecution. Nevertheless he conducted the trial with extreme fairness, bearing in mind that he lived at Lilford, in the Peterborough diocese, and no doubt was personally acquainted with Thomas White, one of the accused. The bishops were acquitted.

Thomas Powys became the Member of Parliament for Ludlow between 1701 and 1713, when he was made a Judge of the Queen's Bench. The following year, Queen Anne died, and George I came to the throne. Powys retired (or more probably was sacked by the new king). He died in April 1719.

Thomas, 4th Baron Lilford (1833-1896)

Ornithologist

The world of discovery owes much to 'amateurs' such as Lord Lilford, who because of their social backgrounds, have the time and the money to pursue their own particular interests, and thus give to the world, knowledge which otherwise would have taken the professionals years to uncover. As such, because of his own passionate interest, Lord Lilford is rightly looked upon as the father of British ornithology.

Thomas Littleton Powys went to Harrow and then to Christ Church College, Oxford, but left without taking a degree. Passionately interested in natural history, Powys kept a small menagerie whilst at Harrow, and a larger one at Oxford, which is perhaps why he never graduated, being more interested in his birds and animals than studying.

Being from the landed aristocracy, Powys could afford to travel to indulge his interest of studying birds and animals. In 1853 he went to the Scilly Isles, Wales and Ireland, and between 1856 and 1858, he was cruising the Mediterranean studying the fauna he found. He took time off however, to get married, which he did in 1859 to Emma Brandling.

Between 1864 and 1882 he made numerous trips to Spain and the Mediterranean collecting ornithological data. On one of these trips he discovered a previously unknown and rare species of gull, *Larus audouni*. At his home at Lilford Hall, he constructed a wonderful set of aviaries, and stocked them with a large collection of birds.

At the age of 19 in 1852 he had been made a Fellow of the Zoological Society, made a Fellow of the Linnaen Society in 1862, and in 1858, was one of the founders of the British Ornithologists Union, and its President from 1867. He also founded the Northamptonshire Natural History Society.

His eldest son died in 1882, and two years later, his wife died. He married for the second time in 1885, Clementina Hamilton.

The culmination of all his collecting came in 1885, when he started to publish his large and seminal work on British ornithology *Coloured figures of the Birds of the British Isles*. This work took 12 years to complete, and had to be finished by Osbert Salvin after Lord Lilford, as he was by then, died in 1896. Powys also wrote his *Notes of the Birds of Northamptonshire and Neighbourhood* in two volumes in 1895.

Lord Lilford lies under the eastern window of Achurch church. His grave is under the right hand cross, with Lady Lilford to the left.

ALTHORP HOUSE

ON THE ISLAND IN THE OVAL LAKE

Diana, Princess of Wales (1961-1997)

APETHORPE

IN THE PARISH CHURCH OF SAINT LEONARD

Sir Anthony Mildmay (?-1617)

Ambassador to France
Personal friend of Elizabeth I and James I

Anthony Mildmay inherited the manor and estate of Apethorpe when his father, Sir Walter Mildmay, died in 1589. Sir Walter had received Apethorpe as a reward for being one of the Commissioners for the Dissolution of the Monasteries, and had settled at Apethorpe, living the life of a country squire.

The magnificent tomb of Sir Anthony and Lady Mildmay. The rectangular plaque beneath the oval ones, is to the 11th Earl of Westmorland.

Being sent to Peterhouse College, Cambridge (which his father had founded), Anthony Mildmay was present at the college when Elizabeth I visited Cambridge in 1564, and he gave the queen the oration of welcome. Good Queen Bess must have remembered him, because in 1596 she sent him as her ambassador to France, along with the customary knighthood.

Unfortunately for Sir Anthony, Henry IV, normally the most charismatic of French kings, did not get on at all well with him, and continually complained of Mildmay's cold manner. On one famous occasion, the king actually threatened to hit Mildmay before ordering him out of the room. Not surprisingly, Mildmay returned home in 1597, and despite continuous requests by the queen, refused ever again to go back to France.

Being a barrister at Gray's Inn, Mildmay returned to his profession, but obviously still retained a bit of influence as in 1603, he was chosen to provide accommodation to James Stuart on his way south from Scotland, to be crowned King of England. It is clear that the king liked Apethorpe, because Lady Mildmay was renowned as one of the greatest cooks of her day, and it is reported that the king enjoyed his meals immensely, especially his hostess's wonderful confectionery.

Sir Anthony Mildmay died in 1617, and his wife three years later. They were buried together in that most imposing of tombs that dominates the south chapel of Apethorpe church.

Francis, 1st Earl of Westmorland (1580-1629)

Member of Parliament
Present at Coronation of James I
Personal friend of James I

Francis Fane was born in Kent in 1580, and in 1597, at the ridiculously early age of 17, was called to the bar by Lincoln's Inn. He was the Member of Parliament for Kent in 1601, for Maidstone in 1604 and 1620, and the Member for Peterborough in 1624.

Francis Fane had married Mary Mildmay, daughter of Sir Anthony Mildmay of Apethorpe. As such, he was at Apethorpe when James Stuart stopped there in the spring of 1603, on his way south to be crowned James I of England. The two men obviously hit it off straight away, and Francis Fane was to remain a close friend of James I all his life. Francis accompanied James to London, and was present at the coronation, where James created him a Knight of the Bath.

In 1617, Francis succeeded to the Apethorpe estate when his father-in-law died. And in 1623, as a further royal favour, he was created 1st Earl of

Westmorland, and Baron Burghersh, which came to be used by the eldest sons as a courtesy title.

Francis Fane died in March 1629, and was buried in the Mildmay/Fane family vault at Apethorpe. There is, however, no monument to him there, although there is one at his birthplace of Mereworth in Kent.

Mildmay, 2nd Earl of Westmorland (1602-1666)

Member of Parliament
Personal friend of Charles I
Confined to The Tower during the Civil War
Poet and Playwright
Spy for Charles II in exile?

Educated at Emmanuel College, Cambridge, Mildmay Fane gained his MA in 1619, when he was just 17. A year later he was in parliament as the Member for Peterborough. Those were the days of the 'pocket boroughs', where the 'owner' of the seat (his father) could give it to anybody he wanted - no elections in those days. And these were also the days of James I's difficulties with parliament, and so the 1620 parliament only lasted a year before being disbanded.

King James died in 1625, to be succeeded by his son, as Charles I. Mildmay Fane attended the coronation, and like his father, was created a Knight of the Bath. The two men were on such friendly terms, that Charles was godfather to Mildmay's son, Charles (later 3rd Earl of Westmorland, and also buried at Apethorpe) in 1634.

The period 1629 to 1640 is known as 'the eleven years tyranny', when Charles I tried to run the country without calling a parliament. He failed, and when the inevitable civil war broke out, Mildmay Fane, quite naturally, sided with the king. Because of this, he was arrested by parliamentarian forces in 1642, and clapped into The Tower. He was released in 1643 under house arrest in London, but only after his estates were confiscated on top of a £2000 fine,

In 1644, he took what was called 'The Covenant', which was an undertaking to oppose the king's ideas for church reform. This obviously pleased the parliamentarians, and his estates were restored and he returned to Apethorpe.

Having thus dropped out of political life, he turned to literature. He was a friend of the old poet Robert Herrick, the clergyman poet, and it was on Herrick's advice that he began writing. At Apethorpe he privately published several plays (still in existence) and volumes of poetry called *Otia Sacra* and *Fugitive Poetry*, which contained word puzzles and acrostics in Latin and English commenting on the political situation he saw around him.

However, at the Restoration of the Monarchy in 1660, his anti-royalist lapses seem to have been overlooked, and he was made lord Lieutenant of Northamptonshire, and in 1662, £50 was granted to him out of the Secret service money. So, during the Commonwealth, was he spying, and sending reports over to Charles II in exile in Holland? We will never know for sure, but that would explain why he was treated so leniently by the restored Charles II.

Mildmay Fane, 2nd Earl of Westmorland married twice, and had twelve children in total. He died in February 1666, and was buried in the family vault at Apethorpe.

John, 10th Earl of Westmorland (1759-1841)

Member of Parliament
Lord Lieutenant of Ireland
Long life personal friend of Pitt the Younger
Eloped to Gretna Green

What more romantic and scandalous thing can you do but elope to Gretna Green? John Fane and Sarah Childs did in 1782, when he was 23 and she was just 19. He was by then the Earl of Westmorland, having succeeded in 1774, but for an Earl to elope, albeit with a rich heiress like Sarah Childs, was a scandal that kept the chattering classes of Georgian drawing rooms tittle-tattling for months. The marriage turned out to be a happy one, and they had six children before Sarah died in 1793. He married secondly Jane Saunders, who provided four more children, and outlived her husband by 16 years.

Whilst at Emmanuel College, Oxford, John Fane met fellow undergraduate William Pitt the Younger. They were to remain firm friends until Pitt died in 1806.

John Fane had succeeded as 10th Earl of Westmorland when he was 15 in 1774, and as a member of the aristocratic ruling classes, his entering politics was as taken for granted as night following day. In 1789, Pitt, who was then

Prime Minister, made Fane his Paymaster General and a Member of the Privy Council.

In 1790, he was made Lord Lieutenant of Ireland, but was recalled by Pitt because Fane opposed Catholic emancipation. But he was immediately made Master of the Horse, and in 1798, still with Pitt as Prime Minister, he was made Lord Privy Seal. He remained as that for 30 years, except during a minor change of government in 1806. He was Recorder of Lyme Regis, and Lord Lieutenant of Northamptonshire in 1828.

He had to retire from politics because of failing eyesight. And eventually he became completely blind. John Fane died in 1841. He and his two wives are buried in the family vault at Apethorpe.

John, 11th Earl of Westmorland (1784-1859)

Member of Parliament
Soldier, who as ADC to General Don fought in the Hanover, Sicily and Egyptian campaigns
ADC to the Duke of Wellington in the Peninsular War
Ambassador to Italy, Germany and Austria
Composer of operas, cantatas and much other music
Founder of the Royal Academy of Music
Nephew-in-law to the Duke of Wellington

When reading the lifetime achievements of John Fane, 11th Earl of Westmorland, it is easy to exclaim "what a man!", although, as the eldest son of the 10th Earl, his path through life was smoothed somewhat by his enviable social background. Born in London in 1784, John went to Harrow and then to Trinity College, Cambridge, taking his BA in 1805, proceeding to MA in 1808.

The family's 'pocket borough' parliamentary seat of Lyme Regis was given to him in 1806, a seat he held until 1816. He could not have attended many sessions however, because in 1805, an army commission had been purchased for him, and he became a Lieutenant in the Northamptonshire Militia, and thence to the 11th Regiment of Foot. He subsequently served in the 7th, 23rd, 91st and 63rd Regiments, and the 3rd Dragoons.

His army service saw him as the ADC to General Sir George Don in the Hanover campaign of 1805, and in the Sicily and Egypt campaigns of 1806-

1807. He was present at the siege and storming of Rosetta, in the British reconquest of Egypt after the Napoleonic occupation.

And then on to the Peninsular War to curb Napoleon's excesses in Spain. As ADC to the Duke of Wellington, he was present at the Battles of Rolica, Vimiero and Busaco, and witnessed the remarkable display of the 48th Regiment in winning the Battle of Talavera. The 48th Regiment was to become the Northamptonshire Regiment, the county of the Fanes for the previous 300 years.

It must have been John Fane's closeness to the Duke of Wellington, that he met the great man's niece, Priscilla Wellesley-Pole. She was already quite a renowned and accomplished artist, and they married in 1811.

Being sent as an Envoy to Florence in 1814, he was much involved in the diplomacy leading up to, and surrounding, the Congress of Vienna, at which the victorious nations carved up the map of Europe after the defeat of Napoleon. With Europe at peace, Fane returned to England.

In 1822, he was made a Member of the Privy Council, and in that same year, proposed what would probably be his most memorable achievement. Because John Fane proposed the formation of an academy of music.

Always a keen musician, John Fane, an accomplished violinist, was also a prolific composer. His works include seven operas and three cantatas, masses, services and hymns, anthems and madrigals, all of which were published, as well as much unpublished work. This proposal from such an eminent public figure, directly led to the formation of the Royal Academy of Music in March 1823, with John Fane a founder member and leading light.

Succeeding to the Earldom in 1841 on the death of his father, he was sent as Ambassador to Berlin where he remained for ten years. During his time in Germany, he was promoted to General and awarded the GCB. And in 1851, he was sent as Ambassador to Austria at Vienna, where in 1855 he was a Special Plenipotentiary to the great Conference of Vienna. No meeting has been recorded as ever taking place, but with Fane's musical interests, it is inconceivable to believe that, whilst in Vienna, he would not have met the great Johann Strauss.

Retiring from public life, the Earl of Westmorland returned to Apethorpe, where he died in October 1859. So much was thought of him, that on the news of his death, all the military bands that were stationed in Berlin at the time, assembled and played Beethoven's *Funeral March* in his honour. He was buried in the family vault at Apethorpe, where 20 years later, his beloved Priscilla, was laid to rest with him.

Priscilla, Countess of Westmorland (1793-1879)

Exhibited artist
Niece of the Duke of Wellington

Priscilla Wellesley-Pole was the daughter of the Earl of Mornington (of Crescent fame), the brother of the great Duke of Wellington. She married John Fane in 1811, and came to live at Apethorpe.

Already an accomplished artist, as Lady Burghersh (Lord Burghersh was John Fane's courtesy title before succeeding to the Earldom) she was given numerous public exhibitions of her paintings and engravings between 1833 and 1841. As Countess of Westmorland, she had two public exhibitions in 1842 and 1857.

Although John and Priscilla Fane seemed to have all the material possessions, they were not immune from the tragedies of life. Their young son, John Arthur, was only six months old when he died in 1810. He was buried in the family vault at Apethorpe, and his touching memorial can be seen in the Fane chapel.

John Arthur Fane, aged six months.

Francis, 12th Earl of Westmorland (1825-1891)

Soldier, Colonel of the Coldstream Guards ADC to Lord Raglan in the Crimea War

Francis Fane succeeded as the 12th Earl of Westmorland in 1859. Never so distinguished as his father, Francis pursued a military career with the Coldstream Guards, and was ADC to Lord Raglan, the Supreme Commander during the Crimean War. As such, he was at Lord Raglan's side when he witnessed the now immortal 'Charge of the Light Brigade' at Balaclava in October 1854.

He died in 1891, and was the last Fane to be buried in the family vault before the estate was sold out of the family after a residence of 300 years.

ASHBY SAINT LEGERS

IN THE CHURCH AND CHURCHYARD OF SAINT LEODEGARIUS

William Catesby (?-1485)

Chancellor of the Exchequer
The 'Cat' to Richard III
Speaker of Parliament
Fought and captured at the Battle of Bosworth
Executed at Leicester

William Catesby, taken from the brass inlay on his tomb.

Richard III was evidently not very popular, neither as a king nor as a man. Consequently he tended to surround himself with, and give preferment to, people he knew well. Even when he usurped power and became King of England in 1483, he continued to do just that, and he named three of his favourites as his closest advisors: Sir Richard Ratcliffe, Francis, Lord Lovell – and William Catesby.

William Catesby was a lawyer, and his patron was William, Lord Hastings. The story goes that Lord Hastings was plotting against Richard, who at the time, was Duke of Gloucester and Regent of England, and it was Catesby who drew Richard's attention to it. Richard met Hastings at a meeting in The Tower of London in June 1483, had him seized, and literally within minutes had his head lopped off on Tower Green. As a reward, Richard, when he usurped the throne a few days later, made Catesby his Chancellor of the Exchequer. And the House of Commons, no doubt wanting to ingratiate itself with Richard, elected Catesby as Speaker of the House in early 1484.

So began Richard's short and unhappy reign. The fact that he was not popular, and the common people were none too impressed with him nor his cronies, was summed up in that most famous of historical rhymes which was nailed to the front door of Saint Paul's Cathedral in July 1484.

The Cat, the Rat and Lovell our Dog
Rule all England under the Hog.

The 'Cat' is Catesby. The 'Rat' is Ratcliffe, and Lovell is described as the 'Dog' because his coat of arms bore the crest of a dog. The 'Hog' is Richard himself, because his personal badge was a wild boar.

It is interesting to note, that of these four, three came from Northamptonshire. Richard himself was born at Fotheringhay, Catesby was born at Ashby Saint Legers, and Lord Lovell was from the old Northamptonshire family from Titchmarsh.

On Monday 22 August 1485, the Hog, flanked by the Cat, the Rat and the Dog, all stood on Bosworth Field in Leicestershire, for the battle against the contender for the throne, Henry Tudor. As we know, the Hog was killed, according to Shakespeare calling for his horse.

The Rat was killed, and the Dog escaped and was never heard of again. The Cat was captured alive, taken to Leicester, and beheaded two days later. He desired in his will to be buried in his birthplace, and this is what was done. His body lies underneath the High Altar in the church of Saint Leodegarius at Ashby Saint Legers.

The final resting place of William Catesby, beneath the High Altar at Ashby Saint Legers.

Ivor, 1st Viscount Wimbourne (1873-1939)

Member of Parliament
Paymaster General
Viceroy of Ireland during the Easter Rebellion
President of the National Liberal Party
Cousin of Winston Churchill
Captained winning Polo team against America

Ivor Churchill Guest was the son of the 1st Lord Wimbourne, and being from the upper classes, went to Eton and then to Trinity College, Cambridge. His background destined him either for politics, the army, or the church. Ivor chose politics.

He stood for election to parliament for the Plymouth constituency in 1898, and lost, but two years later was returned for Plymouth in a by-election, and was re-elected unopposed at the General Election of 1901. This was as a Conservative.

But disagreeing with Joseph Chamberlain's attempts at tariff reforms (to give preferential treatment to some trading partners, rather than a free market) in 1903, Guest, together with his cousin, a certain Winston Churchill, swapped parties and became Liberals. The Liberal Party's opposition to the Conservatives' policy of tariff reform gave them a landslide in the 1906 General Election, and Guest was returned as the Liberal Member for Cardiff.

Ivor Guest was made a Privy Councillor, and elevated to the peerage as Baron Ashby Saint Legers both in 1910. He became Paymaster General in 1910 as well, and stopped in that for two years. In 1914, however, his father died, and he became the 2nd Baron Wimbourne.

At the outbreak of the Great War, he was sent to Ireland on the staff of Lieutenant General Sir Bryan Mahon, the commander of the Irish military divisions. In 1915, however, the Prime Minister, Herbert Asquith, made him Lord Lieutenant and Viceroy of Ireland.

In Ireland, he was a popular figure. That is, until the Easter Rising of 1916, when, finding that he was not as in tune with the Irish as he thought, proposed the arrest of all the 'rebel' leaders. The arrests were never actually made, as the Chief Secretary was absent at that point, but the idea of such arrests caused a public outcry. The inevitable public enquiry followed, but Lord Wimbourne managed to justify himself, and he was exonerated, and remained in Ireland.

In 1918, the British government wanted to bring in conscription in Ireland. Wimbourne did not agree with this, and so was promptly brought back, being replaced by John, Lord French in May 1918. Lord French was obviously seen as more flexible than Lord Wimbourne, and it was to be Lord French who oversaw the implementation of the notorious 'Black and Tans' special police in Ireland, a move which set back relations between the two countries a hundred years. Lord Wimbourne must have realised that he was well out of it, but as a 'reward' for his services, was elevated to Viscount in 1918.

From then on, however, he tended to drop out of politics and concentrated on business, and as such helped to bring about a settlement of the National Strike of 1926. He was also elected as the first President of the National Liberal Party.

He was a keen Polo player, and in 1914, had led and captained the English team that beat the Americans in America, apparently a rare event. He had married in 1902, Alice the daughter of Lord Ebury. Ivor, 1st Viscount Wimbourne died in June 1939, and was buried in a small enclave to the side of Ashby Saint Legers main churchyard.

The monument to Ivor, Viscount Wimbourne.

AYNHO

IN THE CHURCH AND CHURCHYARD OF SAINT MICHAEL

The Cartwright family of Aynho has produced many distinguished men and women over the years. It would be impossible to mention all of them, so only the contributions of William, Fairfax and Frederick will be set out in detail. However, this is not to belittle the rest of the family, and the following is a list of those family members worthy of note, who are buried either in the family vault inside the church, or in the churchyard

Richard Cartwright (1563-1637) Barrister
William Cartwright (1634-1676) MP for East Retford
Thomas Cartwright (1671-1748) High Sheriff and MP for Northamptonshire
William Cartwright (?-1768) MP for Northamptonshire
William Cartwright (1754-1827) Equerry to King George III
William Ralph Cartwright (1771-1847) MP for Northamptonshire
William Cornwallis Cartwright (1825-1890) MP for Northamptonshire

William Cartwright (1797-1873)

Fought at Waterloo and captured Napoleon's dinner service
First and most influential Inspector of Constabulary

William Cartwright was born in February 1797 into the long established Aynho family. After Eton he was sent to the Royal Military College at Marlow in Buckinghamshire (later moved to Sandhurst) in 1809, and then commissioned into the 61st Regiment of the Line. He fought with the regiment in the latter stages of the bitterly fought Peninsular War, and saw much fighting in the actions in the Pyrenees and around the towns of Nivelle and Nive from June to December 1813.

Just two years later he transferred to the much more fashionable cavalry, in this case, the 10th Hussars. On Sunday 18 June 1815, the 10th Hussars were in the 6th Cavalry Brigade assembled on the field of Waterloo.

On that day, it fell to the cavalry to disperse the French attack on the centre of the British line, launched at 1 o'clock in the afternoon by Marshal d'Erlon. The attack had been repulsed by Sir Thomas Picton, and the cavalry finished off the job. Unfortunately, their charge carried too far, and they were themselves subjected to attack with many casualties. Of the 390 men of the 10th Hussars at the start of the day, 94 were either killed or wounded, nearly a quarter of them.

William Cartwright, survivor of Waterloo, and the first Inspector of Constabulary.

However, William Cartwright survived without a scratch, and after the charge found himself near to the French camp, and it was there that he helped himself to one of Napoleon's dinner services. He managed to get this back to England, and it remained a treasured possession of the Cartwright family for many years. Not bad for a young lad, for remember in 1815, William Cartwright was still only 18 years old.

Cartwright retired from the army in 1822 with the rank of Major. As was the custom of the times, even in retirement, promotion followed automatically, and eventually he became a Major General in 1856, even though he had not worn uniform for over 30 years.

In 1822 he had married a London heiress, Mary Ann Jones, and after buying the Manor House at Flore settled down to the life of a country squire. He involved himself in local politics, and became interested in the Poor Law administration.

Because it was considered that policing was a local responsibility rather than national, no government had bothered itself much with any policing matters. There had been an attempt in 1839 to get a rural constabulary, but because of the political situation of the time, the County Police Act of that year, only gave county magistrates the powers to form a police force for their county only if they wished, there was no compulsion. Only about half of the 56 English and Welsh counties bothered, but Northamptonshire had been one, and the Northamptonshire County Constabulary was formed in 1840.

It was not until 1853, that Lord Palmerston, that live wire of Victorian politics, ordered a Royal Commission into policing. The result was the County and Borough Police Act of 1856, where county and borough police forces were made compulsory. The Act also set up the Inspectorate of Constabulary to see that all police forces were of efficient standard.

The very first Inspector of Constabulary to be appointed, in August 1856, was William Cartwright. In September, he was joined by John Woodford, for 16 years Chief Constable of Lancashire; and Edward Willis, Chief Constable of Manchester for 15 years.

But ironically, it was to be the only non-policeman of the three, William Cartwright, who was to have the greatest, and longest lasting influence on policing policy of this country. Many of the ideas (such as proper pension schemes, national pay structure, detective departments and so on) put forward by Cartwright were adopted, and are still with us. If William Cartwright were to come back and see the police service of today, he would recognise it as being not too different from when he left the Inspectorate.

He retired in 1869, when he was 72. He had just seen his son, Fairfax, elected as Member for South Northamptonshire. Aubrey, his other son, had been killed at the Battle of Inkerman in the Crimean War 15 years earlier. Mary Ann Cartwright had died in 1860, and William gave the organ in Flore church in her memory, where a brass plaque marks the event.

William Cartwright died in his London home in June 1873, and was buried in Aynho churchyard alongside his beloved 'Marianne'.

Fairfax William Cartwright (1823-1881)
Captain in a regiment of Lancers in the Austrian army
Major in the British army in the Crimean War
Member of Parliament
Member of Select Committee on Police Pensions

The son of William and Mary Ann Cartwright, Fairfax Cartwright went to Eton and Christ Church College, Oxford. After graduation in 1845, he held a Fellowship at All Souls College.

Perhaps the academic life did not suit, or perhaps he wanted adventure, as he must have heard time and time again, his father's telling of his exploits in the Peninsular War and at Waterloo, but he abandoned Oxford and joined the Austrian army in 1848. Why the Austrian army is not clear, but he was commissioned into Archduke Charles' Regiment of Lancers, and went straight into the cauldron of European politics that was 1848.

War and revolution rocked Europe during that year, and Austria-Hungary had its fair share, from the 'Holy War' against Italy, through to the Hapsburg's overthrow in Hungary followed by their victorious restoration. As a member of the Austrian army, Fairfax Cartwright must have seen it all.

It was only the British involvement in the Crimean War, that persuaded him to resign his Austrian commission, and take a British commission, which took him into the Crimean War. He survived the war, whilst his brother Aubrey did not, being killed at the Battle of Inkerman. Fairfax finished the war as a Major.

He returned to England to the family estates, and entered into local politics. In 1868, he decided to go national, and was elected as Member of Parliament for South Northamptonshire.

Being the son of the first Inspector of Constabulary, Fairfax Cartwright was the ideal person to sit on the Select Committee looking into police pensions. It was Richard Cross, arguably the most influential of the Victorian Home Secretaries, who established the Select Committee in 1872.

The report was published in 1877, and Fairfax Cartwright was a leading light in the attempt to get legislation passed based on the report. He never succeeded, as he died whilst holding office in 1881. Incredibly, it took four attempts, spread over 13 years, before the police service received a standardised national pension by virtue of the Police Act 1890.

Fairfax Cartwright never married, and he was buried in the same grave as his parents in Aynho churchyard.

Sir Frederick Cartwright (1857-1928)

Ambassador to Austria-Hungary on the eve of the Great War

Frederick Leighton Cartwright certainly saw the world. Entering the Diplomatic Service in 1881 as an Attaché, he was sent to Berlin. He subsequently served in Stockholm, Tehran, Madrid, Vienna, Rome, Mexico City, Lisbon and Munich. Along the way, he was promoted from Attaché up to First Secretary. Whilst in Rome in 1898, he had married Maria, the daughter of the Marchese Chigi-Zondodari, and they had one son.

His highest appointment however, was as Ambassador to Austria-Hungary from 1908 to1913. Perhaps he could see what was coming, but he retired in 1913 at the age of 56, and thus missed the diplomatic manoeuvrings of the 1914 July Crisis, in which, as British Ambassador to Austria-Hungary, he would have been a central figure.

Throughout his career, he was awarded with the MVO in 1903, promoted to GCVO in 1909; KCMG in 1908 and promoted GCMG in 1914; and was made a member of the Privy Council in 1908. He died in 1928, and was buried in the Cartwright corner of Aynho churchyard.

The Cartwright corner in Aynho churchyard. The cross is to Sir Frederick, and the table tomb to William, Mary Anne and Fairfax.

BARNWELL

IN THE PARISH CHURCHYARD OF SAINT ANDREW

Thomas Bell (1783-1862)
Author, Local Historian and Poet

Little is known of Thomas Bell before he came to Barnwell, except that he was born in King's Lynn. He married a Barnwell girl, and stayed in the village for the rest of his life, running a private school. He may have been in the army in India, because in his autobiographical poem *The Cadet*, he says he stayed 'for twice seven years and more…by Ganges sacred shore'.

Some detective work is called for here. In 1851, a medal to the survivors of the Indian campaigns was issued, and if Thomas Bell had been a soldier in India, he would have received this medal. On the roll of recipients, there is only one Thomas Bell mentioned – a Private Thomas Bell of the 1st Regiment of Foot, or the Royal Regiment – who received the medal with the clasps (the 'bars' on the medal naming the battles the recipient had been in) *Ava* and *Nagpore*. The clasp *Nagpore* was for the battle which ended the Third Mahratta War when a British force captured the city of Nagpore being defended by its Rajah in December 1817. The clasp *Ava* was for general policing duties in the Ava district of India and Burma during the years 1824 to 1826.

Is this Thomas Bell the Thomas Bell that is buried at Barnwell? Who knows for sure, but the evidence (admittedly only circumstantial) nevertheless points that way, and the chronology seems to fit. And in any case, why spoil a good story, as we imagine his young pupils being kept enthralled as Bell told them tales of the bloodthirsty battles and adventures he had seen in the far away dusty heat of India.

Anyway, we do know that Thomas Bell was in Barnwell during the late 1820s, because he married Martha, a local girl, and settled at Barnwell. He ran a 'gentlemen's boarding school' at Barnwell for the rest of his life, dying in 1862 aged 79.

His first book *The Ruins of Liveden* was published in 1847. It is a local history book with many articles, including some on the Tresham family and the Gunpowder Plot, and included the eponymous poem *The Ruins of Liveden.*

His second book *The Rural Album* was published in 1853. It is an anthology of poems and local history articles.

The third and last book *Winter Evenings at Home* was published in 1856, and is an anthology of prose and poetry. Bell also contributed the notes on village histories that appeared in William Whellan's *History, Gazetteer and Directory of Northamptonshire* published in 1849.

That the life of a village schoolmaster was hard indeed, must be inferred from a verse from his poem *The Village Schoolmaster* from his book The *Rural Album*, surely written from deep personal knowledge.

Bent by age, by sorrows wasted,
Worn his frame, and dim his eye;
Threadbare garments plainly showing
What his frugal means supply.
Coarse his fare, and that but scanty;
From his fate too proud to shrink,
Bread his food with little added,
Water from the spring his drink.
Hope extinguish'd in his breast
Longing for eternal rest.

The tombstone of Thomas and Martha Bell in Saint Andrew's churchyard.

IN THE CHAPEL OF ALL SAINTS

Not now used as a church, All Saints is now the mortuary chapel of that branch of the great Northamptonshire family of Montagu, which became the Earls of Sandwich. For 240 years from 1622, in addition to those described below, generations of Montagus have been buried here, including the 3rd, 5th and 6th Earls of Sandwich, Viscounts Hinchinbrooke, and their families.

Sir Sydney Montagu (?-1644)
Paulina, Lady Montagu (?-c1650)
Uncle and Aunt to Samuel Pepys, the famous diarist

Sir Sydney Montagu settled in Barnwell in the 1590s, and from him comes that branch of the huge and influential Northamptonshire family of Montagu, which became the Earls of Sandwich. Sydney must have already been well connected because he became the Groom to the Bedchamber of King James I. For his services he was knighted in 1616.

Remaining at Court, he was made the Master of the Court of Bequests to Charles I. The Court of Bequests was where the king heard personal petitions, and the Master controlled who should (and more importantly, who should not) have access to the king.

Because of this position, he was obviously on the king's side when the Great Civil War broke out. But, in the 'Long Parliament' of 1640, he had been the Member for Huntingdon, which had been Oliver Cromwell's seat (in the 'Long Parliament' Cromwell sat for Cambridge), and so in 1642, for refusing to take the oath of loyalty to parliament, Montagu was arrested and committed to The Tower.

This broke his health, and he died in 1644. He was buried in the Montagu family vault in the church of Barnwell All Saints, which in those days was a separate parish to Barnwell St Andrew, hence the two churches. They have long since been combined.

But probably his greater claim to fame lies in his marriage, because he married Paulina Pepys of Cottenham in Cambridgeshire. Paulina had a

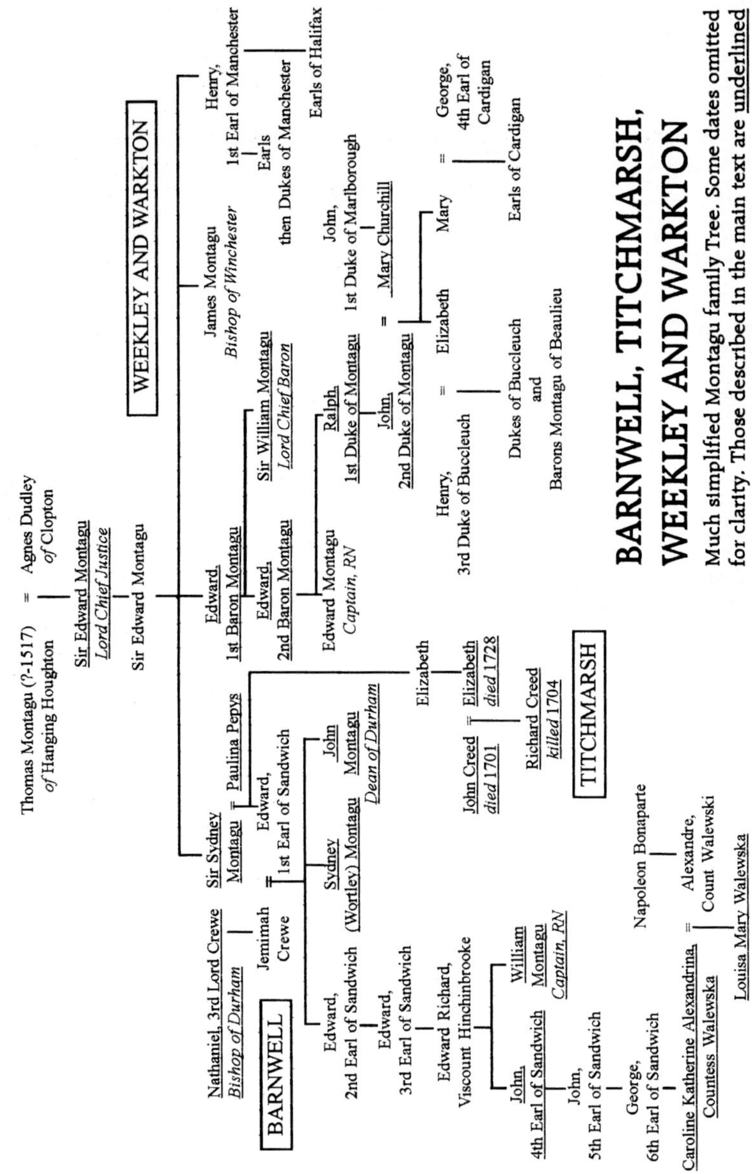

BARNWELL, TITCHMARSH, WEEKLEY AND WARKTON

Much simplified Montagu family Tree. Some dates omitted for clarity. Those described in the main text are underlined

younger brother, Thomas, and Thomas was the father of Samuel, the famous diarist. Although Pepys' Uncle Sidney and Aunt Paulina both died before the famous diary was started, their son, and therefore Pepys' cousin, Edward, later to become the 1st Earl of Sandwich, is mentioned numerous times.

The Montagu family chapel. The brass plaque records the names of all the Montagus buried in the underground vault.

John Montagu (1655-1728)
Dean of Durham

John Montagu was the fourth son of Edward Montagu, 1st Earl of Sandwich, and like many of the youngest sons of the aristocracy, entered the church. He graduated from Trinity College, Cambridge and proceeded MA in 1673. He then became a Fellow of Trinity and remained there until 1680.

His mother was Jemimah, the daughter of Nathaniel, 3rd Lord Crewe, who had been Bishop of Durham since 1674 (*see* Steane, where he is buried). And what better way to use influence than to benefit members of your own family.

John Montagu became Master of Sherburn Hospital in Durham in 1680, and three years later, a Canon of Durham, as well as Master of Trinity.

He was made DD by Royal Warrant in 1686, and became Vice-Chancellor of Cambridge a year later. He resigned all these in 1699 to become Dean of Durham under his grandfather who was still Bishop. The Bishop died in 1722, but John continued as Dean until he died in 1728. He was unmarried and was buried in the family vault at Barnwell.

William Montagu (1720-1757)

Captain in the Royal Navy
Member of Parliament

If youngest sons of the aristocracy entered the church, their elder brothers (except the eldest, who got the title) went into the military, or in William Montagu's case, the navy. Brother to the infamous 4th Earl of Sandwich, William, known as 'Mad Montagu' packed more into 37 years of life than others do in twice that.

There is not room for a blow by blow account of his career, but just a list of his ships. In 1740 he was Lieutenant in HMS *Defiance* at the Battle of Cartagena; on HMS *Launceston* in the Leeward Island, and promoted Commander to HMS *Mercury* in Antigua in 1744. He narrowly escaped court-martial in Antigua when he fired on a rowing boat which had refused to answer, but which only contained one man, who subsequently died of the wound he received when 'Mad Montagu' had fired at him. By the influence of his Admiral, Sir Peter Warren, and the incompetence of the indicting officer, Montagu escaped. He was promoted Captain in HMS *Mermaid*, then to HMS *Prince Edward* in 1745,and then onto the 50 gun ship of the line HMS *Bristol* in July 1746 in the Squadron of Admiral Sir George Anson.

In the action of 3 May 1747, called the Battle of Finisterre, HMS *Bristol* engaged the French ship *Invincible*. Anson in HMS *Pembroke* tried to intervene but was rebuked by Montagu who continued his attack, crippled the *Invincible*, then went straight on to capture the *Diamante*. But in the meantime *Invincible* had surrendered to Anson. Anson in his later report, took all the credit and never mentioned the real victor, Montagu – it was thought at the time to be jealousy. For his part, Anson received a peerage, and Montagu got nothing.

Returning to England, Montagu was put in charge of HMS *Cumberland* at Chatham, and virtually retired from active service.

In November 1775, he became Member of Parliament for Huntingdon, and in February 1752, Member for Bossiney in Cornwall.

He had married Charlotte Nailour, but they had no children. Both William and Charlotte are buried in the family vault at Barnwell.

John, 4th Earl of Sandwich (1718-1792)

First Lord of the Admiralty on two occasions
Ambassador to Breda and Aix la Chapelle
Had the Sandwich Islands named after him
Inventor of 'The Sandwich'

Earl of Sandwich when he was aged 11, John Montagu was grandson of the 3rd Earl. His father, Richard, Viscount Hinchinbrooke, had died in 1722, seven years before *his* father.

John was educated at Eton and Trinity College, Cambridge, and as was usual for a member of the aristocracy of the time, he went on the 'Grand Tour' between 1737 and 1739. On his return, being from the ruling classes, John entered politics automatically, and became involved in what was known as the 'Bedford Gang', which had John Russell, Duke of Bedford as its leader.

In 1746 he was Plenipotentiary to Breda, and then at Aix la Chapelle in 1748, where he took part in arranging the great Treaty of Aix la Chapelle which gave peace between France and England. It was for the firework display at the London celebrations of this Treaty that Handel wrote his *Music for the Royal Fireworks*.

No doubt because of his performance here, the Prime Minister, Henry Pelham, brought him home and made him a Lord of the Admiralty in the so-called 'Broad Bottomed Ministry'. Because he wanted to reduce the national debt, Pelham wanted savings, so Sandwich instituted stringent money saving reforms in the navy. In 1751, he was dismissed for various reasons, and he was not to hold office for another 17 years. During this period, he perhaps showed his character in what was known as 'The Wilkes Affair'.

In 1767, John Wilkes, the controversial writer and thinker of the day, published his *Essay on Woman*. This was considered to be pornographic, and was attacked in the Lords. Eventually Wilkes was indicted and prosecuted. It was the Earl of Sandwich who was one of the leaders of the attack and earned him the nickname of 'Jemmy Twitcher' named after a character in *The*

Beggars' Opera who was two-faced and betrayed his friends. Wilkes, during all this time was noticeably absent, and could not defend himself from the vitriolic attacks of his once great friend, the Earl of Sandwich.

In William Pitt's government of 1768, Sandwich was appointed Postmaster General, but in 1771, when Lord North came upon the scene as Prime Minister, Sandwich was reinstated as first Lord of the Admiralty. He was to serve for 11 years until Lord North resigned, and during this time, Sandwich undertook dealings which can only be described as corrupt.

Under the left hand tombstone, lies the inventor of the sandwich.

Of the vast sums allocated to the navy, very little was actually used for its proper purpose. So when the 1775 American War of Independence broke out, aggravated in 1778 by France and Spain's entry into the war on America's side, the British navy was entirely inadequate, with rotting ships and empty storehouses. Consequently, the British navy lost control of the seas, and Sandwich and North came under severe criticism.

Lord North fell as Prime Minister in 1782, taking Sandwich with him, who then retired from public life. Both John and Dorothy, 4th Earl and Countess of Sandwich are buried at Barnwell.

However, the name of the Earl of Sandwich is perhaps better remembered nowadays for two reasons. In 1778 when Captain Cook 'discovered' some South Sea Islands, he called them after the then First Lord of the Admiralty, and the islands became the Sandwich Islands. Keeping this name until the mid nineteenth century, they are now known as Hawaii, and in 1959 became the 50th state of the USA.

But the most famous way that John Montagu is remembered is, of course, for the sandwich. He invented the snack because he wanted quick and instant sustenance without having the tiresomeness of leaving the gaming table. Sandwiches are now universally known, and their originator is buried at Barnwell under an ornate slap of black marble.

Caroline Katherine Alexandrina, Countess Walewska (1811-1834)

Daughter in law of Napoleon Bonaparte

Louisa Mary Walewska (1834-1837)

Granddaughter of Napoleon Bonaparte

Nobody could deny that Napoleon was one of the great figures of history, and will always be remembered. Already married to the equally famous Josephine by 1806, Napoleon was in Poland in December of that year, and whilst there, he met Maria, Countess Walewska. She was an 18 year old temptress (he was twice her age at 37) married to the Polish Count Walewski, who was four times her age at 77. She had already borne him a son, and had had the privilege of being educated by the father of the great Polish composer Chopin.

The inevitable happened, and Maria Walewska became the second biggest love of Napoleon's life. Apparently the 77 year old Count knew all about it, but did nothing, and in 1809, Maria became pregnant by Napoleon.

Napoleon was proud to acknowledge fatherhood, mainly because he had now squashed rumours that he could not sire children. Josephine had not given him any, and she would be divorced within the year. When Maria gave birth to Alexandre in 1810, Napoleon was ecstatic, and boasted that one day Alexandre would be king of Poland. The old Count Walewski was complaisant in the extreme and allowed Alexandre to take the surname of Walewski.

Napoleon continued to acknowledge Alexandre as his son, and he was brought up and educated as such. In 1815, Alexandre and his mother were among Napoleon's entourage when he abdicated after his Waterloo defeat.

After Napoleon's abdication, the Bonaparte family was scattered throughout Europe, and Alexandre found himself in England. It was here that he met Lady Caroline Montagu, the daughter of the 6th Earl of Sandwich. They were married in December 1831. Caroline therefore became Countess Walewska, and thus the daughter in law of Napoleon Bonaparte.

Their daughter Louisa Mary was born in 1834, but Caroline never recovered from the birth and died in April 1834. She was only 23, and Alexandre was 24. Caroline Katherine Alexandrina, Countess Walewska was buried in her family's vault at Barnwell.

Louisa Mary, the granddaughter of Napoleon, always a sickly child, never gained the strength to live, and she died in 1837 aged three. She was buried alongside her mother at Barnwell.

Count Walewski married again, became French Ambassador to Britain, and died in 1868, aged 58.

BARTON SEAGRAVE

IN THE CHURCH OF SAINT BOTOLPH

John Bridges (1666-1724)
Historian of Northamptonshire

Born in Barton Seagrave in the year of the Great Fire of London, John Bridges was called to the bar by Lincoln's Inn. He entered government service and was a solicitor to the Customs and Excise by 1695; a Commissioner of Excise in 1712; and a Cashier of Excise by 1695. He was also governor of the Bridewell, and of Bethlehem Hospital, the famous 'Bedlam'.

But that is not why we remember him. His great service to the county of his birth was his pioneering *History of Northamptonshire*.

Always interested in history, he was elected a Fellow of the Society of Antiquaries in 1718, after years of collecting information about the county. But by his premature death at the age of 58, his *History* had still not been published. He was brought home and buried in his native village.

However, his manuscripts were well known, and non-publication was seen as unacceptable. Thus in 1760, William Cartwright of Aynho formed a Committee to get the *History* into print. Volume I was published in 1762, and the first part of Volume II in 1769. But it was not until 1791 that the work was finally completed.

The story now comes to 1847, when the Kettering printers, Thomas and William Dash, father and son, reprinted it, with lots of additions, in five volumes. When William Dash died in 1883 (and was buried in London Road Cemetery, Kettering) his copy of Bridges' *History of Northamptonshire* was presented to the British Museum.

The plaque to John Bridges, above the north door.

BLATHERWYCKE

❁

IN THE UNUSED CHURCH OF THE HOLY TRINITY

❁

Thomas Randolph (1605-1635)

Poet and Playwright
Friend and adopted 'son' of Ben Jonson

Thomas Randolph died at the age of 30 when he was visiting the Stafford family of Blatherwycke. He had just returned from London, and was heavily in debt and in poor health.

Having been born at Newnham near to Daventry, Thomas went to Westminster School and Trinity College, Cambridge where he graduated, and was elected a Fellow. He took his MA degree in 1632. He had shown literary promise at an early age, and apparently had written a poem on the Incarnation when he was ten. He was noted at Cambridge for his poems in Greek and Latin.

But London was calling him, and he arrived there in 1632 where he straightway gatecrashed a gathering over which the great and virtual poet laureate of the day, Ben Jonson, was holding court. Eventually a great friendship grew up between these two men, and Jonson 'adopted' Randolph as his 'son'.

Under the tutelage of Jonson, Randolph put his intellectual and poetic gifts to work. He wrote numbers of works, and in 1632, his comedy *The Jealous Lovers* was published. One poem from this play *A Charm Song* was thought good enough by Benjamin Britten to set to music and include in his song cycle *A Charm of Lullabies* in 1947.

However, the fleshpots of the capital beckoned, and he spent a couple of years indulging the sins of the flesh - drinking, gambling, brawling and fornicating. A poem of his, published posthumously, describes the loss of the little finger of his left hand which he obviously lost in a tavern brawl somewhere.

By 1634, heavily in debt by losing at the gaming tables, and no doubt totally riddled with some form of venereal disease, Randolph had to take time to recover in the country. Hence his visit to Blatherwycke. But it was too late. He died, officially of small pox, but that may be a euphemism, in 1635 when he was only 30.

Three years after his death, two of his plays *Amyntas* and *The Muse's Looking-Glasse* were published to great acclaim. He had been looked upon as one of the most promising poets and dramatists of his time. Not to be, however, and he was buried in Blatherwycke church where Sir Christopher Hatton of Kirby Hall paid £10 to have a monument erected to his memory.

Anthony Williams (?-1836)

Black Slave

Charles Bacchus lies at Culworth, and Anthony Williams lies buried in Blatherwycke churchyard. Both were black slaves 'owned' by the land owning gentry in keeping with the fashion of the times. But Anthony Williams' story has more than a twist of tragedy.

The memorial to Thomas Randolph in Blatherwycke church.

He was the slave to Henry O'Brien the Lord of the Manor. Judging by his epitaph, he may have come from the West Indies, or from India itself, and Anthony Williams was probably not his given name either.

In June 1836, O'Brien was fishing in a boat on Blatherwycke Lake, taking Williams along with him. Suddenly the boat overturned and the two men were pitched into the water. Despite attempts at rescue by Williams, O'Brien was drowned. Williams was saved, but died a few days later from the effects. The inscription on his gravestone in the churchyard sums everything up, and hints at a personal story that we will never get within a million miles of guessing.

Here a poor wanderer hath found a grave
Who death embraced when struggling with the wave
His home far off in the broad Indian main
He left to rid himself of slavery's chain
Friendless and comfortless he passed the sea,
On Albion's shores to seek for liberty
Yet vain his search for aye with toiling brow
He never found his freedom until now

The partially hidden tombstone to Anthony Williams is on the left, behind the Rose Bay Willow Herb, and faces away from the church.

BRACKLEY

IN THE CHURCHYARD OF SAINT PETER

Mary Leapor (1722-1746)
Poetess

Born in Marston Saint Lawrence in 1722, Mary's father was gardener to Sir John Blencowe (*see* Marston Saint Lawrence). After Sir John died in 1726, the family moved to Brackley. Mary taught herself to read and write, and acquired a few books, mostly by Dryden and Pope.

Mary was 'in service' in what is believed to be Edgcote House, the home of Sir Richard Chauncy. Edgcote House is believed to be she got the inspiration for one of her best known poems *Crumble Hall*. Unfortunately we cannot check the details 'of the goodly Row of oaken Pillars – where a giant Show of mimic Pears and carv'd Pomegranates twine', because Edgcote House was completely rebuilt in 1747, the year after Mary died of measles at the young age of 24. She was buried in Brackley churchyard in an unknown grave.

Such was the quality of her verse, that several influential persons wanted to publish it after her death, notably David Garrick, the famous actor. And her poetry is still generally reckoned, by those who know these things, to be amongst the best. Two volumes of her poetry have been published. One authority even ranks her alongside Dryden and Clare as the best of the Northamptonshire poets. As such, she is still remembered today, having an entry in the *Dictionary of National Biography.* The following is an extract from *Crumble Hall*, written at a time when all nouns in English were written with capital letters, as German is today.

We count the Stairs and to the Right ascend,
Where on the Walls the gorgeous Colours blend.
There doughty George bestrides the goodly Steed;
The Dragon's slaughter'd and the Virgin freed;
And there (but lately rescu'd from their Fears)
The Nymph and serious Ptolemy appears:
Their awkward Limbs unwieldy are display'd;
And, like a Milk-wench, glares the royal Maid.

BRIGSTOCK

IN THE CHURCH OF SAINT ANDREW

Reverend Talbot Keene (1735-1824)

Poet

After Trinity College, Cambridge, Keene, an Irishman, was ordained by John, Bishop of Lincoln. In 1773, he became Vicar of Brigstock and Stanion, and stopped there for the rest of his life, another 51 years. He died in February 1824 aged 89, and was buried in Brigstock church, with a memorial tablet in the south aisle.

He was a renowned poet, and in 1787, published a book of verse *Miscellaneous Pieces: Original and Collected.* One of these poems, *House Rules*, must surely sum up his attitude to life, because it could not have been written otherwise.

Behold the man who speaks the truth... The memorial to the Reverend Talbot Keene.

Short Rules to be observed by all
Who on the B-------k Vicar call.

Whoe'r within this roof doth come,
Let him the robe of mirth put on,
For brow austere and looks demure,
The matter of it can't endure.
If he should be in studious fit,
Why! In the study he may sit:
But if inclin'd to laugh and talk,
Then in the parlour let him walk,
And in the wheel of each narration
Put in his spoke of conversation:
Let those who thus shall honour me,
Be as at home, and just as free.
Know then, a flower in ev'ry room
Here grows, in full eternal bloom:
Hearts-ease, 'tis call'd: and may each guest
luck off the leaf he likes the best.

Robert Smith (Vernon), 1st Baron Lyveden (1800-1873)

Member of Parliament
Under Secretary of State for War at the outbreak of the Crimean War
President of the Board of Control during the Indian Mutiny

Robert Smith's father, Robert Percy Smith, was the Advocate General of Bengal, and after making his fortune in India, returned to England and became a Member of Parliament. Robert, senior, was the brother of the famous Reverend Sydney Smith, that live wire of the Victorian theological and literary scene. Coming from such a social background, Robert, junior could hardly fail. He was sent to Eton and then to Christ Church College, Oxford where he graduated in Classics in 1822.

A year later he married Lady Emma Fitzpatrick, a daughter of the Earl of Upper Ossory. And thus introduced to Irish life, accepted the Earl's pocket borough, and became the Member of Parliament for Tralee in 1829.

Earl Grey (of tea fame) was the Prime Minister at the time, and Smith became Junior Lord of the Treasury in 1830, a job he held until Lord Melbourne became Prime Minister in 1834, when he became Joint Secretary of the Board of Control. The Board of Control was the government department that looked after the affairs of India. When Sir Robert Peel took over in 1841, Smith was moved, and became Under Secretary of State for War.

Lord John Russell did not give him a job when he formed his ministry in 1846, but the Earl of Derby did in 1852, and Smith returned to being Under Secretary of State for War. As such, he saw the start of the Crimean War in 1854.

The lovely marble table tomb of Lord Lyveden

But it was Lord Palmerston, that most energetic of Victorian politicians, who gave Smith his most prestigious job, when he made him President of the Board of Control in 1855. This put him in complete control of all the affairs of the Indian sub-continent. So it was Smith who had to handle the outbreak and aftermath of the great Indian Mutiny of 1857-1858, the occurrence of which had shaken British complacency of Indian affairs to the roots. So much so, that in 1858, the whole Board of Control was scrapped, and a new department created under a Secretary of State for India.

This meant the end for Smith. He had been in politics for 29 years, which was half his life, and it was obvious after the Mutiny crisis and the India Office reorganisation, that it was time to go. He thus retired from active politics. To compensate for this, he received the customary reward for retiring politicians – a peerage. He became the 1st Baron Lyveden, and it was then he changed his surname to Vernon, which is the name by which he is now remembered.

His wife's family had connections with Northamptonshire (*see* Grafton Underwood) and Lord Lyveden came to live the life of a country squire at Fermyn Woods Hall, Brigstock. He filled his time by editing and publishing two volumes of the letters of Horace Walpole and his son. He was awarded the GCB in 1872. Robert Vernon, 1st Lord Lyveden died in November 1873 and his magnificent tomb is inside Saint Andrew's church.

BRIXWORTH

IN THE CHURCH OF ALL SAINTS

Saint Boniface (680-755)

English monk who is the patron saint of Germany

Or to be more accurate, just a throat bone. Or to be more accurate still, *it is believed* to be a throat bone of Saint Boniface.

In 1809, a stone reliquary was found in Brixworth church, and in this was the bone, and a piece of parchment, which when the reliquary was opened immediately crumbled into dust. This parchment must have contained the name of the saint whose bone it was, and the mystery will now never be solved.

Saint Boniface was born in Crediton in Devonshire in 680, and after entering the monastic life, felt the call to missionary work. He visited Pope Gregory II in Rome, who asked him to convert the Germanic tribes, and consecrated him a bishop in 723. In 755 he was martyred by heathen tribesmen and was buried in Fulda monastery, which is just to the north east of Frankfurt.

There were seven Councils of Clovesho held between 742 and 803. The most important being the one in 747, which concerned itself with ecclesiastical discipline, and ordering that the liturgy used in the Church of England conformed with the Roman Rite. It is known that Saint Boniface had a great influence at this Council.

Nobody knows for certain the whereabouts of Clovesho, but David Parsons, in a booklet *The Mystery of the Brixworth Relic*, available in the church, argues that Clovesho *could* be Brixworth. If that is true, then it is possible that when Saint Boniface died in 755, a bone of the Saint was sent to the monastery at Brixworth as a relic.

The ledge where the Reliquary with the bone of Saint Boniface was kept, which is now sensibly in a safer place, far away from the light fingered.

BROUGHTON

IN THE CHURCH OF SAINT ANDREW

Robert Bolton (1572-1631)

Religious Author

The remarkable memorial to Robert Bolton, believed to be a true likeness of him, probably taken from a death mask.

Born in Blackburn, Bolton attended Lincoln College, Oxford in 1592. Apparently nothing short of a genius, he became fluent in Latin, Greek and Hebrew. In 1596, he transferred to Brasenose College, and graduated BA. He remained at Brasenose as a Fellow, and proceeded MA in 1602. As a lecturer in Logic and Philosophy, Bolton was chosen to give an address to the new king, James I when he visited, who apparently was exceedingly impressed with Bolton's oratory.

Although tending towards Roman Catholicism, Bolton was converted to Anglicanism, received the BD degree in 1609, and was ordained. He became Rector of Broughton in 1610 and remained there for the rest of his life. When he was instituted to Broughton, Doctor King, the Bishop of London, said to Sir Augustine Nicholls, the patron of Broughton "Sir, you have deprived the University of its brightest ornament".

Because of his immense learning, he wrote many theological books, and became one of the leading religious thinkers of his day. He died in 1631, and is buried in the chancel.

BUGBROOKE

IN THE CHURCH OF SAINT MICHAEL

Reverend William Tresham (?-1569)

Notable Recusant

From the Latin *recuso*, I refuse, Recusancy was the term given to the specific refusal of Roman Catholics to attend the Protestant services of the Church of England. This had started during the reign of Edward VI (1547-1553) and was to last for just over 200 years. Church going had been made compulsory, and savage penalties, from fines to execution, were given for Recusancy. However, as time went on, enforcement tended to tail off, and was finally abandoned in the 1770s. But in the early years, Recusancy was harshly punished. William Tresham was one of the famous Recusants.

Born in Newton near Geddington, William went to Merton College, Oxford, and by 1532 had the degrees of MA and DD. He was made Vice-Chancellor of Oxford in 1532, and Henry VIII made him one of the first Canons of the newly founded Christ Church College.

Also a Canon of both Ely and Lincoln, Henry made him one of the first Canons of the new Bishopric of Oxford. At the same time, he was Rector of both Bugbrooke and Towcester. Multiple church livings (it was called 'plurality') like this were common in those times. So all in all, William Tresham was highly regarded as one of the pillars of the church, and soon no doubt, would have been made a bishop somewhere.

So what went wrong? The answer is not known. All that is known is that William Tresham refused to take the oath of allegiance to Elizabeth I in 1559, and turned Recusant. The reason probably has something to do with the fact that Elizabeth started returning the country to Protestantism after the Catholic years of her half-sister Mary.

As a punishment, William Tresham was deprived of every single one of his livings, except Towcester, and was placed under a sort of house arrest in the custody of the Archbishop of Canterbury, Matthew (the famous 'Nosey') Parker. But on giving his word to behave himself, he was released back to Towcester and lived a quiet subdued life until he died in 1569.

There appears to be some doubt as to where he is buried. *The Dictionary of National Biography* argues that as at the time of his death he was only the Rector of Towcester, then he would logically be buried in Towcester. But the Reverend Henry Longden in his stupendous *Northamptonshire and Rutland Clergy*, states categorically, that although there is no memorial stone in the church, or entry in the parish register, Tresham is buried in Bugbrooke. He cites Alice Saunders of Bugbrooke who states quite clearly in her Will of 1575 that she wanted to be buried in the chancel of Bugbrooke church 'between the burial of my brother Doctor Tressham and my sister Kynesman'.

For a simplified Tresham family tree, *see* Rushton.

BURTON LATIMER

THE NEW CEMETRY NEXT TO THE PARISH CHURCH

Louisa Sophia Johnson (1865-1893)

Murder victim of Richard Sabey

Louisa Johnson arrived at her sister's house at Ise Brook Cottage, Finedon on Monday 6 February 1893, bringing with her a tiny baby. She had just left Liverpool Workhouse where she had been forced to live, when the legal wife of the man she had been living with had turned up on the doorstep and had thrown her out into the cold.

For what reason this man, Richard Sabey, followed Louisa from Liverpool to Finedon, can only now be guessed at. But at his trial he did admit to feeling jealous that Louisa might marry another man.

Arriving at Ise Brook Cottage on Wednesday 8 February, Sabey waited for an opportunity to talk to Louisa. At 5.30pm, wishing to draw water from the well, Louisa appeared and was confronted by Sabey.

What was said at that fatal meeting is unknown. All we have to go on is the evidence of Edward Partridge, a Finedon baker, who saw Sabey and Louisa walking along the road towards Burton Latimer. Partridge saw Sabey put his arm around Louisa in what appeared to be a friendly gesture. But suddenly Sabey whipped out a knife. Louisa struggled.

"He's trying to kill me" she screamed, and Sabey instantly cut her throat. Louisa managed to break free, and seeing four ironstone workers returning from work, started to run towards them. The wounds must have been dreadful, because she collapsed in a pool of blood and died before she could reach the men.

Sabey took to his heels in the opposite direction, making his way across the field on the banks of the Ise Brook. But he was captured a few minutes later by James Burley, one of the ironstone labourers, who found him skulking down besides a hedge.

Poor Louisa's body was taken to the *Red Cow* public house at Burton Latimer, and buried a few days later. Her memorial is a simple cast iron headstone, which now leans up against a wall as though it has been uprooted, and so may not indicate the exact position where Louisa was buried.

Richard Sabey was found guilty of wilful murder and was hanged at Northampton Borough Gaol on Tuesday 18 July 1893. For his grave, *see* Northampton, the Towcester Road Cemetery.

The cast iron memorial to Louisa Johnson

CASTLE ASHBY

IN THE CHURCH OF SAINT MARY MAGDALENE

Spencer, 2nd Marquis of Northampton (1790-1851)

Took over the Northampton seat from Spencer Perceval
Scientist and poet
Friend and supporter of William Wilberforce

The only Prime Minister to be murdered, Spencer Perceval was shot in the House of Commons on Monday 11 May 1812. Coming from the same family as the Marquises of Northampton (the Comptons), Perceval had been Member of Parliament for Northampton since 1796.

Northampton was a pocket borough of the Compton family, so Spencer Compton filled the vacancy left by Spencer Perceval. During his time in the Commons, he became a great friend, and supporter, of William Wilberforce in his anti-slavery campaign.

He married Margaret Douglas-Maclean-Clephane in 1815, and in 1820, having given up politics, which obviously did not appeal to him much, the couple moved to Italy. Whilst there, his house became the centre of ex-patriot society.

In 1828, he succeeded his father as 2nd Marquis of Northampton. Two years later his wife died, and he returned to England. Although he took his seat in the House of Lords, his heart was not in it, and he had an unremarkable career. But he was interested in science, and became the first President of the Geological Society, and President of the Royal Society between 1838 and 1848.

He was also a sensitive poet. In his book *The Tribute: A Collection of Miscellaneous unpublished Poems, by Various Authors*, which he published in 1837 in aid of the family of the late Reverend Edward Smedley, he included some of his own poems, and some of his wife's, who was also a poet. Although written in 1814, her book *Irene, a poem in six Cantos* was published posthumously in 1833. She came from a wealthy Scottish family, and her godfather was Sir Walter Scott.

Spencer Compton, 2nd Marquis of Northampton died suddenly in January 1851, and was buried in Castle Ashby church next to his wife.

Margaret Compton. Extract from *Irene*

Parting is ill to bear-ev'n when we leave
Some town or city on a distant shore,
The heart flies back a moment's space to grieve,
And sighs to hear the knell of Never more!

Spencer Compton. Extract from *Cowper's Oak and the Emperor Butterfly*

A Butterfly one summer's day
Sat on an old oak's topmost spray-
A Butterfly that but of late
Had left the chrysalis's state:
Emerging from that narrow room
Of sleep, imprisonment and gloom,
For a brief space he flutters round,
Then settles on the verdant ground:
About impertinently stares,
And gives himself most mighty airs.
Ungrateful to his foster oak,
At length contemptuously he spoke:

The striking tomb of Spencer Compton in Castle Ashby church.

And the memorial to Margaret Compton

CATESBY

IN THE CEMETERY OF CATESBY PRIORY

(Saint) Margaret of Catesby (?-1257)

Sister to Saint Edmund, Archbishop of Canterbury

Sometime about the year 1199, a saintly mother lies on her deathbed. Her three children are there, a son and two daughters. The mother commits the care of the two sisters to the brother, and leaves a sum of money to enable them to enter a fashionable nunnery. The brother, an ordained priest, would have none of this and looks for a nunnery that will take his sisters with only their piety to recommend them. He chooses the Cistercian nunnery at Catesby Priory, where the Prioress receives them willingly. The brother, Edmund Rich, is a lecturer of Divinity at Oxford and Paris, and eventually, in 1234, becomes Archbishop of Canterbury. His reign is a stormy one, but by his piety overcomes all.

Looking down to Lower Catesby from the cemetery at Upper Catesby. The site of the priory cemetery is unsure, but would lie in one of the fields in the middle distance.

In 1240 he dies, and his belongings are sent to his sisters at Catesby. Soon miracles are being associated with these articles, and in 1248, he is canonised as Saint Edmund.

Margaret his sister becomes the Prioress of Catesby. She dies in 1257, being buried in the cemetery at the Priory.

She was described as a woman of 'great holiness', and soon after her burial, miracles were said to be happening at her tomb. Because of this she is sometimes referred to as Saint Margaret of Catesby, but she has never been officially canonised.

CHARLTON

IN THE CHARLTON VILLAGE CEMETERY

F.E.Smith, 1st Earl of Birkenhead (1872-1930)

Member of Parliament
Solicitor General
As Attorney General, prosecuted Sir Roger Casement
Lord High Chancellor
Secretary of State for India

Better known as F.E.Smith, Lord Birkenhead was born in the town from which he took his title. After graduating from Wadham College, Oxford, he was made a Fellow and Lecturer in Jurisprudence at Merton College in 1896, and was called to the bar by Gray's Inn in 1899. But he also craved the political life, and after two defeats he finally became a Member of Parliament for Liverpool Walton in 1906.

Because of his maiden speech, which apparently was so brilliantly unforgettable that he was immediately marked out as one of the political firebrands to watch out for, his parliamentary rise was inexorable. By 1911 he was a Privy Councillor, by 1915 Solicitor General, and then Attorney General. It was in 1916 that he demonstrated this extraordinary oratory in the trial of Sir Roger Casement.

Roger Casement had been arrested in Ireland when he was landed from a German U-boat at Tralee. He was tried for treason, and the case for the prosecution was led by the Attorney General, Sir Frederick Smith, as he then was, having been knighted in 1915. F.E.'s job was to convince the jury that Casement meant to start the Sinn Fein rebellion. He succeeded. Casement was found guilty and hanged.

After the war, F.E., by then 1st Baron Furneaux (he had married Margaret Furneaux in 1901) was made Lord High Chancellor at the early age of 47. He became a great authority on legal matters, and ruled on many famous cases.

By 1922 however, the coalition government of the 'Welsh Wizard', Lloyd George, finally tumbled, and F.E. lost his job. To compensate however, he was promoted in the peerage, and became the 1st Earl of Birkenhead.

But two years later, after turbulent depression years and three changes of government, Stanley Baldwin became Prime Minister, and made Lord Birkenhead the Secretary of State for India. Almost certainly ill at ease with this portfolio, Lord Birkenhead resigned in 1928, and returned to legal practice.

F.E.Smith, Lord Birkenhead, died at the age of 58, and was buried in the little village cemetery of Charlton where he had his country estate. He was succeeded to the Earldom by his son.

For a much deeper evaluation of this charismatic man, arguably one of the greatest figures of this century, a choice of many biographies is available.

The memorials to the Earls of Birkenhead in Charlton cemetery. The 1st Earl's tomb is on the right.

CLIPSTON

IN THE GRAVEYARD OF THE BAPTIST CHAPEL

Thomas Jarman (1776-1861)

'The Northamptonshire Composer of Sacred Music'

Thomas Jarman's day job was as a tailor. But in his spare time, he was the Clipston Baptist Chapel organist and choirmaster. He was also a prolific composer, and every single piece was written to be performed by himself and his choir in the Baptist Chapel. All in all, he composed over 1500 psalm and hymn tunes, and over 100 pieces of devotional music, many of which found their way into published anthologies of sacred music. Perhaps his best known tune is *Lyngham*, sung to the words 'Oh for a thousand tongues to sing'.

He died in 1861, and quite naturally, was buried in the grounds of the Chapel he had served for well over 70 years.

The tombstone to Thomas Jarman, in need of restoration.

COURTEENHALL

IN THE CHURCH AND CHURCHYARD OF SAINTS PETER AND PAUL

Generations of the Wake family are buried in Courteenhall. But, as with the Cartwrights of Aynho, although the family produced the following noteworthy members, only the lives of Sir Herward, the 13th Baronet and his sister, Joan, will be fully described.

Sir William, 8th Baronet (1742-1785) MP for Bedford
Sir Charles, 10th Baronet (1791-1864) and Lady Wake (1800-1888) brother in law, and sister, of Archibald Tait, Archbishop of Canterbury
Sir Herewald, 12th Baronet (1852-1916) Founder member of the Northamptonshire County Cricket Club, July 1878
Sir Baldwin Wake, KBE (1882-1951) Vice Admiral

Sir Hereward Wake, 13th Baronet (1876-1963)

Soldier, one of the 'Old Contemptibles'
Present on the First Day of the Somme
ADC to Lord Roberts, VC during the Boer War
ADC to King George V
Royal Humane Society Bronze Medallist for Gallantry

Until the introduction of a proper scheme, the awarding of medals to members of the armed forces for acts of bravery, was left to private societies. The Victoria Cross was introduced in 1856, but this was for gallantry in the face of the enemy. So for brave conduct outside this remit, there were no official awards. Thus a number of private societies awarded their own medals, and amongst the foremost of these was the Royal Humane Society.

Hereward Wake was awarded the RHS Bronze Medal when he was serving with the King's Royal Rifle Corps in the Boer War in South Africa. On Christmas Eve 1901 at Bosman's Spruit in the Transvaal, he had dived into the swollen river and rescued one of his men who had been swept away whilst crossing the river bridge, which at that time was under water.

The RHS Silver and Bronze Medals were prized, and were given for acts of bravery that nowadays would almost certainly merit the award of the George Cross or George Medal. And being 'unofficial' (that is, *not* given by the Sovereign), the RHS Medals were easily distinguishable by being worn on the right, rather than left, breast.

Whilst in the Boer War, Hereward Wake also received the Distinguished Service Order (DSO), and had the honour of being an ADC to the Supreme Commander, that most famous of Victorian soldiers, Lord Roberts of Kandahar, VC.

Hereward Wake had been commissioned into the 60th Regiment, the King's Royal Rifle Corps, in 1897 after Eton and Sandhurst. And being a regular soldier, was a member of the British Expeditionary Force that went to Flanders' Fields in August 1914.

Kaiser Wilhelm's brusque dismissal of the BEF as 'that contemptible little army', inadvertently backfired on him. Forever afterwards being proudly known as the 'Old Contemptibles', the British Expeditionary Force proved not so contemptible when it stopped, and then reversed, the German advance into France.

The Great War eventually bogged down into trench warfare, but in 1916, the Generals tried to break the deadlock. A massive attack was to take place. The date chosen was Saturday 1 July 1916, and the place - the Rover Somme.

The 'First Day of the Somme' was the blackest and most dreadful day that the British Army has ever encountered. Of the 62,000 men who went 'over the top' at 7.30am that day, an incredible 57,000 of them were killed or wounded. Hereward Wake survived.

Hereward Wake retired in 1937. Along the way he had also been awarded the CMG in 1918, the CB in 1933, the French Legion d'Honneur, and the Italian Order of the Crown. He was a Major General, and had been an ADC to King George V in 1931 and 1932.

Coming out of retirement for the Second World War, he became a King's Messenger and then was in command of the Northamptonshire Home Guard, before retiring for the second time in 1945.

During his second retirement, he wrote the history of the King's Royal Rifle Corps, along with W. F. Deedes, now Lord Deedes, KBE, ex-editor of *The Daily Telegraph*.

In 1962, he celebrated his Golden Wedding, having married Margaret 'Daisy' Benson in 1912. He died in August 1963, was cremated, and his ashes buried (in an unmarked spot) in the second Wake enclave of Courteenhall parish churchyard. In 1976, Daisy's ashes were buried alongside his.

Joan Wake (1884-1974)

Local Historian
Founder of the Northamptonshire Record Society
Founder of the Northamptonshire County Record Office
Founder and editor of *Northamptonshire Past and Present*

The study of the local history of Northamptonshire would not have been as advanced without the efforts of Joan Wake. Coming from the old Northamptonshire family of the Wakes of Courteenhall, Joan Wake was another of the gifted 'amateurs' who seem to give so much more to their fields of expertise than any professional seems to do. Joan Wake's consuming passion was the preservation of any document to do with the history of Northamptonshire.

Coming from well-to-do landed gentry, she was privately educated by governesses at Courteenhall, the family home. Up to the age of 30 she had led the leisurely work-free life of a county lady of her class, with plenty of continental travelling.

But she craved more. In 1913, she went on a two-year course at the London School of Economics studying palaeography and medieval history. She came out top in her final examination in 1915, but then went straight in to war work with the Northamptonshire District Nursing Association.

It was after the war that her real work began. She had talked with a family friend, Professor (later Sir Frank) Stenton of Reading University, who drew Joan's attention to the Lincolnshire Record Society which had been founded in 1910. He said that local history documents needed to be preserved before they all disappeared.

In October 1920, Joan Wake was the prime mover in the foundation of the Northamptonshire Record Society. But this was different to the Lincolnshire Society which only printed translations of documents. The Northamptonshire Society would be different in that it would *collect together, and preserve in an archive,* any Northamptonshire local history document.

Joan Wake, because of who she was, personally knew all the landed gentry and aristocracy of the county, and using this influence, collected together those estate papers which the families were willing to deposit, in an archive at County Hall. Thus Northamptonshire established one of (if not *the*) first of the County Record Offices.

Eventually with the influx of more and more material, the County Hall rooms became too small, and the County Record Office was moved to Lamport Hall in 1947. And when that became too small, it was moved to Delapre Abbey in Northampton, and when that became too small, it finally moved to its present-day wonderful and specially built home in Wootton Park. Joan Wake would have been amazed, and pleased, at the state of things as they are today.

She also started the Record Society's series of annual volumes, instantly recognisable in their green bindings, and edited several of these. In 1948, she established *Northamptonshire Past and Present,* the annual learned magazine of the Northamptonshire Record Society, which she also edited for a number of years, herself contributing many articles (some under pseudonyms, notably 'Tales of Whittlebury Forest' by 'Wymersley Bush').

Joan Wake was especially delighted by the award of two honorary university degrees, which she looked upon as 'acceptance' of her work by academia. She became an Oxford MA in 1953, and a Leicester LLD in 1959, and was also awarded Fellowships of the Royal Historical Society, and Society of Antiquaries. In 1960 she was honoured for her work, by being created a Commander of the Most Excellent Order of the British Empire (CBE). Joan Wake never married, and died in 1974, being buried in the second Wake enclave of Courteenhall parish churchyard.

The Wake family enclave. From left to right, Joan Wake, Admiral Sir Baldwin Wake, and Sir Herewald Wake, 12th Baronet. The ashes of Sir Herward, 13th Baronet and of Lady Wake are also buried here, but with no memorial stone.

CRANFORD

IN THE UNUSED CHURCH OF SAINT ANDREW

Matilda (Maud) Fossbrook (fl 1420s)

Nursemaid to Henry VI

Possible witness to trial and burning of Joan of Arc?

The Fossbrook family held the manor of Cranford for several generations. John Fossbrook died in 1418, leaving a widow, Matilda, also known as Maud. How or why she came to be the nursemaid to Henry VI is unknown, but probably as a well connected widow of the locality, she had connections at the great Royal household at Fotheringhay castle just a few miles away.

The Fossbrook brass in Cranford Saint Andrew.

But we know for a fact that she was Henry's nursemaid, because her monumental brass in Cranford Saint Andrew church says so. Henry VI was born in December 1421 at Windsor castle. He became King of England in September 1422 when his father Henry V died; and King of France a month later when his grandfather, Charles VI of France, died.

We can imagine Matilda fussing over the boy king at his coronation in Westminster Abbey in November 1429, when he was only eight. And can we also assume that she went to France with him in 1431, when he was ten? If she did, then she could have attended the trial of Joan of Arc which Henry VI had to attend in the spring of 1431 at Rouen, and possibly even saw the burning of Joan in May of that year. And did she still fuss over the ten year old when he was crowned King of France in Notre Dame Cathedral in Paris in the December of that same interesting year?

Pure speculation, of course, but it could have happened, and is not beyond the realms of possibility. For all this, she was paid £10 per year, but this was increased to £20 after she complained.

When she died is unknown, but she was laid to rest beside her husband in Cranford church. The translation of the monumental brass reads 'Here lie John Fossbrok Esquire who died the 7th day of the month October in the year of our Lord 1418 and Matilda his wife who was dry nurse to the lord King Henry the Sixth. To the souls of whom may God be merciful. Amen'

Reverend Nathaniel Whiting (1612-1682)

Poet and Playwright

Although ordained into the Church of England in 1639, Whiting could not accept its teachings until the Commonwealth put its own particular brand of Puritanism into practice. He replaced the ejected incumbent at Lowick in 1645, and was instituted as intruding minister at Aldwincle All Saints the same year. He was also the Headmaster at Aldwincle Grammar School.

With the Restoration of the Monarchy in 1660, the backlash restored all the incumbents who the Puritans had ejected. Whiting was therefore thrown out of his livings at Lowick and Aldwincle and lost his post of Headmaster at Aldwincle.

Not to be outdone, he set up a 'church' at Cranford in 1662 where he remained for the rest of his life. Apparently he was a very godly man with a knack for comforting the sick, and by his manner gained many converts. He died at Cranford in 1682 'of a violent fit of the wind'. He was 70 years old, and was buried in Cranford Saint Andrew church in a grave that is now unknown.

But the reason that Nathaniel Whiting is most remembered, is for his poems, and a remarkable play. Whilst at Queen's College, Cambridge, he was noted for poetry in Greek and Latin. But his best known work is *Le Hore di Recreatione, or, The Pleasant Historie of Albino and Bellama*, published in 1637. It is a massive work, 4,000 lines long, and in effect it is a novel told in verse. Some of it is quite bawdy and near the knuckle (at one point a man is in a nunnery disguised as a nun – you can guess the rest), and not at all what you would expect from a straight-laced Puritan. However, it was considered good enough to be printed in 1921 (and reprinted in 1968) in the series *Minor Poets of the Caroline Period* by Professor George Saintsbury.

CRICK

IN THE CHURCHYARD OF SAINT MARGARET

George Smith (1831-1895)

Philanthropist

Influenced Lord Shaftesbury over juveniles working in brickyards

Brought regulation to barges and canal boats

George Smith was no feather bed philanthropist. He knew what hard work was like. At the age of nine, he had had to start work in the brickyards of the Potteries, working 13 hours a day and pulling loads of 40 pounds.

But he was determined to make something of himself, and brought a few books to educate himself. He pulled himself up, and at the age of 24 was manager of a brickyard at Humberstone in Staffordshire. Wanting to discover new seams of clay he went to Coalville, and did just that. Unfortunately, he did not keep the news to himself, and others cashed in on it as well. So he did not reap the full reward, although he made a comfortable living.

But the working conditions of the young boys and girls appalled him. He discovered one young boy who weighed just 53 pounds having to pull a weight of 40 pounds, and knowing that they deserved a better life than this, burned to do something about it. In 1863, he was backed in his endeavours at improvement by Robert Baker, the Inspector of Factories. His book *Cry of Children* was published in 1871, which came to the notice of the great Lord Shaftesbury himself, already famous for his protection of factory workers, chimney sweeps and miners. As a direct result of Lord Shaftesbury's involvement, an Act of Parliament was passed regarding the inspecting of brickyards, and the regulation of the juveniles and female labour working there.

But this was dangerous stuff, and Smith's employers bitterly resented his interference with their profits. They promptly sacked him.

So Smith turned his attention to the canal people, and what he found shocked him as much as the plight of the brickyard workers had done. Immorality and drunkenness were rife, with un-educated children being totally unprotected from this seedy existence.

In 1874 he published an article in the *Fortnightly Review* and a year later, another of his great books *Our Canal Population: a Cry from the Cabins* appeared. As with the brickyards, powerful friends took this up and in 1878 a Canal Boats Bill was introduced into parliament. But this was too loosely worded to be of much use, and it failed.

In 1884 however, he did succeed, and the Canal Boats Act was passed. This provided for registration of all canal boats to a particular place so that children could receive compulsory education; it regulated sanitary conditions on board; and it appointed an Inspector of Canal Boats to oversee the workings of the Act.

Since being sacked, he had lived in great poverty, as he could not get a job. But as soon as the Canal Boats Act was passed, he received a government grant. He brought a house at Crick.

He then tried to regulate the country's gypsies as well. But this crusade proved a failure. Despite his book *Gypsy Life* of 1880 and a Moveable Dwellings Bill introduced into parliament, no reforming Act was ever achieved.

In 1886 a 'George Smith of Coalville Society' for the furtherance of his philanthropic works was established. George Smith married twice, Mary Mayfield, and after her death, Mary Lehman. He had three children.

George Smith died in June 1895 and was buried in Crick churchyard. He knew all about poverty and appalling working conditions from hard personal experience, and he never stopped working so that other people need not.

'Boats' Smith's memorial in Crick churchyard.

CULWORTH

IN THE CHURCHYARD OF SAINT MARY

Charles Bacchus (1746-1762)

An African Slave

In the early to mid eighteenth century, British trade with her colonies ensured a plentiful supply of slaves. Over 50,000 black slaves a year were transported from Africa to the sugar plantations of the West Indies. These shipments sometimes called into English ports, and it became very fashionable for aristocratic households to have pre-teenage Negro boys as domestic servants, which they viewed as 'playthings', 'toys' and 'status symbols'.

The grave of an African slave, on the south side of Culworth church

Charles Bacchus was obviously one such status symbol, and the name Charles Bacchus was given to him by his 'owners' – probably the D'Anvers family of baronets of Culworth – for 'own' him they did. However, there is just one good side, because Charles, as a status symbol, would have led a fairly pampered life, which was preferable to the life he would have had, breaking his back on the sugar plantations.

We cannot begin to know his real name, or where he came from. All we know is that he died aged 16 in an England of cold, cloud and damp, far away from his own African sunshine.

DEENE

IN THE CHURCH AND CHURCHYARD OF SAINT PETER

Sir Robert Brudenell (1461-1531)

Member of Parliament
Judge of the King's Bench
Chief Justice of the Common Pleas
Privy Councillor to Henry VIII

Robert Brudenell was educated in law at Cambridge and by 1490 was a barrister, and a Member of Parliament by 1503. In 1504 he was made a Sergeant of Law (what we would call a QC) and in April 1507 became a Judge of the King's Bench, together with the customary knighthood. On the accession of Henry VIII in 1509, he transferred to the Common Pleas, and was made a member of the Privy Council. The year 1521 saw him promoted to be the Chief Justice of the Common Pleas. In the meantime, he had bought Deene Park, which remains the family's home to this day. In 1529, he was a Commissioner to survey the lands of Leicestershire for the Duchy of Lancaster. He married twice, Margaret Wyville, and Phillipa Powre. His magnificent tomb in the Brudenell chapel in the south chancel, has his effigy dressed in judge's robes, lying between his two wives.

Anne, 1st Duchess of Richmond (?-1722)

Daughter in law to Charles II

Anne, Duchess of Richmond was a Brudenell, her father being Francis, Lord Brudenell, which is why she is buried at Deene. Already widowed, she had married a certain Charles Lennox in January 1693. But this Charles Lennox was no ordinary Charles Lennox, because he was the illegitimate son of King Charles II by his French mistress, Louise de Kerouaille, who had been created Duchess of Portsmouth. Charles Lennox (1672-1723) was created Duke of Richmond when he was three years old by his father, and went on to have a distinguished career in public service. And being half French, with a French title as well, was personally acquainted with the 'Sun King' himself, Louis XIV.

Anne and Charles' only son became the 2nd Duke of Richmond in 1723, who was the father of the four Lennox sisters, the subjects of the BBC television series *The Aristocrats*. So that makes Anne the great grandmother of Charles James Fox; and if Lady Sarah Lennox's romance with King George III had come to anything, would have been grandmother of the queen as well.

Anne, Duchess of Richmond, daughter in law to Charles II, died in 1722 and was buried in her family chapel in Deene church.

James, 7th Earl of Cardigan (1797-1868)
'Cardigan of the Light Brigade'

Half a league, half a league,
Half a league onward,
All in the valley of Death
Rode the Six Hundred.
Theirs not to reason why
Theirs but to do or die.

The Charge of the Light Brigade Alfred, Lord Tennyson

So many books have been written on James Brudenell, Earl of Cardigan and the Charge of the Light Brigade at Balaclava, that it is impossible to add anything new. His ancestral home, Deene Park, is well worth a visit on its open days, because there you will see the uniform he wore during the Charge, and the preserved head of Ronald, the horse he rode.

Whatever else may be said of Lord Cardigan, his bravery cannot be denied. He did himself what he asked his men to do, and he rode with his Light Brigade up the 'valley of Death' with cannon fire from three sides, through the Russian guns at the end, and returned the same way.

And here he lies, in Deene church, in a magnificent table tomb sculptured by Queen Victoria's favourite sculptor, Sir Joseph Boehm. His second wife lies with him, her head inclined towards him. His mother, the 6th Countess of Cardigan who died in 1826, also lies in the chapel, not far away.

'Cardigan of Balaclava'.

Reginald, 1st Viscount Dilhorne (1905-1980)

Member of Parliament for 19 years
Attorney General
Lead the prosecution against Doctor Bodkin Adams, alleged serial murderer
Lord High Chancellor

Reginald Edward Manningham-Buller was the son of Sir Mervyn Manningham-Buller, the 3rd baronet and Member of Parliament for Kettering and Northampton. After Eton and Magdalen College, Oxford, Reginald was called to the bar by the Inner Temple in 1927.

During the Second World War, he served in the Judge Advocate's Department, but in 1943 was elected unopposed to parliament as the Member for Daventry. He held this seat until 1962, although after reorganisation in 1950, it had been renamed South Northamptonshire. After the war, he was appointed QC in 1946, Solicitor General in 1951, and then Attorney General in 1954. It was while he was Attorney General, in January 1957, that he led the prosecution against Doctor John Bodkin Adams.

Doctor Adams, an Eastbourne general practitioner, had been arrested in 1956 on suspicion of hastening to their deaths his elderly lady patients, who just happened to have left him a lot of money in their wills. Certainly well over 100 wills were eventually traced naming him as a beneficiary.

The prosecution failed for various reasons, not least being a brilliant defence counsel, and the fact that Doctor Adams never took the witness stand. He was not forced to do this, but it was fairly unprecedented, and robbed the prosecution of questioning him. Doctor Adams was acquitted, but there were/are some still convinced of his guilt. Adams himself died in 1983. The Bodkin Adams case became world famous, and numerous books on it are still available.

Harold Macmillan reshuffled his Cabinet in 1962, in what has come to be known as 'The Night of the Long Knives', and it was in this reshuffle that Manningham-Buller was elevated to the peerage as the 1st Baron Dilhorne, and became the Lord High Chancellor. He advised Macmillan and his successor Sir Alec Douglas-Home on the various topics of the time, including the notorious Vassall and Profumo Affairs.

He retired in 1964, and was promoted to Viscount. In retirement he became a Lord of Appeal in Ordinary. He had married Lady Mary Lindsay, the daughter of the Earl of Crawford, and their son is the present Viscount Dilhorne. Their daughter is now Mrs Edmund Brudenell of Deene Park.

Reginald, 1st Viscount Dilhorne was buried in Deene churchyard.

The grave of Reginald, Viscount Dilhorne, Lord High Chancellor, on the north side of Deene churchyard.

DESBOROUGH

IN THE CHURCH OF SAINT GILES

Ferdinando Poulton (1536-1617)

Legal Historian
Rumoured to be involved with the Gunpowder Plot

Coming from the family which had been Lords of the Manor of Desborough for generations, Ferdinando Poulton was probably the best known of them. He was educated at both Oxford and Cambridge and was called to the bar by Lincoln's Inn in June 1559. He practised as a lawyer, but his greatest achievement is his book *Statutes at Large 1215-1560*, the year he published them.

The *Statutes* is a collection of laws and commentaries, and Poulton is generally considered to be one of the most thorough of the early English legal historians. His work was continued by Pickering, Tomlin and Raithby, and by perhaps the most famous of them all, Halsbury, whose work is still used today.

Those are the facts about Ferdinando. However, there is just one more thing to say.

He was a devout Roman Catholic and as such was no lover of the political situation under James I. The story goes that the Gunpowder Plot was devised at Desborough either by Ferdinando himself, or by one of his tenants.

Robert Catesby, as a fellow Roman Catholic and fellow county landowner, visited Poulton regularly. On one occasion, Poulton's servant got wind of his master's discontent and possibly his thoughts about getting rid of the king, and mentioned this to Catesby's servant. But the servant added that Poulton, although he thought along such lines, would never carry it through. Catesby's servant however, said that his master would, and he would tell him at the earliest opportunity. The rest, they say, is history.

Fanciful rubbish? Who is to say, but for some time afterwards, it is a documented historical fact that a cottage in Desborough was regarded by the locals as being the place where the Plot was hatched. Poulton, however, was never in any way implicated by the purge which followed the discovery of the Plot, and he lived happily on for another 12 years. He died in 1617, and was buried in the chancel of Desborough (Anglican) Church.

DINGLEY

IN THE CHURCH YARD OF ALL SAINTS

Ethel, Countess Beatty (1874-1932)

Daughter of the inventor of the department store system
Wife of Earl Beatty, co-victor of the Battle of Jutland

Ethel Field was an extremely wealthy American heiress. Her father was the famous Marshall Field (1835-1906) of Chicago. It was Marshall Field who in 1865 had pioneered the department store system, by founding Marshall Field and Co., the world's first, and for a long time, largest, department store in the world.

She had married an Englishman, Arthur Tree when she was 16 and had come to live in England. However, despite having a son, Ronald, the marriage foundered.

The now almost indecipherable tomb of the Countess Beatty.

And then she met David Beatty. He was by then a dashing Captain in the Royal Navy, and the spark between them was obvious. Much to the opposition of both families, Ethel Tree divorced her husband and married David Beatty in 1901.

Even in Edward VII's liberal times, a divorced woman was frowned upon. It was only her immense wealth that eventually provided the means to overcome this, and she was eventually accepted at Court, which was what she had set her heart upon.

The life of this woman is fascinating. Alleged to have had character defects brought about by a spoilt upbringing by enormously wealthy parents, her life with Beatty was far from easy. However, there is no doubt that Earl Beatty, as he became, was devoted to her, and when she died in July 1932 at Dingley Hall, which the couple had brought, he was distraught. At the funeral in Dingley churchyard, apparently it was the only time that Captain William Grint, Beatty's Flag Officer, had seen tears in his Admiral's eyes.

Countess Beatty was buried in a double grave, the idea being that Earl Beatty should be buried there also. Not to be however, as, befitting a national hero, he was buried in Saint Paul's Cathedral just four years later. This rather sad separation is recorded on Countess Beatty's Grave.

EAST CARLTON

IN THE CHURCH OF SAINT PETER

Sir Geoffrey Palmer, 1st Baronet (1598-1670)

Member of the Long Parliament
Prosecutor of the Earl of Strafford
Attorney General

Whilst one Northamptonshire man, Sir Richard Lane, was Strafford's defence counsel, another, Geoffrey Palmer, was his prosecutor. Palmer had been elected to the Long Parliament in 1640 as the Member for Stamford, after being called to the bar by the Middle Temple.

Thomas Wentworth, the 1st Earl of Strafford, was Charles I's favourite. He was Charles' agent in Ireland and was vigorous in Ireland and Scotland in obtaining money for the king by whatever means he could think of, which of course, deeply upset the locals. He was Charles' advisor, and it was Strafford who urged the king more and more to despotic action.

His inevitable downfall came when he urged the king to send the parliamentary leaders to The Tower, when Charles' regime was on the point of collapse in 1640. In revenge, Wentworth was arrested by parliament, and was placed on trial for his life in March 1641. Charles then completely disowned Strafford and abandoned him.

Sir Geoffrey Palmer was entrusted with the prosecution of Strafford. But he failed. It was only the brilliant and spirited oratory of Strafford's defence counsel, Sir Richard Lane, which stopped him from being beheaded. Charles however, eventually had to agree to Strafford's execution in May 1641, because of enormous political pressure.

Incidentally, Sir Richard Lane was a Northamptonshire man, living at Kingsthorpe. He was a staunch royalist, who eventually died in exile in Jersey. His wife, however, stopped at Kingsthorpe, where she is buried in the chancel of the church, although her tombstone has long since vanished.

So Geoffrey Palmer was on the same side as Parliament. Or was he?

In 1641 he disagreed with John Hampden in a debate in the House of Commons, and apparently bloodshed was only avoided by the intervention of other Members. Nor surprisingly, he was thrown into The Tower for a year, and when released, went to join the king at Oxford. King Charles held his own parliament whilst he was besieged at Oxford, and Palmer sat in this, and was with the king throughout the siege. When Oxford surrendered in June 1646, all Palmer's estates were confiscated, and he was fined.

We next hear of him in June 1655 when he was imprisoned for three months for trying to raise a regiment against Parliament. Thankfully in 1660, the monarchy was restored. Geoffrey Palmer was knighted, and then made a Baronet by Charles II who made him Attorney General in 1660. He remained as Attorney General for the rest of his life.

He was a good law reporter. He edited the Law Reports of the King's Bench from 1619 until 1629, and these are noted for their accuracy. He married Margaret Moore and they had four sons and three daughters. He died in 1670 and was buried in the church of his country estate.

The imposing monument to Charles II's Attorney General in East Carlton church.

EAST HADDON

THE NEW CEMETERY, HOLDENBY ROAD

Annie Pritchard (1860-1892)

Murder victim of Andrew George McRae

Annie Pritchard lived with her family in Birmingham. In 1892 she was 32 years old and unmarried, which is probably why in March of that year, when she was nearly five months pregnant she was forced to move away before enough of her condition showed to scandalise her unknowing family. The baby's father was Andrew George McRae, a 36 year old married man, with children, who lived close to the Pritchard home.

By his later actions, we can assume that McRae was none too pleased with Annie's condition. He was trapped. What could be done? He had to devise a plan whereby he could be rid of Annie and her baby in such a way as she would not be missed. His plan was ingenious.

McRae's brother, Edward, owned his own bacon curing business in a warehouse in Dychurch Lane, Northampton, plus a stall on Northampton market. It was an easy matter for Andrew to leave his family in Birmingham and come to Northampton on the pretext of working for his brother. This he did, taking lodgings in Saint John Street. He then arranged for Annie to come and join him, and she arrived in March 1892.

Before leaving home, however, Annie had told her parents, in a story obviously concocted by McRae, that she was going to Liverpool to marry a man called Anderson. But when she arrived at Northampton railway station, she persuaded a stranger who was travelling to Liverpool, to post a letter when she arrived there.

In this letter Annie said that she had arrived safely in Liverpool, but that the man Anderson, was taking her to live in New York. In this way, McRae hoped that Annie would appear to her family to be in America, and so would not be missed, probably for several years.

Posing as man and wife, Annie Pritchard and Andrew McRae thus set up home in Saint John Street, Northampton, and there in June 1892, Annie was delivered of their baby. McRae was now faced with getting rid of Annie and her baby.

At 8pm on the evening of Wednesday 20 July 1892, McRae got Annie to leave Saint John Street with him on the pretext of seeking new lodgings in Derby Road. This was the last time she was seen alive.

On Sunday 7 August near to the village of East Haddon, the headless and armless torso of a young woman was found in a sack dumped in a ditch. The sack bore the words *E.McRae*. These sacks were fairly commonplace, and so not much notice was taken of it at first.

Eventually however, at the request of the County Constabulary, the Northampton Borough Police (there were two separate forces in those days) searched the McRae warehouse in Dychurch Lane. And what they found convinced them that here was the murder scene, because in the copper used for curing bacon, were found traces of human hair and fat, and human bones in the fire underneath.

The case against Andrew McRae was overwhelming. It was thought that he had murdered Annie and her baby at Dychurch Lane on the evening of Wednesday 20 July, and in the copper had boiled down the body of the baby, together with Annie's head and arms.

Because he could not destroy the whole of Annie's body, or had become so revolted by his ghoulish task, he had taken the remains of Annie, wrapped them in a sack, and hidden them for some days before dumping them by the side of one of the main roads leading away from Northampton. This happened to be at East Haddon. What remained of Annie Pritchard was buried in the new cemetery at East Haddon, and a headstone erected by 'friends and sympathisers'.

Protesting his innocence, Andrew McRae was hanged at Northampton Borough Gaol on Tuesday 10 January 1893. For where he is buried, *see* Northampton's Towcester Road Cemetery.

What remains of Annie Pritchard lie under this stone at East Haddon.

EASTON MAUDIT

IN THE CHURCH OF SAINTS PETER AND PAUL

Sir Christopher Yelverton (1535?-1612)

Speaker of the House of Commons
Justice of the King's Bench
Knew Francis Bacon and probably Shakespeare
Prepared treason cases against the
Earls of Essex and Southampton
Wrote the House of Commons Prayer

Almighty God, by whom alone all kings reign and princes decree justice, and from whom alone cometh all counsel, wisdom and understanding:

We, Thine unworthy servants, here gathered together in Thy name, do most humbly beseech Thee to send down Thy heavenly wisdom from above, to direct and guide us in all our consultations:

And grant that, we having Thy fear always before our eyes, and laying aside all private interests, prejudices and partial affections, the result of all our counsels may be the glory of Thy blessed name, the maintenance of true religion and justice, and the safety, honour and happiness of the King, the public welfare, peace, and tranquillity of the realm, and the uniting and knitting together of the hearts of all persons and estates within the same in true Christian love and charity one towards another, through Jesus Christ our Lord and Saviour.

This is the prayer written by Christopher Yelverton which still opens every session of parliament. I wonder how many of our professional politicians actually listen to it, let alone take any notice of it. Perhaps if they did, the country would be better managed.

Christopher Yelverton was a barrister, and first entered parliament as Member for Brackley in 1562, and then variously for Northampton and Northamptonshire in the six parliaments to the end of Elizabeth's reign. In the 1597 parliament, he was elected Speaker of the House, and the session is famous for the queen vetoing no less than 48 Bills.

As the Queen's Sergeant (her own private barrister) in 1598, Yelverton prepared the treason case against the Earls of Essex and Southampton. Essex, the queen's former favourite, was found guilty of plotting against the queen, and was beheaded. Southampton was found guilty and imprisoned.

King James made Yelverton a Judge of the King's Bench and gave him the KCB in 1603. Sir Christopher Yelverton died in 1612, and was buried at his country seat of Easton Maudit.

In his youth, whilst studying to be a barrister at Gray's Inn, he had written and acted in a little play with Francis Bacon, a fellow student. There is a belief that Yelverton also knew Shakespeare, who moved in the same circles as Bacon, and that he saw the great man act in one of his plays *The Comedy of Errors*. Perhaps Christopher Yelverton, were he alive today, could shed some light on who actually wrote Shakespeare's plays, Bacon or Shakespeare.

Sir Henry Yelverton (1566-1629)

Member of the Addled Parliament
Attorney General
Imprisoned in The Tower
Judge of Common Pleas

One of the definitions of addled is 'barren' or 'empty', and the parliament of 1614 would be aptly named the Addled Parliament because it passed no laws whatsoever. In fact it only sat for two months.

The king, James I, wanted more money so he had called parliament together so that it could vote him some. But parliament did not play ball. It refused to pass tax raising laws until the king stopped extorting money on customs duties, which by some legal chicanery, he had done so since 1606. In a huff, the king dissolved parliament, and would not call it together again for another seven years. As the Member for Northamptonshire, Henry Yelverton had sat in the Addled Parliament.

Always very fickle in his political allegiances, Henry Yelverton was only made Attorney General in 1617 after a lot of 'to-ing and fro-ing' between the king and Francis Bacon (by then Lord Chancellor) who was unsure of his allegiance. And in 1620, Bacon was proved right.

Yelverton was suspended and tried by the House of Lords. As Attorney General, he had granted the City of London a charter, which contained certain conditions to which the House of Commons objected. He was thrown into The Tower of London and stopped there for a year. When he was released, he retired to his country seat at Easton Maudit.

But in 1625, Charles I came to the throne. He remembered Yelverton and promoted him to be a Judge of the Court of Common Pleas, where he stopped until he died in 1629. He was buried in the family vault in Easton Maudit church, next to his father, Sir Christoher Yelverton.

The impressively restored monuments to the Yelvertons.

Thomas Morton (1564-1659)

Ambassador to the Emperor of Germany
Bishop of Chester, Lichfield and Durham
Imprisoned for refusing to surrender the diocese of Durham
Lived in the Yelverton household after release
Author of the infamous *Book of Sports*

The *Book of Sports* was probably one of the most divisive books ever written. Thomas Morton had written the book whilst Bishop of Chester, and it was issued by James I in 1618. It caused a storm. It said that it was acceptable to play games and sports on Sundays after church services. Naturally the Puritans and Calvanists were horrified, and the resulting religious split just emphasised the differences that would later become some of the causes of the Great Civil War.

Morton had been consecrated Bishop of Chester in 1616. Previously he had been to St. John's College, Cambridge, gaining MA and DD degrees, and had been a lecturer there. He had been chosen to accompany Lord Eure as ambassador to Denmark and to the Emperor of Germany, and when he returned in 1606, he was made Dean of Gloucester, and chaplain to the king. Three years later, he was transferred to be Dean of Winchester and Canon of York, before going to Chester, where he penned his bombshell the *Book of Sports*.

This, however, was not his first book. In 1605 he wrote *Apologia Catholica* which was anti-Catholic, and which had brought him to the notice of the king in the first place. He followed this by *Catholic Appeal* in 1609. His one aim was to bring Nonconformists and Recusants (*see* Bugbrooke) back to the Church of England. He was translated to the diocese of Lichfield and Coventry in 1618, and then to the much richer diocese of Durham in 1632.

The only indication that a Bishop is buried here, is the Coat of Arms of Bishop Morton on a pillar next to the Yelverton tombs.

When the Great Civil War came along, he was naturally a Royalist, and because of his views, also a target for the Parliamentarians. He was seized in 1641 and imprisoned without trial for four months. But Parliament had another go at him in 1645. Parliament claimed to have dismissed him from Durham, but Morton refused to hand over the seal of the diocese, and for his defiance was clapped into gaol again. He was released in 1648, and turned out of his London house.

It was at this point that he met Sir Christopher Yelverton, who seeing his plight, offered him a home at Easton Maudit. Morton accepted, came to Easton Maudit, and stayed for the rest of his life, acting as a tutor to the Yelverton children. He always considered himself to be Bishop of Durham, despite what Parliament said.

Ironically, he outlived Oliver Cromwell, who died in 1658. Thomas Morton died in 1659, at the age of 94, and was buried in the Yelverton family vault.

Derek Nimmo (1930-1999)

Stage, Screen and Television Actor and Director

Although probably best remembered for his television series of *All Gas and Gaiters* and *Oh! Brother,* that was only a tiny part of the work of Derek Nimmo. Numerous West End starring roles, and world wide theatre tours, both as actor and director, also made Derek Nimmo a star for over 40 years. And who could forget his radio broadcasts, especially *Just a Minute*, where he continually 'clashed' with chairman Nicholas Parsons.

Derek Robert Nimmo was buried in the churchyard of Easton Maudit, where he had lived for many years.

The grave of Derek Nimmo, with the wooden cross.

EASTON NESTON

IN THE CHURCH OF SAINT MARY

Richard Fermor (?-1552)

Cloth Merchant to Cardinal Wolsey
Imprisoned as a Roman Catholic and property confiscated
Restored for having employed Will Somers, Henry VIII's favourite jester

The table tomb to Richard Fermor in Easton Neston church. The central bust above, is the only memorial to Sir William Fermor.

Of all the reasons to be remembered for in history, surely there can be none better than getting all your belongings back for having once employed the king's current favourite court jester. Richard Fermor of Easton Neston can claim just that.

By 1530, Fermor was a wealthy man. He was a wool and cloth merchant of Welsh descent, who in 1513 had obtained a licence to export wool. Trade flourished and he branched out into cloth, and became Cardinal Wolsey's cloth merchant. In 1529, he supplied the good Cardinal with cloth to the value of £124 8s 9d, a substantial sum for the times, and in 1530 he was rich enough to buy Easton Neston House and the estate that went with it.

Richard Fermor, however was a staunch Roman Catholic. During Henry VIII's religious upheavals of the early 1530s, when England became Protestant, Fermor's priest/confessor was gaoled, and Richard took a gift of money and clothing to the priest whilst he was in prison. The authorities were unimpressed by this, and because Richard Fermor was a wealthy man, a Statute of Praemunire was unleashed against him.

A Statute of Praemunire, (so named after the first words, in Latin, on the arrest warrant, *Praemunire facias* meaning *let the below named be forewarned*) was an arrest for allegedly asserting the supremacy of the Pope over the King of England. Richard was tried in 1540, and not surprisingly was found guilty. He was clapped into the Marshallsea prison and all his property confiscated.

He was released soon afterwards, but he was placed under a type of 'house arrest' at Wappenham. It was a chance remark of Fermor's that he had once employed Will Somers as a jester, who was now Henry VIII's favourite funny-man, that Henry got to hear of this, and repented, and put the wheels into motion for a return of Fermor's property. Henry died in 1547, but the wheels continued to turn, and in 1550, Richard Fermor got all his property and estate back again. He returned to Easton Neston and died there in 1552. His table tomb is in the chancel of the church of Saint Mary.

Sir William Fermor, 1st Baronet (1623-1661)

Personal friend of Charles I
Privy Councillor and Member of Parliament
Created a KCB at Charles II's coronation

William Fermor was loyal to Charles I, who had made him a Baronet and a Privy Councillor in 1641, and had given him an army command during the Civil War. During the Commonwealth, Fermor lived at Easton Neston, but being wealthy, was continually bled by Parliament. He had to pay £1400 per year for the privilege of living in his own home. In 1651, the authorities found that he had received a £300 dowry five years before, so they made him hand that over as well.

The Restoration of the Monarchy in 1660 gave blessed relief. He was reinstated as Privy Councillor and was elected as Member of Parliament for Brackley in 1661, in the so-call Pensioners Parliament, because it would sit for 18 years.

Charles II's coronation took place in April 1661, and during the ceremony William Fermor was created a Knight Commander of the Order of the Bath. But within a month, he was dead, at the age of 38. He was buried in the family vault at Easton Neston.

William, 1st Baron Leominster (?-1711)

Member of Parliament
Builder of Easton Neston House

Becoming the 2nd Baronet in 1661 when his father died, William Fermor was also Member of Parliament for Northampton in 1671 and 1679. So rich and influential did he become that he was created 1st Baron Leominster in 1692.

But it is for building Easton Neston House for which he is remembered. Commissioning Nicholas Hawksmoor in 1700 as the architect, Fermor created one of the finest stately homes in England. If you are able, go and see it, the West Front is wonderful.

One of history's ironies is that the builder of such a magnificent house has no church memorial. William Fermor, 1st Baron Leominster died in 1711, and was buried in the family vault.

Henrietta Louisa, Countess of Pomfret (?-1761)

Grand daughter of Judge Jeffreys
(of the 'Bloody Assizes' fame)
Benefactress to Oxford University

Henrietta Louisa Jeffreys was the grand daughter of the infamous Judge George Jeffreys of the 1685 'Bloody Assizes'. He died in 1689, and so it is possible that she never knew him. She became a Lady of the Bedchamber to Queen Caroline (of Ansbach, wife of George II) and at court, she met, and married, Thomas Fermor, 2nd Lord Leominster, soon to become the 1st Earl of Pomfret.

Coming to live at Easton Neston, her son, after his father's death, spent all the family money, so that he was forced to sell the art collection which his father had built up. Henrietta, however, loathed to see a set of statues go, so she bequeathed them to Oxford University. They are still there to this day.

She died in 1761 and again, there is no memorial in Easton Neston church, where she lies in the family vault. But there is a memorial to her in Saint Mary's Church, Oxford which remembers her donation to the University.

She wrote a life of Van Dyck, and a large number of letters. However, not very complimentary things about her literary prowess were said by Walpole and Lady Mary Montagu at the time, and by the *Dictionary of National Biography* of today.

Thomas, 4th Earl of Pomfret (1770-1833)
General who fought in the Peninsular War

Thomas William Fermor was an army man, and remained so all his life. His brother, George, was the 3rd Earl of Pomfret, who died without issue in 1830, so Thomas was only Earl of Pomfret for the last three of his 63 years.

Joining the 3rd Foot Guards (later the Scots Guards) as an Ensign in 1791, Thomas remained with this regiment for the rest of his life. His battle honours are many: Valenciennes and Lincelles in the Flanders Campaign of 1793; the Helder Expedition of 1799; the Egyptian campaigns; and thence into the last part of the Peninsular War, being present at the Battle of Salamanca in July 1812. For his part in the Peninsular War, he was awarded a Portuguese knighthood with the award of the 5th Class in the Order of the Tower and The Sword.

He had risen through the ranks automatically, as was the custom of the time. Lieutenant in 1794, Lieutenant Colonel by 1800, Major General in 1813 and Lieutenant General in 1825.

Thomas Fermor was also a Fellow of the Royal Society and a Fellow of the Society of Antiquaries. He died in June 1833, and was buried in the family vault at Easton Neston. His brass memorial plaque is on the north wall of the Lady Chapel.

The brass plaque to Thomas, 4th Earl of Pomfret in the Lady Chapel at Easton Neston.

ECTON

IN THE CHURCHYARD OF SAINT MARY MAGDALENE

Thomas (?-1702) and Eleanor (?-1711) Franklin

Uncle and Aunt to Benjamin Franklin

The Franklin tombstone has the plaque in front of it. The cherry tree was planted by a direct descendant of Benjamin Franklin.

Benjamin Franklin stands alongside George Washington as one of the founding fathers of the United States of America. Reading his life story is highly recommended. For generations, the Franklin family were the Ecton blacksmiths, and the great Benjamin Franklin himself, on his numerous visits back to Ecton traced his Franklin ancestors back in the Ecton registers to 1555.

Thomas and Josiah Franklin were brothers. In 1682 Joshua emigrated to America taking his wife with him. On the death of his wife, he married again, and Benjamin was the fifteenth of seventeen children, being born in 1706 in Boston. Thomas stayed in Ecton, and married his Eleanor. And here they lie, uncle and aunt to one of America's great heroes.

EVENLEY

IN THE CHURCH OF SAINT GEORGE

Sir Creswell Levinz (1627-1701)

Judge of Common Pleas
Attorney General
Prosecuting counsel against the Popish Plotters
Sat on the commission which sent Lord Russell for trial for the Rye House Plot
Fellow judge of Lord Jefferies at 'The Bloody Assizes'
Defence counsel for the Seven Bishops

Few men can lay claim to being involved in all four of the great episodes of national importance of the late seventeenth century. But Sir Creswell Levinz can. Born in Evenley, he left Cambridge with no degree, but was called to the bar by Gray's Inn in 1661. He must have been well thought of because in October 1678 he was knighted.

The Popish Plot of 1678-79 was devised by Titus Oates who spread the rumour that the English Catholics were going to murder the king, Charles II, and all the government, and replace them with a Catholic ministry. Totally false, of course, but the rumour was fanned by Titus Oates and his cronies. The inevitable backlash saw many English Catholics rounded up, tried and executed. Sir Creswell Levinz tried four of the supposed conspirators, including William Ireland, the Procurator of the Diocese of London, who was executed after being found guilty on the perjured evidence of Titus Oates himself. On the strength of his performance during the crisis of the Popish Plot, Levinz was made Attorney General.

In 1683, there was uncovered a plot to assassinate Charles II and his brother the Duke of York, later James II, at a place near to Hoddesdon in Hertfordshire called the Rye House. The Rye House Plot obviously never succeeded and was the work of only minor figures. But the government took the opportunity of getting rid of a few enemies, and implicated a lot of important political figures of the time. Included, was the son of the Earl (later Duke) of Bedford, William, Lord Russell. A commission was set up to examine the evidence against him.

Not surprisingly, he was committed for trial, and duly executed in July 1683. Creswell Levinz sat on the initial commission which sent Lord Russell for trial and ultimate death.

This Rye House Plot spawned the next crisis, known as Monmouth's Rebellion. Charles II's illegitimate son, James Scott, 1st Duke of Monmouth, a Protestant, landed from Holland in June 1685 after the Duke of York succeeded to the throne as James II. The Rye House Plot had tried to get rid of him, and the Monmouth Rebellion tried to do likewise. It failed. The Duke of Monmouth's army was defeated at the Battle of Sedgemoor (incidentally the last battle fought on English soil), Monmouth was captured and executed, and his followers hunted down. When they had all been rounded up, they were put on trial in the towns of the Western Assize Circuit, Bodmin, Exeter, Dorchester, Bristol, Winchester, Taunton, Wells, Devizes and Salisbury. The most notorious of the judges was, of course, Judge Jefferies, and during the 1685 Summer Assizes, several hundred 'rebels' were transported, and over 300 more were sentenced to death by being hung, drawn and quartered. Not for nothing are these Assizes called 'The Bloody Assizes'. Judge Jefferies, as the Lord Chief Justice of the time, was the chief judge, but he was ably assisted by Sir Creswell Levinz, who joined him on the Western Circuit, and also tried some of the rebels in London (*see* Weekley, where Sir William Montagu was another 'Bloody Assizes' judge).

But this was the last of Levinz's work for the Crown. The following year, he was sacked as a judge. The new king, James II, being Catholic, had tried to use what was called 'the dispensing power', which the king thought gave him the right to grant individuals immunity from certain laws. James was using this to advance his own followers and so rid the government of Protestants and replace them with Catholics. Levinz thought the 'dispensing power' was illegal, which, of course, upset the king, and he was dismissed.

Returning to private practice, he then changed sides and became the defence counsel in the next constitutional crisis, the trial of the Seven Bishops. In one of those historical coincidences, the prosecuting counsel against the bishops, was another man with Northamptonshire connections, Sir Thomas Powys, who was Attorney General at the time. For a description of the Seven Bishops case, *see* Achurch, Sir Thomas Powys. Powys' heart was not in his job, and the bishops were acquitted.

Sir Creswell Levinz continued at the bar and appeared in several notable cases. He had married Elizabeth Livesay in 1670, and they lived in the family estate at Evenley. He died in January 1701, and was buried in Evenley church. A splendid monument was erected over his grave, but was subsequently moved into its present position in the tower.

The almost life size statue to Sir Creswell Levinz in Evenley parish church.

FAWSLEY

IN THE CHURCH OF SAINT MARY

Edmund Knightley (?-1542)

Commissioner in the Suppression of the Monasteries

Edmund Knightley knew only too well the fickle nature of Henry VIII. Edmund was a Sergeant at Law (today known as a QC) but he had been foolish enough to oppose Henry VIII's claim to some property in 1532. And for doing so, was promptly clapped into the Fleet prison.

But whilst there, he wrote to Henry's current favourite, Thomas Cromwell, begging for release. This was obviously granted, because the next we know, Edmund became a member of Thomas's Commission to suppress the monasteries of 1535.

Edmund had married the sister of the Earl of Oxford, and that, coupled with his seat on the Commission, gave him a certain social standing and wealth. He started building his country hall on his estate at Fawsley in 1537. He died in 1542 being buried in the church of the family estate.

Well worth a visit for the monuments alone...

Richard Knightley (?-1639)

Arch Puritan and anti-royalist
Imprisoned for refusal to support the forced loan
Friends with Cromwell, Pym, Hesilrigge and Hampden

The first parliament of Charles I's reign lasted only from May to August 1625, and Richard Knightley sat for Northamptonshire. He made no secret of his Puritanism and his anti-royal feelings. When parliament was dissolved without granting the king any money, Knightley was directed to search all the Catholic houses in the county, in an attempt to waylay any money should the king try to get hold of it. Whilst searching Harrowden Hall, the home of the staunchly Catholic Vaux family, Knightley was seriously assaulted by Lord Vaux, and had to withdraw rather hurriedly.

Charles I was so concerned over Knightley's hostility, that in 1626, he made him Sheriff of Northamptonshire. This was to stop him sitting in parliament again, as county sheriffs were not eligible to sit.

...Fawsley church is packed with monuments to generations of the Knightley family

The king still wanted money, so he resorted to the tactic of the 'forced loan'. In 1627 in the famous 'Five Knights' case, Charles demanded a loan from five provincial knights, who refused, and were imprisoned. One of the knights was Sir Edmund Hampden (*see* Abingdon). Knightley, being the sheriff of the county of one of the knights, was expected to back the king. Not surprisingly, he did not. And not surprisingly either, he was promptly arrested. Despite making a defiant speech before the Privy Council, Knightley was imprisoned in the Fleet.

When he was released a few months later, not being sheriff any more, he returned to parliament as Member for Northamptonshire in March 1628. This parliament would be destined to last for a year, before being dissolved by the king, who would then try to reign without it for 11 years – the so called '11 years tyranny'.

It was in this parliament that Knightley formed close friendships with all the major players of parliament at that time, Cromwell, Pym, Hesilrigge and Hampden. Richard Knightley died in November 1639, and so did not witness the agonies of the country during the Great Civil War. He was buried in the family church at Fawsley, leaving no heirs.

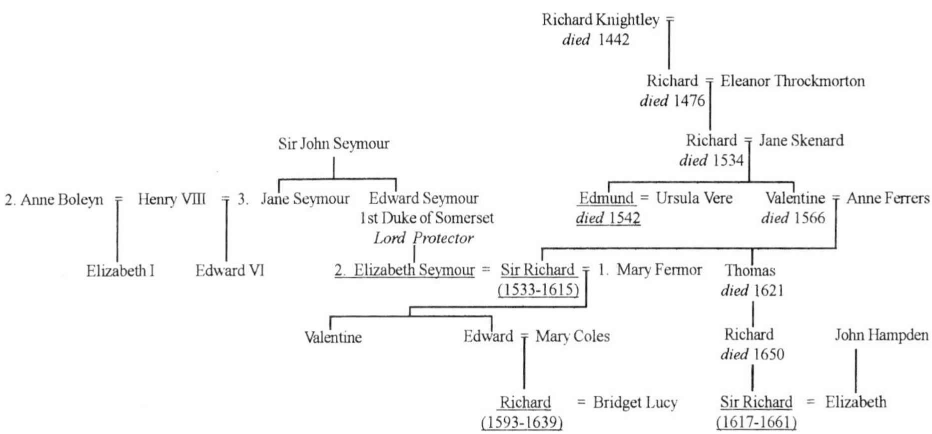

FAWSLEY AND NORTON

Much simplified Knightley family tree. Some dates omitted for clarity
Those described in the text are underlined

Sir Richard Knightley (1617-1661)

Member of the 'Short' and 'Long' Parliaments
Son in law of Hampden and friend of Cromwell
Secluded Member in 'Pride's Purge'
On Council for Restoration of Monarchy
Knighted at coronation of Charles II

Richard Knightley was a strong supporter of parliament, and had sat as Member for Northamptonshire in both the 'Short Parliament' of April to May 1640, and in the 'Long Parliament', which started in November 1640, and would continue until April 1653. He was a great friend of Cromwell, Pym and Hampden, indeed he was John Hampden's son in law, having married Hampden's daughter, Elizabeth.

Although supporting Parliament throughout the Great Civil War, he strongly disagreed with the trial of the king, and made his views known. And this led him to being ejected from the House in the famous 'Pride's Purge' of December 1648 (*see* Steane).

He was back in the first parliament after Oliver Cromwell's death in 1658, when it was apparent that Richard Cromwell did not want to go the way of his father. Knightley, because of his known views, was chosen to sit on the Council of State which arranged for Charles II to return from exile and restore the monarchy. And for his services, attended Charles II's coronation where he was awarded with the KCB.

Sir Richard Knightley died in June 1661, and was buried in the family church at Fawsley.

John Dod (1555-1645)

Nonconformist
Brother in law to Oliver Cromwell

Rector of Hanwell, Oxfordshire in 1585, John Dod was suspended for his arch Puritanical views in 1604. He was given shelter by the Puritan family of Knightley at Fawsley, and in 1637, became Vicar of Fawsley. His grandson, John Wilkins, then Vicar, was moving on to pastures new (he eventually became the Bishop of Chester) and it was natural for John Dod to take over the living. John Dod had married Robina, the sister of Oliver Cromwell, but died in 1645, before seeing his brother in law become the Lord Protector of England.

John Dod was a noted and popular author. His book *The Plain Exposition of the 10 Commandments* caused him to be known as 'Decalogue Dod' and his sayings were often quoted by the masses, what we would call today 'catch phrases'.

His most famous work however, was probably his *Sermon on Malt*. The story goes that Dod, a notorious teetotaller, forever preaching on the evils of the demon drink, was seized one day by some drunken students. They swore he would not be released until he had preached a sermon. Dod tried to use a couple of religious texts, but the students stopped him. Finally in exasperation Dod asked *them* to give him a subject. And some joker suggested 'Malt', as malt was a chief ingredient for brewing. The text is too long to be given in full, but Dod resorted to the initials of the word 'Malt' to drive his message home, and leave the drunks suitably chastened. The gist of the sermon is:

M stands for the Moral. The Moral of this sermon is to teach good manners, therefore my **M**asters, **A**ll of you **L**isten to my **T**ext
A stands for Allegorical, when you say one thing and mean another, so when you say Malt you really mean that you make Malt your
Meat, and **A**pparel, your **L**iberty and your **T**ext
L stands for Literal, which means according to the letter. So Malt means
Much **A**le-**L**ittle **T**hrift
T is the Theological, which means the effect Malt produces. And it produces two kinds, the present day life, and the after life. The effect Malt produces in this life is **M**urder in some; **A**dultery in others;
Licentiousness in all; and **T**reason for many.
In the after life, the effects of too much Malt are
Misery; **A**nguish; **L**amentation; and **T**orment.

'Decalogue' Dod died in 1645 aged 90, and was buried in the church at Fawsley

FINEDON

THE PARISH CHURCH OF SAINT MARY

Catherine Dolben (nee Sheldon) (1626-1706)

Niece of Gilbert Sheldon, Archbishop of Canterbury
Wife of John Dolben, Archbishop of York

The east end of Finedon church. The Dolben family vault is under the east window, and the Paul family vault is under the window of the south transept.

Catherine Sheldon was the daughter of Ralph Sheldon of Stanton in Derbyshire, who was a brother of Gilbert Sheldon. Because his religious views did not coincide with the Commonwealth, Gilbert Sheldon had been held under arrest in Oxford. Whilst at Oxford with her uncle, Catherine Sheldon met and married the Reverend John Dolben in 1657. Dolben, who had returned to his studies at Oxford after the Civil War (he had fought on the Royalist side, and had been wounded at Marston Moor), had just been ordained.

After the Restoration of the Monarchy, Catherine's uncle became Bishop of Rochester, and her husband became Rector of Newington, Oxford. In 1662 her husband became a Prebendary of Saint Paul's Cathedral, and Dean of Westminster; and a year later Gilbert Sheldon became Archbishop of Canterbury. And in 1666, no doubt because of his uncle-in-law's influence, John Dolben was consecrated Bishop of Rochester.

Gilbert Sheldon died in 1677, and in 1683, John Dolben became Archbishop of York. He died of smallpox three years later and is buried in York Minster.

Catherine's two sons, Gilbert and John, had married the two Mulso sisters, co-heiresses of Tanfield Mulso of Finedon, and Catherine spent her widowhood at Finedon. She died in August 1706, and was buried in the newly constructed Dolben family vault underneath the east window.

Sir Gilbert Dolben, 1st Baronet (1658-1722)

Son of John Dolben, Archbishop of York
Member of Parliament
Judge of the Common Pleas of Ireland
Instigator of the Abdication of James II

Being the son of a bishop (his father was then Bishop of Rochester), Gilbert Dolben went to Oxford University, but left without taking a degree. He was called to the bar by the Inner Temple in 1681.

In February 1685, Charles II died, and in May, his brother, as James II, called his first Parliament, something that Charles had not done for the previous four years. Gilbert Dolben sat as Member for Ripon, as by then his father was Archbishop of York, and Ripon was obviously a 'pocket borough' in the gift of the Archbishop.

That Parliament was dissolved in July 1687, and was not called again until January 1689. In the meantime great things had been happening, which historians now call 'The Glorious Revolution', which ended with King James actually fleeing the country at the dead of night.

Gilbert Dolben, now the Member for Peterborough, straightaway argued that James II in leaving England as he did, constituted abdication. This was the general mood, and Parliament did indeed force James to abdicate, asking instead his sister and brother-in-law to be the new monarchs. They accepted, and became William III and Mary II.

Gilbert Dolben continued in politics until 1713, both as Member for Peterborough and then for Yarmouth on the Isle of Wight. In 1701, he was made a Judge of the Common Pleas in the Irish courts, and in 1704 received a baronetcy. He died in 1722 and was buried in the Dolben vault.

John Dolben (1662-1710)

Son of the Archbishop of York
Member of Parliament after dissipated youth
Instigated impeachment of the Reverend Henry Sacheverell for Treason

John Dolben is the prime example of a rich young man debauching his inheritance away, but then seeing the light and making good. Born at Oxford in 1662, he was sent to Christ Church College, but left without a degree. He was called to the bar, but obviously his heart was not in it, and he took to gambling and womanising with the wrong crowd. This was not helped when his father (John Dolben, Archbishop of York) died when he was 24, leaving him a large inheritance, the majority of which went in the same fashion.

John and his brother Gilbert, married the Mulso sisters, Elizabeth and Anne, co-heiresses of Tanfield Mulso of Finedon. Marriage however, seems not to have changed our John, and his uncle (Sir William Dolben, a distinguished judge) exasperated at his nephew's conduct, packed him off to the West Indies to see if that would calm him down. It did not, and when John returned to England, he soon fell into his old ways.

William Dolben appealed to his old friend, Jonathan Trelawney, at that time Bishop of Exeter (and the Trelawney of the *Song of the Cornishmen*, 'And shall Trelawney die, here's 20,000 Cornishmen will know the reason why'). The bishop in despair, and 'in hopes of a transition of his character' gave Dolben what was obviously one of the Exeter diocese's 'pocket boroughs', that of Liskeard in Cornwall.

So John Dolben entered Parliament in 1707, and this did indeed transform him, because he became a committed and energetic politician.

In 1709, a certain Doctor Henry Sacheverell preached sermons in Saint Paul's Cathedral that severely criticised the government over handling of church matters, and actually advocated violence against political and church leaders. This caused quite a stir in an age when religious interest was far greater a talking point than it is today.

In December 1709, it was John Dolben who first drew the attention of the House of Commons to Sacheverell's sermons. Straightaway, Parliament condemned Sacheverell's ideas as seditious libel and treason. Dolben was put in charge of the impeachment process, and he chaired the Committee of Impeachment, and then delivered the Articles of Impeachment to the House of Lords. So successful was Dolben, that Sacheverell was found guilty and imprisoned. But in doing so, Dolben's health was broken, and he died in May 1710, much to the great delight of Sacheverell's followers. John Dolben was buried in the family vault at Finedon.

Sir William Dolben, 3rd Baronet (1727-1814)

Member of Parliament for 38 years
Personal friend and supporter of William Wilberforce

Educated at Christ Church College, Oxford, William Dolben at the age of 29 became the 3rd Baronet on the death of his father (the Reverend Sir John Dolben, Vicar of Finedon, and also buried in the Dolben vault). In 1768, Sir William entered Parliament as Member for Oxford University, which in those days sent Members to Parliament, a practice which continued until quite recently.

Sir William Dolben sat for Oxford University through seven Parliaments, a total of 38 years, ending in 1806 at the age of 79. During this time, he was a personal friend and supporter of William Wilberforce, and continually supported him in his attempts to abolish slavery. Wilberforce tried no less than seven times to get anti-slavery legislation passed, which eventually he did in 1807. Sir William Dolben died in 1814 aged 87.

IN THE CHURCHYARD EXTENSION, CHURCH HILL

Digby Mackworth-Dolben (1848-1867)

Poet

Frances Dolben of the Finedon family had married William Mackworth, and, as there were no male heirs to carry on the Dolben name, had changed the family surname to Mackworth-Dolben. Digby Augustus Stewart Mackworth-

Dolben was their third and youngest son. Educated at Eton, he made friends there with the future Poet Laureate, Robert Bridges.

Leaning strongly towards Roman Catholicism, Digby had made his mind up to convert Finedon Hall into a monastery. His poetry was steeped in his beliefs, and he was widely admired by Bridges, and Gerard Manley-Hopkins amongst others. Bridges later arranged all of Mackworth-Dolben's poetry into a volume published by the Oxford University Press.

Digby Mackworth-Dolben was drowned in a boating accident in June 1867 in the River Welland at Luffenham. He was buried in the family vault at Finedon. But in 1892, his body (together with that of his elder brother Herbert, a Commander in the Royal Navy who had died of tuberculosis in 1870) was moved to a new grave in the churchyard extension opposite the church in Church Hill.

The final resting place of Digby Mackworth-Dolben in the cemetery opposite the church.

From Bridges' edition of Mackworth-Dolben's Collected Poems of 1911:

A Prayer

From falsehood and error,
From darkness and terror,
From all that is evil,
From the power of the devil,
From the fire and the doom,
From the judgement to come-
Sweet Jesu, deliver
Thy servants for ever.

Reverend Samuel Woodfield Paul (1778-1847)
Reverend George Woodfield Paul (1820-1911)
Father and Son, Vicars of Finedon for over 100 years

Samuel Paul was Vicar of Finedon from 5 April 1810 until his death on 1 August 1847. His son, George, already a curate under his father, became Vicar on his father's death, and remained for 63 years, until he died on 7 April 1911.

Thus father and son between them held the living of Finedon for 101 years and 2 days, a record very rare, if not unique, and which in today's climate is certain never to be repeated. Samuel is buried in the Paul family vault under the south transept, whilst son George is buried in the churchyard extension, on the opposite side from the church on Church Hill.

The grave of the Reverend George Paul, in the cemetery opposite Finedon church, where he was Vicar for 63 years.

Arthur George Henfrey (1867-1929)
England International footballer
Captain of Northamptonshire County Cricket team

An all round sportsman, Arthur Henfrey, born at Finedon, became a 'blue' at Cambridge University in athletics and cricket. But above all, his first love was football.

Founded in 1882, The Corinthians Football Club was comprised of players from the universities and public schools, and Arthur Henfrey was a regular team member, playing and touring with them for ten years. And so good was he that he was chosen to play for England, in the centre forward position (or 'striker' for those under 35 years of age).

The Henfrey family plot, in the cemetery opposite Finedon church, and which gives no indication that an England International footballer lies here.

In all, Henfrey was capped five times, and scored goals in every appearance:

Saturday 5 March 1892 at Wrexham: Wales 0 England 2
Monday 18 March 1895 at Queen's Club, Kensington: England 1 Wales 1
Saturday 9 March 1895 at Derby: England 9 Ireland 0
Monday 16 March 1896 at Cardiff: Wales 1 England 9
Saturday 4 April 1896 at Glasgow: Scotland 2 England 1

And whilst all that was going on, he was also a member of the Northamptonshire County Cricket team, appearing in every season between 1886 and 1899, and captained the side twice, in 1895 and 1896. He was a batsman, and made two scores above 90.

He had taught briefly at Wellingborough School, of which he was an Old Boy, before returning to Finedon to involve himself in the family boot and shoe business. He remained at Finedon for the rest of his life, and forayed into local politics. Despite two attempts, he was never elected to the County Council, but was on the Finedon Urban District Council, when there was such a thing, for several years.

Arthur Henfrey died in October 1929. Ironically, he was buried in his family grave in the old cemetery, and there is no headstone to him.

FOTHERINGHAY

IN THE CHURCH OF SAINT MARY AND ALL SAINTS

Mary, Countess of Pembroke (?-1377)

Widowed on her wedding day
Founder of Pembroke College, Cambridge

Unhappiness seems to surround Fotheringhay. Not only have we the touching story of Mary Stuart, Queen of Scotland who was beheaded there, but two hundred years before that, another melancholic woman lived and was buried there. She was Mary, Countess of Pembroke.

Born Mary de St Pol, she had married Aymer de Valence, Earl of Pembroke when he was on an ambassadorial visit to the court of Charles IV of France in 1324. On their wedding day, Aymer took part in a knightly joust, as was the custom. And he was killed. Aymer and Mary had been married just three hours.

She spent the next 53 years as a widow, refusing to marry again. In 1331, her uncle, John, Earl of Richmond (himself the nephew of Edward I) obtained leave of the king at the time, Edward III, to grant Fotheringhay, which was a Royal manor, to Mary for life. She lived here in widowhood engaged in pious deeds. She was immensely rich and endowed a College at Cambridge, which she named Pembroke College in honour of her husband.

Mary, Countess of Pembroke died in 1377, and was buried in the church at Fotheringhay, which is not the present building, although the site is the same. Her grave has been lost.

Edward, 2nd Duke of York (1373-1415)

Grandson of Edward III
Cousin of Richard II
Died at the Battle of Agincourt

Imagine if you will, approaching Fotheringhay church up the long gravel path. Suddenly music is heard. Not the modern, simplistic and naïve 'thump-

FOTHERINGHAY

Much Simplified Plantagenet Family Tree

Those buried at Fotheringhay shown in **BOLD CAPITALS**

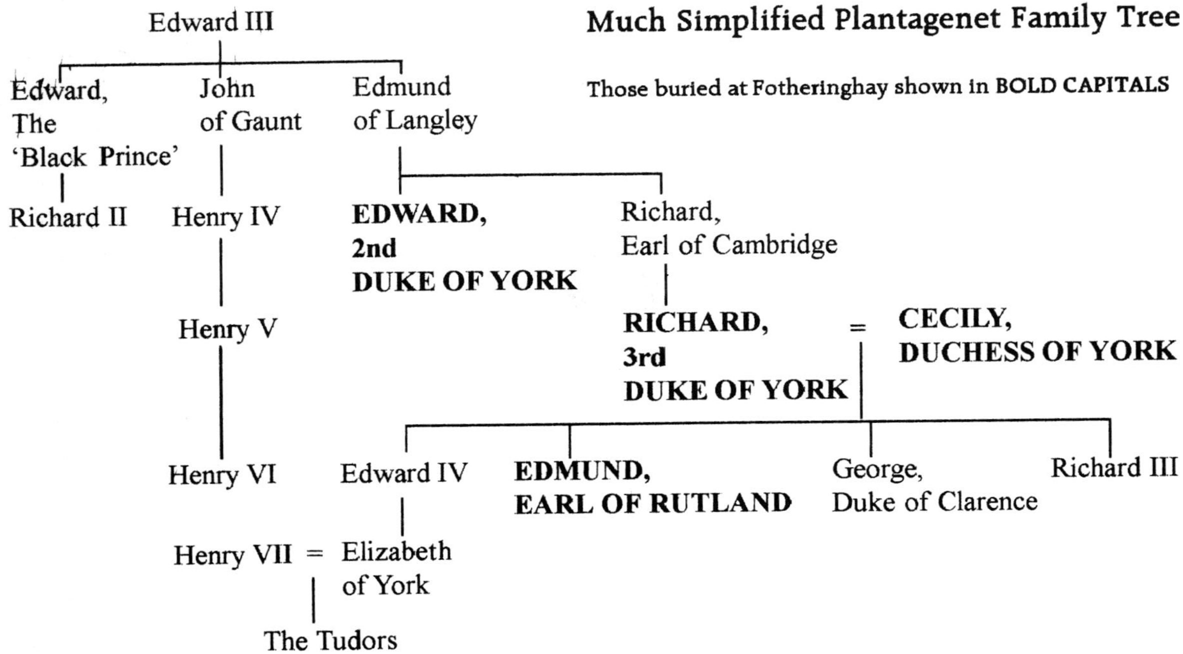

thump-thump' rubbish, but something 'different' – 'older' sounding.

In the past few years, there have been reports by perfectly sane and sober people of hearing medieval music coming from Fotheringhay church. But on entering, the church is always empty. It is thought that the sound of trumpets and drums is the ghostly echoes of the funeral of Edward, Duke of York, who was buried at Fotheringhay, after dying at Agincourt.

Edward's father, Edmund of Langley was the fourth son of Edward III, which makes Edward nephew to both the 'Black Prince' and John of Gaunt. Being a medieval prince, he was much involved in the intrigues and machinations of medieval England. Not only that, but honours were given to him automatically: KG in 1387; Earl of Rutland 1390; Admiral of the Fleet 1392 (he was 19); Earl of Cork 1396.

In 1388, his cousin Richard II, had lost a civil war which had put his opponents (called the Lords Appellant) in charge of what was to be called 'The Merciless Parliament'. By execution, exile and other general nastiness, this Parliament gradually got rid of Richard's allies. By 1397, however, Richard had sufficiently recovered to attack the Lords Appellant and dispose of them. He was helped by his cousin Edward of York, who was consequently given large amounts of land, created Duke of Albermarle and given the office of Constable of England.

But within a couple of years, Richard was deposed by another cousin, Henry of Bollingbrooke (and one of the Lords Appellant) who took the throne as Henry IV. So Edward was deprived of all his offices.

But in 1402, Edward's father died, and he became the 2nd Duke of York, much too much a powerful figure for Henry IV to tamper with any further, and Edward gradually regained some of his offices.

Henry IV died in 1413 to be succeeded by his son Henry V. Henry restored Edward to all his remaining titles, and gave him an army command.

The Battle of Agincourt on Friday 25 October 1415 ranks alongside Waterloo as one of the great victories of all time. The much bigger French army was annihilated, Henry V became an instant hero, and went on to capture the whole of Normandy.

But there were some English casualties, and Edward, Duke of York was one. He was put in command of the English right flank. But his death is somewhat bizarre, as he was pulled out from underneath a pile of corpses. He had not been killed, but had either suffocated or had died of a heart attack.

His body was brought home to Fotheringhay and was buried in the choir of the Collegiate Church, to funeral music of trumpet and drums. Music, it seems, which can still be heard today.

Richard, 3rd Duke of York (1411-1460)
Heir presumptive and Lord Protector of England
Father of two English Kings
'Started' the Wars of the Roses
Killed at the Battle of Wakefield

Being descended on his father's and mother's side from Edward III, Richard, who became Duke of York when he was three, would have had the greatest claim on the English throne had Henry V died childless. But Henry had a son, who became Henry VI when he was only six months old. And there we have the seeds of the Wars of the Roses.

Although seeming to serve the king (who in fact was his second cousin once removed) by being Henry's governor in France, by 1440 the king and the court regarded Richard with suspicion as they thought he had his eye upon the throne. So in 1447, he was made Lieutenant of Ireland. Richard, who wanted to stop in France at the hub of things, saw this as banishment. But he went to Ireland, nevertheless, and there was starved of money by the Exchequer.

In the meantime, France had managed to recover Normandy. Outraged at this, and because he had lost a lot of valuable property there, Richard promptly came back to England in September 1450. Incidentally, it was at this point that William Tresham the Chancellor of the Duchy of Lancaster whilst secretly on his way to meet him, was murdered at Moulton (*see* Sywell). Henry had no intention of letting Richard get his toe back in the door, but Parliament wanted Richard to be regarded as Heir Presumptive.

Henry characteristically did nothing, and Richard tried to force the issue by raising an army against him in 1452. But Fate intervened. Henry quite suddenly went into a bout of temporary insanity.

Faced with this, the court had to give in to the demands of Richard. They made him Lord Protector of England and Heir Presumptive. This was 1453. Two years later, Henry recovered, and promptly dismissed Richard. It was this act that caused the Wars of the Roses – Richard of York against Henry VI of Lancaster.

It was Richard who won the first battle of the Wars, Saint Albans in 1455. He was reappointed Lord Protector, but Henry took this away three months later. Things went badly, and in November 1459, Richard was proclaimed a traitor, and he fled to Ireland. But after the Earl of Warwick had captured Henry at the Battle of Northampton (near to the present day site of Delapre

Abbey) in 1460, Richard returned, and Parliament again proclaimed him Heir Presumptive.

Marching north to meet a fresh challenge from the Lancastrian forces, Richard was killed at the Battle of Wakefield. After death, his body was decapitated, and his head stuck on a pole in York with a paper crown upon it. He was buried at Pontefract, but his widowed Duchess of York later removed his remains (and those of his son Edmund) to Fotheringhay.

Edmund, Earl of Rutland (1443-1460)

Brother to Edward IV and Richard III
Killed at the Battle of Wakefield

Born in Rouen in France, Edmund was created Earl of Rutland when he was three. Possibly he had no choice, but he had followed his father, Richard, Duke of York, in his attempts upon the throne.

Edmund went with his father to Ireland in 1459, and returned to England with him a year later. He, also, was killed at the Battle of Wakefield. He was just 17. His remains, along with those of his father, were removed to Fotheringhay.

Cecily, Duchess of York (1415-1495)

The 'Rose of Raby'
Mother of two English Kings

Cecily, or Cecilia, Neville, was the daughter of Ralph, 1st Earl of Westmorland. Her mother was a daughter of John of Gaunt, which makes her the great granddaughter of Edward III. She was born at Raby Castle in Durham and was called the 'Rose of Raby'. She had married Richard, Duke of York in 1438 and eventually had 14 children, eight of whom died in infancy.

She certainly saw the ups and downs of life. She had seen a husband and son killed at the Battle of Wakefield. She also saw another son become Edward IV, get deposed, become king again, but die peacefully in 1483.And she saw another son, George, Duke of Clarence, murdered by drowning in a butt of malmsey in 1478. Her greatest tragedy, though, was to see her only remaining son become Richard III, only to die horribly and despised on the Field of Bosworth. But happily, she then saw her grand daughter become queen of

England and start off another dynasty by giving birth to her great grandson in 1491. And it was this great grandson who became probably the best known of all the English kings, Henry VIII.

Cecily, the 'Rose of Raby' saw it all. She died in a Benedictine nunnery in Hertfordshire, aged 80 in 1495. She was buried alongside her husband and son at Fotheringhay.

The Plantagenet monuments on either side of the High Altar

GAYTON

IN THE CHURCH OF SAINT MARY

George Butler (1774-1853)
Headmaster of Harrow school for 24 years

Being a Headmaster for 24 years between 1805 and 1829, George Butler must have influenced thousands of schoolboys. And coming from one of the two most famous British public schools, these are the generations that built and administered the British Empire when it was at its dazzling height. His son Henry also grew up to be Headmaster of Harrow, and was lucky enough to be the Headmaster when a certain Winston Churchill started there.

Born in London in July 1774, George was the son of the Reverend Weedon Butler who was secretary to the notorious Reverend William Dodd. Dodd was struck off the list of Royal Chaplains when he was caught trying to solicit for preferment by toadying to the Lord Chancellor, and then rapidly going downhill, was executed for forgery in 1777, one of the few clergymen to be executed for non ecclesiastical crimes. This seems not to have affected Weedon, and he went on to be the Preacher at Pimlico Chapel and keep a school in London's West End.

Weedon's son, George, was apparently nearing genius level. At Cambridge he was Senior Wrangler in 1794. The Senior Wrangler was the student who gained the highest marks in the final examinations for mathematics, followed by the Second Wrangler who got the next highest marks, and so on. He was fluent in French, German and Italian, was proficient in physics and chemistry, and on top of all that, was an all round sportsman as well.

He was ordained in 1804, taking the BD degree, and a year later the DD degree. It was in that year he became Headmaster of Harrow, where he remained for 24 years.

In 1814, he became the Rector of Gayton, which is in the gift of his Cambridge college, Sidney Sussex. Four years later, he married Sarah Gray of London.

Starting to suffer from heart and eyesight problems, Butler gave up the Headmastership of Harrow in 1829, and returned to Gayton to live the life of a country parson. He became the Chancellor of the Diocese in 1836, and in 1842, the Dean of Peterborough, but his health deteriorated so much, that he eventually became totally blind.

Whilst sitting at the dinner table in the Deanery at Peterborough in 1853, at the age of 79, he suffered a stroke, and died within ten minutes. George Butler was buried in Gayton church, where he had been the Rector for 39 years.

The monument to George Butler, above the fourteenth century tombs of Scholastica de Gayton, and Mabila de Murdak

GRAFTON UNDERWOOD

IN THE CHURCH OF SAINT JAMES

Richard, 1st Baron Gowran (?-1727)

Royal Navy captain
Present at the Battle of Vigo Bay

By marrying the daughter of Sir John Robinson of Cranford. That is the explanation of why an Irish sea captain comes to be buried at Grafton Underwood, almost as far away from both the sea and Ireland as it is possible to get.

Richard Fitzpatrick had joined the Royal Navy, and by 1687 with the rank of Commander was captain of HMS *Richmond*. He remained in the Navy until 1702, by which time he had worked himself up the chain of command, and was now a Captain of HMS *Ranelagh* an 80 gun ship of the line, and had been involved in many battles and campaigns.

The War of the Spanish Succession broke out in 1700 when Charles II of Spain died, and nobody could agree on who should inherit his possessions. The English allied themselves with the Dutch against the French and Spanish.

During an expedition of 1702, Richard Fitzpatrick in command of HMS *Ranelagh*, was part of the Anglo-Dutch fleet which captured a vast amount of Spanish gold and silver bullion at the Battle of Vigo Bay. All this was brought back to England where it was used to mint coins. In commemoration, all the coins minted with this bullion have the word 'Vigo' underneath the head of Queen Anne. These coins are still available to collectors.

Entering politics after leaving the Navy, Fitzpatrick was Member of Parliament for Harristown, and then for Queen's County in the Irish parliament. For this, in 1715, he was created the 1st Baron Gowran in the Irish peerage. He married Anne Robinson and came to live in Grafton Underwood.

He died in 1727 and was buried in what was to become the family vault at Grafton Underwood. His son became the Earl of Upper Ossory, and his grandson, another Richard Fitzpatrick, became one of the political live wires of the eighteenth century, forming a life-long friendship with that most charismatic of politicians Charles James Fox.

The monument to Lord Gowran...

...which is opposite to another one for him, which claims his descent from the Sir Barnaby Fitzpatrick who killed the Irish rebel Rory O'Moore when he attacked The Pale around Dublin in 1577/78.

GREAT ADDINGTON

IN THE CHURCH OF ALL SAINTS

Sir Henry Vere (?-1516)

'Cousin' to Henry VII

Fought at the Battle of Bosworth 1485

Sir Henry Vere lies in his tomb at Great Addington. His effigy on the tomb is dressed in armour, which is supposed to be a copy of the armour he wore when he was fighting in the Battle of Bosworth in August 1485. The Battle of Bosworth is where Henry Tudor defeated Richard III, and then took the crown as Henry VII, the first Tudor monarch. Henry Vere obviously fought on Henry's side, because they were distantly related. The two were 'cousins', or to be more accurate, 'step-cousins, once removed' would be a better description.

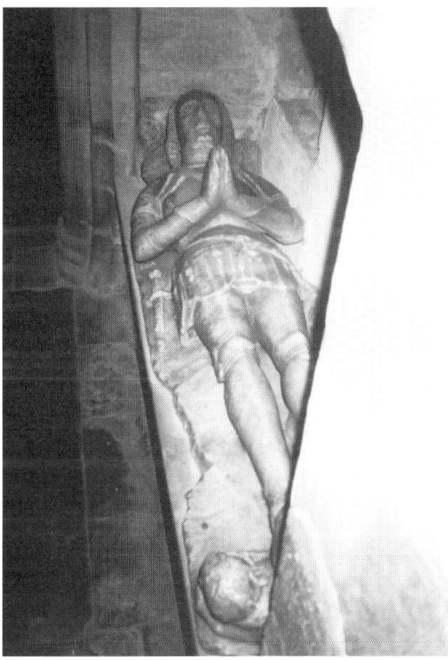

Henry de Vere in the armour he wore at thc Battlc of Bosworth.

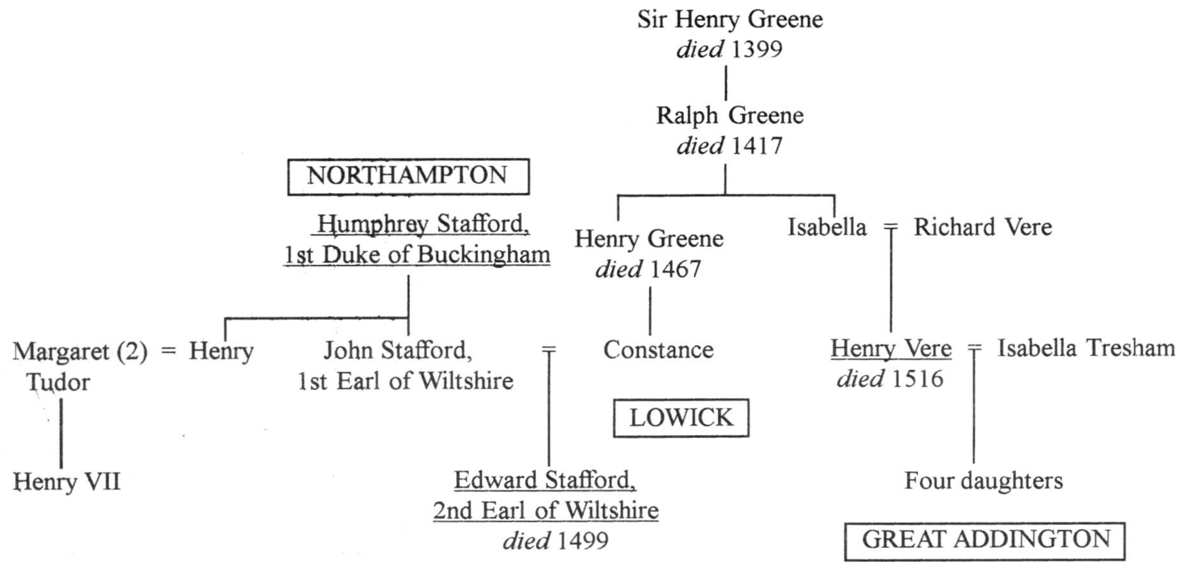

GREAT ADDINGTON, LOWICK AND NORTHAMPTON

Much simplified Greene, Vere and Stafford family tree. Some dates omitted for clarity
Those described in the text are underlined

GREAT BILLING

IN THE CHURCH AND CHURCHYARD OF SAINT ANDREW

Henry, 7th Earl of Thomond (?-1691)

A descendant of Brian Baru, King of the Irish

Henry O'Brien's father, the 6th Earl of Thomond, came from Ireland to England to fight on the side of Charles II during the turbulence of the 17th century. As a result he received an English peerage to add to his Irish one; he became the Marquis of Billing, and received the Manor of Billing as well. His son, Henry, 7th Earl of Thomond and 2nd Marquis of Billing remained in England and was buried in Saint Andrew's church after he died in 1691.

This memorial to the Earl of Thomond is probably not the greatest example of the sculptors' art.

Thomond is a part of Ireland, and as befits the name, the O'Briens claim descent from the best known of all the Irish kings, the chief king himself, Brian Baru (926-1014). It was Brian who having united all of Ireland under his rule in 1001, then turned his attention to ridding Ireland of the Danes. He was partly successful at the Battle of Clontarf in 1014, but was murdered soon afterwards.

IN THE ROMAN CATHOLIC ENCLAVE OF THE CHURCHYARD

Gervase Elwes (1866-1921)

World renowned singer
Friend of Brahms, Elgar, Vaughan-Williams, Percy Grainger and Sir Henry Wood

"He was one of those rare souls to whom ideals of art were indistinguishable or inseparable from ideals of living" wrote the obituarist of *The Observer* in 1921. A few years earlier, *The Times* had said of Gervase Elwes "that he gave another of those recitals that made people wonder how it is a song can be so perfectly satisfying a thing". Gervase Elwes was regarded by many as the leading tenor of his day, his most famous role being the tenor lead in Elgar's *Dream of Gerontius*. And when a bizarre accident robbed the world of his voice at the age of 55, the shock of this loss was profound.

Gervase Henry Cary-Elwes was born at Billing in November 1866, the son of Valentine Cary-Elwes. Billing had been in the Cary-Elwes family since 1795, and they were well respected by their tenants despite converting to Roman Catholicism in 1874. After The Oratory School in Birmingham, Gervase went to Eton and then to Christ Church College, Oxford, but left with no degree.

He entered the Diplomatic Service and went to Munich in 1891. It was there that someone suggested he consider a musical career after they had heard him sing, and suggested that he apply to go to Vienna, the undisputed musical capital of Europe, perhaps the world. He did just that, and obtained a post at the British Embassy in Vienna, and it is there that he became on friendly terms with Johannes Brahms.

The death of his father forced him back to Billing to manage the family estate, but the idea of a singing career never left him. He studied in London and Paris, and after his tutor Henry Russell suggested taking the step, he adopted the stage name of Gervase Elwes and made his professional singing debut on Christmas Eve 1902. His success was instant. Tours of Europe and America followed with regularity, and he became absorbed by the musical life of the country. During those years, he met all the 'greats' of British music.

During the Great War, he gave concerts to the troops in France. Four of his six sons also served in the War, and all survived. He had married Lady Winefride Fielding, daughter of the Earl of Denbigh in 1899, and they had six sons and two daughters.

The 1920 North American Tour began with a concert in Winnipeg, followed by ones in Washington and New York. On Wednesday 12 January 1921, Gervase and Lady Winefride alighted from the train at Boston's Backbay Station. Realising that he had picked up the wrong coat, Gervase turned back and tried to get back on the train. He slipped and fell between the platform and the moving train. He died from his injuries a few hours later.

Dudley Charles Cary-Elwes (1868-1932)
5th Roman Catholic Bishop of Northampton

Brother to Gervase Elwes, Dudley kept the family surname of Cary-Elwes. He was also educated at The Oratory School in Birmingham, but went to Rome to prepare for the Catholic priesthood. He was ordained in 1896, became a Curate at Peterborough, and thence to a Curacy at Luton in 1898. He was Diocesan Inspector of Schools from 1907 and Rector of the Roman Catholic Church at Peterborough from 1910 until 1921.

He had been made a Canon of Northampton in 1912, and when Frederick Keating, 4th Bishop of Northampton died in 1921, Cary-Elwes was consecrated as the 5th Bishop of Northampton. He died in 1932, and was buried next to his brother in Great Billing Roman Catholic cemetery.

Francis Gerard Thomas (1930-1988)
9th Roman Catholic Bishop of Northampton

Born in Stone in Staffordshire, Francis Thomas prepared for the Roman Catholic priesthood at Oscot College, Sutton Coldfield. He was ordained in 1955, and served as a Curate at Saint Peter's, Leamington Spa.

Three years at the Gregorian University in Rome followed, and he returned in 1959 to lecture in Theology at Oscot College, becoming Rector there from 1968 until 1979. In 1979, he was parish priest at the Holy Trinity, Newcastle under Lyme, at the same time as being a Canon and Vicar General of the Diocese of Birmingham. He was consecrated as 9th Bishop of Northampton in 1982 and remained until his death in 1988.

The Roman Catholic cemetery at Great Billing parish church. The large cross is to Gervase Elwes, the central cross is to Bishop Cary-Elwes, and the grave of Bishop Thomas is to the right, just out of shot.

GREAT BRINGTON

IN THE CHURCH OF SAINT MARY

Robert Washington (1544-1620)

Great great great great grandfather of George Washington

Robert Washington was the son of Lawrence Washington of Sulgrave, and who lies in the church there. Robert inherited the manor of Sulgrave in 1584 when his father died.

The grave of Robert Washington and his second wife, in the nave of Great Brington church. These brass tablets are normally protected by wooden covers.

In May 1601, Robert gave a portion of the Sulgrave estate to his son, another Lawrence. Over the next nine years, this Lawrence gradually sold off his share of the Sulgrave estate to his cousin, Lawrence Makepiece. Lawrence Washington then rented the manor of Wicken, where he started living.

Meanwhile his father, Robert, continued to live at Sulgrave. His first wife, Elizabeth (nee Light) had died, and he had married his housekeeper, Anne Fisher. Because his son, Lawrence died four years before he did (in 1616) and was buried at Brington, Robert was not buried with his father at Sulgrave, but with his son at Great Brington.

The grave of Lawrence Washington in the chancel, underneath Victorian choir stalls.

Lawrence Washington (c1568-1616)

Great great great grandfather of George Washington

The Washington family and the Spencer family of Great Brington were related, and when Lawrence Washington sold his portion of Sulgrave manor in 1610, he rented the manor of Wicken, which was owned by his third cousin, Robert,1st Lord Spencer. Lawrence Washington died young, aged 48 in 1616, which was still during his father's lifetime. His younger brother, Robert, and his wife Elizabeth, had farmed in Brington for many years, so because of the family connection there, Lawrence Washington was buried in Great Brington church.

Robert, 1st Baron Spencer (?-1627)

Reputed to be the richest man in Britain

The Stuart monarchs were always on the look out for more money. And what better way to get some, than befriend the richest man in Britain. This is exactly what James I did when he became King of England in 1603.

Sir Robert Spencer (Elizabeth I had knighted him in 1600) was the target, because he was the richest man in Britain, having made his immense wealth from sheep breeding and dealing in wool. So in July 1603, after being king for just three months, James I ennobled Robert Spencer as the 1st Baron Spencer of Wormleighton. Spencer owned Wormleighton, just over the Warwickshire border, as well as Althorp.

Lord Spencer was a warm supporter of Henry Wriothesley, the Earl of Southampton, another of James' favourites. Indeed, his son William married Penelope, Southampton's daughter (or supposed daughter – see below). It is highly possible, that moving in the same circles as the Earl of Southampton, Spencer knew William Shakespeare, who was Southampton's protégé.

Robert Spencer had married Margaret Willoughby of Wollaston, but she died in 1597, just after the birth of their second son William, who was to become the 2nd Lord Spencer. Robert Spencer never married again, and was 30 years a widower. Margaret and Robert Spencer both lie together in the Spencer family vault at Great Brington.

A lovely chapel in a lovely church; the magnificent Spencer family chapel in Great Brington church.

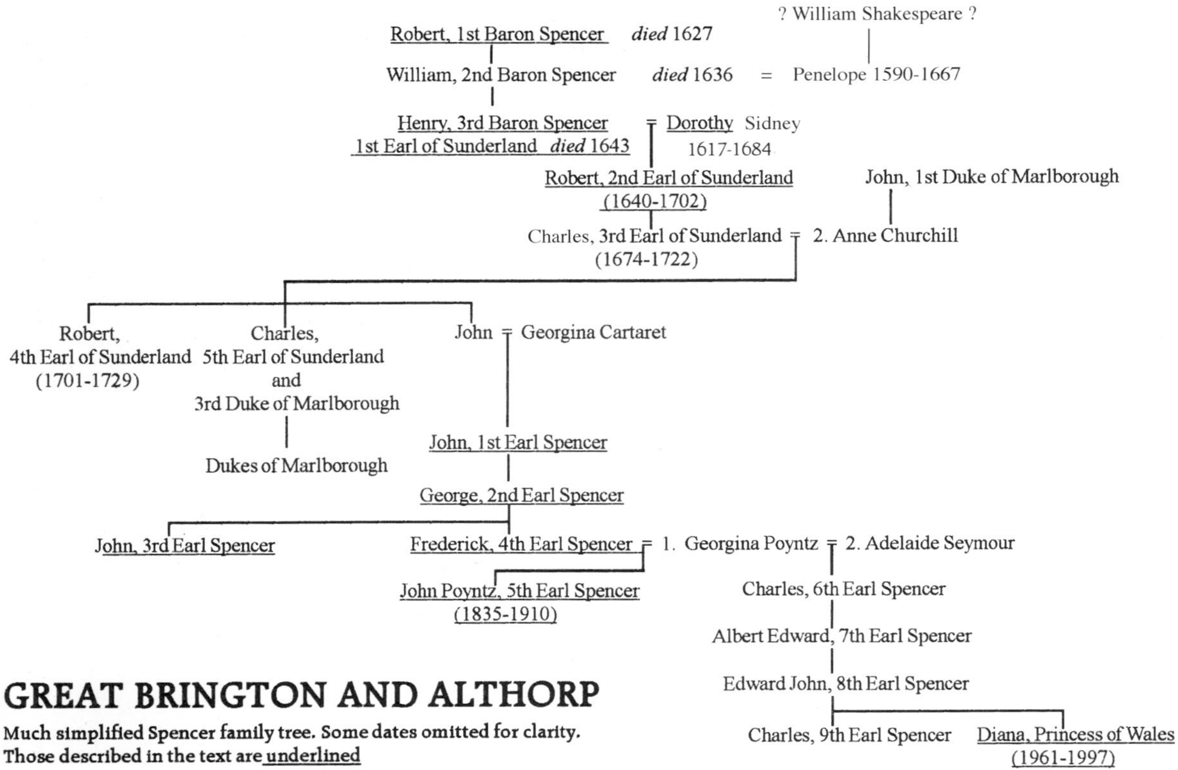

GREAT BRINGTON AND ALTHORP

Much simplified Spencer family tree. Some dates omitted for clarity. Those described in the text are underlined

William, 2nd Baron Spencer (1596?-1636) Penelope, 2nd Baroness Spencer (1598-1667)

? Shakespeare's daughter ?

Do we have here the solution of a mystery that has baffled experts for over 300 years? Nobody knows for certain the identity of Shakespeare's 'Dark Lady' of his sonnets. The latest theory, put forward in the summer of 1999 by Doctor Hildegard Hammerschmidt-Hummel of Mainz University, is that the 'Dark Lady' is Elizabeth Vernon, a lady in waiting to Queen Elizabeth.

Elizabeth Vernon married Henry Wriothesley, the Earl of Southampton in August 1598 just ten weeks before the birth of her daughter Penelope. The Earl of Southampton, remember, was Shakespeare's patron. Doctor Hammerschmidt-Hummel states the Earl of Southampton married Elizabeth Vernon to stop any scandal, but that in reality, Penelope was the daughter of no less than William Shakespeare. Penelope married William Spencer in 1617, and so becomes a direct ancestor of Diana, Princess of Wales.

The Spencer Chapel, from the north aisle.

So do we have buried in Brington William Shakespeare's daughter? Penelope Spencer was a widow for 31 years, and was buried alongside her husband in the Spencer Chapel. Because she had time to arrange these things, the sculptures on the tomb are supposed to be life-like portraits. Can we see a likeness between Penelope's face and that of Shakespeare in the surviving portraits of him? That is for you to decide, but if the theory is proved to be correct, and Penelope is William Shakespeare's daughter, that certainly is an exciting prospect, isn't it?

Henry, 1st Earl of Sunderland (1620-1643)

Killed at the Battle of Newbury

Only 23 when he was killed in the First Battle of Newbury in September 1643, Henry, 3rd Baron Spencer was already married with a son. A favourite of Charles I, he had volunteered to fight for the Cavaliers and the king had made him the Royal Standard Bearer. Spencer believed passionately in the theory of monarchy, although not convinced so much by the person then filling that position. "I would rather be hanged" he wrote "than fight for Parliament". Because of this loyalty, Charles had created him the 1st Earl of Sunderland in June 1643.

Riding with the Royalist cavalry under the command of Prince Rupert, Lord Sunderland was killed in the attack on the centre of the Parliamentary line into the brigade commanded by General Phillip Skippon. Lord Sunderland's heart was taken from his body, and conveyed back to his mother at Althope. It now lies in an urn in the Spencer chapel.

Dorothy, 1st Countess of Sunderland (1617-1684)

Famous beauty painted often by Van Dyck

Lady Dorothy Sidney, daughter of the Earl of Leicester, was, in the modern vernacular, a 'bit of a looker'. The poet Edmund Waller tried his luck with her, and wrote scores of poems to her between 1634 and 1638 at her family home at Penshurst in Kent. In the loveliest of these poems *Go Lovely Rose*, he calls her 'Sacharissa'. But she would have nothing of him, and in 1639 married Henry Spencer. Dorothy and Henry had one son, the notorious Robert, 2nd Earl of Sunderland, before Henry was mown down at Newbury.

Spending her widowhood at Althorp, Dorothy devoted her life to helping distressed clergy and royalists during the Commonwealth, before marrying again in 1652. She moved away to her new husband's home, but when she died in 1684, her body was buried in the Spencer vault at Brington. Her beauty had been made famous by Waller's poems and she was painted several times by Van Dyck, one of these pictures still being at Althorp.

Robert, 2nd Earl of Sunderland (1640-1702)
"The craftiest, most rapacious and most unscrupulous of all the politicians of his age"

In a profession not exactly renowned for its shrinking violets and small egos, what man would not be delighted to be called the "craftiest, most rapacious and most unscrupulous of all the politicians of his age". Robert Spencer, 2nd Earl of Sunderland, were he alive today to read that quotation about him from the *Dictionary of National Biography* would have been ecstatic. But he certainly deserves the description.

Because of his 'dalliances' with Charles II's mistresses, Robert Spencer, Earl of Sunderland since his third birthday, obtained royal preferment. He was sent on diplomatic missions to Madrid and Paris, and in 1679, by the paying of a £6000 'sweetener', he became the Secretary of State for the Northern Department, with a Cabinet position from where he exercised much political power.

But a setback was coming. When Parliament voted to exclude James, Duke of York from the royal succession in 1679, James' brother, Charles II, promptly dissolved Parliament. A General Election was held, Parliament assembled, but again demanded James' exclusion from the succession on the grounds that he was a Catholic. Parliament was dissolved again, was re-elected, and yet again, passed the Exclusion Bill. This time it got to the House of Lords where it was rejected. But Sunderland, for some reason unknown to us, had voted for it, and consequently was out of favour with the king and his brother. He had to grovel to the two royal brothers and eventually regained favour in 1683.

Now seeing that nothing could stop the Duke of York from becoming king (Charles had no legitimate children, although he had 16 of the other sort from eight different women), Sunderland toadied to him. And in 1685, James did indeed succeed, as James II.

Sunderland got his main rivals dismissed and ingratiated himself into the Queen's affections. Consequently he was made Lord President in 1685, and supported James' repeal of the Test Acts (Acts which barred Catholics from holding political office). In 1687, he converted to Catholicism, and was instrumental in getting the case of the Seven Bishops (*see* Achurch, Sir Thomas Powys) to court.

But all the time, he was hedging his bets by secretly intriguing with the Protestant William of Orange. The 'foresight' of this was quickly realised, as things went disastrously wrong when negotiations with the French over a mutually beneficial naval treaty disintegrated around him. Sunderland was blamed by the king, who promptly dismissed him and ordered his arrest. He fled the country to Rotterdam disguised as a woman.

Whilst in Rotterdam, Sunderland continually bombarded William of Orange, destined to be William III of England, with explanations and excuses for his previous conduct. As we say today, laying it on with a trowel. This gift of the gab so convinced William that Sunderland had all the contacts, and could 'pull strings', that when William became king of England in 1688, he invited Sunderland to return with him. Spencer then conveniently reconverted to Protestantism.

Sunderland then became the power behind the throne. Unable to accept office openly because of opposition from people who could *not* forget his past, nevertheless, Sunderland was continually consulted by William over state matters. However, by the spring of 1697, Sunderland and the king felt sufficiently safe, and Sunderland openly accepted the office of Lord Chamberlain. But the resentment this caused was still too strong, and the House of Commons virtually hounded him out of office, and he resigned within a few months.

In effect, this was the end of his political career, although he did retain the wealth he had built up. He lived just a few years more. Whilst on a visit to Althorp, his family home, he was taken violently ill and died. He was buried with his Spencer ancestors in the family vault. There is no monument to him.

George John, 2nd Earl Spencer (1758-1834)

As First Lord of the Admiralty, made Horatio Nelson a hero Home Secretary

George Spencer, when he succeeded as Earl Spencer in 1783, had to leave the House of Commons. He had been the Member for Northampton in 1780, and for Surrey since 1782. Whilst in the Lords, he was much influenced by the views of Edmund Burke, who is supposed to be the father of Conservatism. But be that as it may, William Pitt, when half way through his 17 year term as Prime Minister, made Earl Spencer the First Lord of the Admiralty in 1794. The First Lord, by that period, was always a politician, whilst the professional navy man was the First Sea Lord. Between them, they had control of the Royal Navy.

In his seven years at the Admiralty, because of Earl Spencer's organisational skills, naval administration was greatly improved, just in time to cope with the Napoleonic Wars. But not without some highs and lows in the meantime. The lows were the three great naval mutinies of 1797 (Spithead in April, the Nore and Plymouth in May). These were suppressed and some of the ringleaders hung.

The highs were the three immense triumphs. The battles of Saint Vincent in February 1797 by Sir John Jervis, and Camperdown in October 1799 under Admiral Duncan were much needed victories. But the greatest stroke of genius of Lord Spencer, was when he chose a hitherto undistinguished and 'unknown' naval officer to command a Mediterranean fleet. That officer was Horatio Nelson, and his complete annihilation of the French fleet at the Battle of the Nile in 1798 led to Napoloeon being bottled up in Egypt which gave the rest of Europe a breathing space to combine against him. It made Nelson a hero.

Spencer left the Admiralty when Pitt's government fell in 1801. But when Lord Grenville was reluctantly forced to form a government in March 1806, Spencer became Home Secretary. This government lasted but 13 months before Grenville resigned.

Earl Spencer then retired from active politics, and concentrated on building up the library at Althorp. So vast did it become, that a printed catalogue of it was published, *Bibliotheca Spenceriana*. In 1892, this library formed the basis of the Rylands Library in Manchester. George, 2nd Earl Spencer died in 1834 and was buried in the family vault at great Brington.

John, 3rd Earl Spencer (1782-1845)
The proverbial 'ugly duckling' of politics
Leader of the House of Commons
Chancellor of the Exchequer

From being an embarrassment to his parents, to a politician who won admiration from his opponents for his truthfulness and integrity, it is strange to think that john Spencer's heart was not really in politics. And when in 1834, he succeeded to the Earldom, he promptly gave it up to concentrate on his first love – the country pursuits of hunting with the Pytchley, horse racing and shooting.

Because of his debts and clumsy manners, John Spencer was an embarrassment to his parents who tried to interest him in art and culture. They failed.

Having left Cambridge, Spencer entered politics at the age of 22, obviously because his father wanted him to, as Member for Oakhampton. He was then the Member for Saint Albans in 1806, and throughout this time rarely spoke in debates. But in 1806, Lord Grenville became the Prime Minister, his father became Home Secretary, he became the member for Northamptonshire – and he met Charles James Fox. This meeting with one of the most charismatic figures of politics of the time, transformed him.

Spencer joined the Whig party, and plunged himself into active politics. He devoted himself to the great causes of the time, and was involved so much, that in 1830 he was actually the Leader of the Whigs in the Commons when it was in opposition to the Tory government of the Duke of Wellington.

When Wellington resigned in 1830, the Whig party, under Earl Grey came into power. Spencer was made Leader of the House and Chancellor of the Exchequer. The greatest piece of legislation of that time was the Reform Act of 1832. Thanks to Spencer's rallying of his followers, the Bill was eventually passed, even though it had at one point been rejected by the House of Lords.

But the Whigs were faltering. And when in 1834 Earl Grey resigned, and the short lived government of his Whig successor Lord Melbourne also resigned, allowing Sir Robert Peel to form a Tory government, all corresponded to Spencer's succession to the Earldom, he called it a day. He gave up politics and involved himself on the Althorp estate. He died in 1845 and was succeeded by his brother.

Frederick, 4th Earl Spencer (1798-1857)
Fought at the Battle of Navarino
Lord Steward of the Royal Household

The Battle of Navarino of October 1827 was fought to keep the eastern Mediterranean from being controlled by Egypt and Turkey. The combined fleets of Britain, France and Russia under the British Vice-Admiral, Sir Edward Codrington, totally crushed a combined Turkish and Egyptian fleet. Of 80 enemy ships, only four were left afloat. Frederick Spencer was Captain of HMS *Talbot*, and for his part in the battle was awarded the CB.

Having joined the Royal Navy in 1811, he retired in 1831, and went into politics, becoming Member for Worcestershire and then Midhurst. He succeeded to the Earldom in 1845, and having to leave politics, entered the royal household of Queen Victoria and Prince Albert in 1846, as Lord

Chamberlain. He was made a Knight of the Garter in 1849. Between 1854 and 1857, he was Lord Steward of the Household.

Frederick Spencer married twice, Georgiana Poyntz and Adelaide Seymour. The present line of the Spencers comes from his second wife.

John Poyntz, 5th Earl Spencer (1835-1910)

Viceroy of Ireland
President of the Council
First Lord of the Admiralty
Leader of the House of Lords
Almost became the Prime Minister

The attainments of the 'Red Earl' (from his hair colour, not his politics) are many, and whole books have been written about him. Justice cannot be done in this short space, so if anyone wants to know more, then the Northamptonshire Record Society two volume biography of him *The Letters of the Red Earl* is recommended.

After a lifetime at the heart of political life in this country, he very nearly became Prime Minister in 1894, but Lord Roseberry was chosen instead. So the Spencer family just missed having that one great office of state that still eludes them.

John Spencer was incapacitated by illness and died in 1910. The Earldom went to his half-brother Charles.

GREAT OAKLEY

IN THE CHURCH YARD OF SAINT MICHAEL

Sir Arthur de Capell Broke, 2nd Baronet (1791-1858)

Co-founder of the Royal Geographical Society

By absorbing the Raleigh Travellers' Club of 1827, and the African Association of 1788, the Geographical Society of London came into being in 1830. One of its founder members was Arthur de Capell Broke (he spelt his name with one 'o', whilst the rest of the family spelt it with two). Already an accomplished travel author, his book *A Winter in the North Cape* was the best known of his many books.

The Geographical Society of London was granted a Royal Charter in 1859, thus becoming the Royal Geographical Society. Unfortunately Sir Arthur did not live to see this, as he had died a year previously. He was buried in the family vault at Great Oakley.

The Capell-Brooke tombs in Great Oakley churchyard. The founder of the Royal Geographical Society lies on the extreme left of the picture, nearest the church.

GREAT OXENDEN

IN THE CHURCH OF SAINT HELEN

John Morton (1671-1726)

Naturalist

John Morton's greatest contribution was the *Natural History of Northamptonshire* published in 1712, whilst he was Rector of Great Oxendon. His book is phenomenal. After years of observations, everything he saw was recorded. For instance, he devotes more than 60 pages to the description of fossils, going into great detail on the differences between scallops and ammonites and so on.

This lovely tombstone to John Morton is in the chancel, and so is normally hidden by the high altar.

He was elected a Fellow of the Royal Society in 1703, the year when he was instituted vicar of Weston in Lincolnshire. Previously he had been a curate at Great Oxendon and returned there in 1707 as Rector.

Morton's *History* is one of the great quartet of county histories (along with Bridges', Baker's and Whellan's) into which every student of the county should be continually delving.

GRETTON

IN THE CHURCH OF SAINT JAMES

Christopher, 1st Viscount Hatton (1632-1706)

Governor of Guernsey

It was whilst Christopher Hatton was Governor of Guernsey that he lost his wife and mother in what must surely be one of the cruellest acts of fate imaginable. On the night of 29/30 December 1672, a terrific thunderstorm raged over Cornet Castle, the home of the Governor of Guernsey.

Christopher Hatton and his wife were in bed. Suddenly, a bolt of lightning struck the castle, and somehow found its way to the main gunpowder magazine. In the terrific explosion, Christopher Hatton's wife and mother were killed instantly, and Christopher himself was 'blown out of bed and on to the battlements'.

Christopher Hatton subsequently married twice more, and continued on his army career. He was created a Viscount in 1683, and died at Kirby Hall, being buried in nearby Gretton church in 1706.

The Hatton memorials in Gretton church. The memorial on the right wall, nearest the east window, recalls the horrendous explosion at Guernsey Castle.

GUILSBOROUGH

THE CHURCHYARD EXTENSION OPPOSITE THE CHURCH

Thomas Orde Hastings Lees (1846-1924)

Chief Constable of Northamptonshire 1875-1881
Chief Constable of the Isle of Wight 1890-1899
Personal friend of Queen Victoria
Personal friend of Charles Boycott

Thomas Lees was born at Annadown in County Galway in February 1846, where his father was Rector. His mother was a daughter of Hans, 11th Earl of Huntingdon, and this therefore puts Thomas Lees very much of the upper class. After private education he went to Trinity College, Dublin, taking an MA in law, and qualifying as a barrister.

The Irish Constabulary was at that time (1868), a permanently armed police force, run along military lines. It thus exercised a policy of direct officer entry, and Thomas Lees joined as a Cadet officer in December 1868. He was eventually promoted to Second Sub-Inspector, and served in Longford, Mayo and Tipperary.

He had married Grace Bateman, daughter of Joshua Bateman of Guilsborough, in 1871, and so had become attached to the county of his adoption. Thus, when the position of Chief Constable of Northamptonshire became vacant in 1875, Thomas Lees was chosen. He moved to the Chief Constable's house in Saint Giles' Square, Northampton (which is now the Northampton Tourist Information Office).

In 1880, legislation was passed which gave control of the county gaols to the Home Secretary. The Northamptonshire County Gaol in Saint Giles' Square, thus became redundant, and was closed down. All the prisoners were moved to the Northampton Borough Gaol on The Mounts, and the old prison buildings in Saint Giles' Square were sold.

Unfortunately, this complex also included the Chief Constable's house, and it was sold about Lees' ears without his knowledge. He promptly resigned in a fit of pique.

Returning to being a barrister on the Midland Circuit, he practised for another nine years. During this time, he contested the Borough of Northampton Parliamentary Seat as a Conservative. Unfortunately, this was the time of the famous Bradlaugh-Labouchere rivalry, and he failed to get elected, that honour going to Labouchere.

It was during his campaign, that he received the help of an old friend from his Irish days. Captain Charles Boycott spoke on the hustings for Lees, and on one occasion in Northampton, actually spoke in public about the circumstances of his 'boycotting' a few years before. This is the only time, apparently, that Boycott ever referred to this matter in public.

In 1890, the Isle of Wight County Constabulary was formed, and Thomas Lees was appointed its first Chief Constable. He thus became personally acquainted with Queen Victoria who lived at Osborn house on the island. In 1897, Lees received the Diamond Jubilee Medal personally from the Queen,

The grave of Thomas Lees is to the left. The cross is the memorial to his son, killed in the Great War.

in special thanks for the police handling of the Jubilee celebrations on the island.

Thomas Lees resigned from the Isle of Wight in 1899, and came to live the life of a country squire at Guilsborough. He had two sons and a daughter. His oldest son, Edmund, was in the Border Regiment and was killed on the Western Front in October 1914. His memorial is also in Guilsborough cemetery next to his father's grave. Thomas Lees died in September 1924.

HARDINGSTONE

THE CHURCHYARD OF SAINT EDMUND

An Unknown Man (?-1930)

Murder victim of Alfred Arthur Rouse

James Kellie-MacCallum's (*see* Quinton) final months as Chief Constable of Northamptonshire, were, quite literally, spent in a blaze of nationwide publicity, and all because of the murder of an unknown man at Hardingstone in the early hours of Thursday 6 November 1930. This particular case, attracting immense countrywide news coverage, has come to be called 'The Blazing Car Murder'.

Alfred Arthur Rouse was a commercial traveller. In 1930 he was 36 years old, and had served with distinction during The Great War. The only trouble was, a head wound sustained by a shell burst in 1915 seems to have affected his personality. Although his upbringing with an aunt had been blameless, and he had been happily married, the head wound changed Rouse into a promiscuous rake with an enormous sexual appetite.

In those circumstances, the job of a commercial traveller, taking him to all parts of the country, was tailor made for him, and eventually, over 80 cases of seduction were traced to him. Not surprisingly, this led to many illegitimate births, numerous bigamous marriage ceremonies and several paternity suits.

In 1930, his total income was £8 per week, and from that, he had to pay the mortgage and housekeeping on his proper matrimonial home in London, hire purchase on his car, and existing paternity orders and foster parents' wages for his illegitimate offspring. In short, in the summer of 1930, Rouse was in a financial mess, which was not helped by the news that a girl in London was pregnant by him, and a girl in Wales was pregnant by him for a second time. Something had to be done, and quickly.

He conceived a plan to stage his own apparent death in a car accident, and so disappear to start a new life free from any financial restrictions. His plan fell into halves. First he had to choose a man to take his place, and who was so inconsequential, that he would not be missed by anybody.

The second part was to set fire to his car in an isolated place with a man inside, so that the body would be taken to be that of Rouse himself. He chose

Hardingstone Lane, Northampton, and the date Wednesday 5 November. He thought that yet another bonfire on that date would go unnoticed on the one night of the year when bonfires were commonplace, and so would not attract immediate attention.

The actual mechanics of the murder, his subsequent capture, and trial at the Northamptonshire Assizes in January 1931 are well known, having been described in numerous other books. Alfred Arthur Rouse was hanged at Bedford Gaol in March 1931.

In choosing his 'inconsequential' victim, Rouse succeeded admirably, for even to this day, we still do not know who it was who burnt to death in Rouse's car. Therefore, the only inscription that could be placed on the simple wooden cross when the remains were buried in Hardingstone churchyard, were 'In memory of an unknown man'.

The simple wooden cross of an unknown murder victim.

HARDWICK

IN THE CHURCH OF SAINT LEONARD

Sir Francis Nicholls (?-1621)

Governor of Tilbury Fort at the time of The Armada

Let tyrants fear.
I have always so behaved myself that, under God, I have placed my chiefest strength in the goodwill of my subjects; and therefore I am come...being resolved in the midst and heat of the battle to live or die amongst you all; to lay down for God, my kingdom and my people, my honour and my blood, even in the dust.
I know I have but the body of a weak and feeble woman: but I have the heart and stomach of a king - and a king of England too!

The impressive wall monument to Sir Francis Nicholls

Queen Elizabeth's speech to her troops at Tilbury. The year was 1588, and they were awaiting The Armada of the Duke of Parma. And as Governor of Tilbury Fort at the time, Sir Francis Nicholls would have witnessed Elizabeth in full armour and riding a white horse, riding triumphantly amongst the ranks, exhorting her troops in one of the great stirring calls of history. And it is the same Sir Francis Nicholls who now lies in the peace of Hardwick church far away from those exciting and heady days.

HAZELBECH

IN THE CHURCHYARD OF SAINT MICHAEL

Edwin Lawrence Godkin (1831-1902)

Crusading American journalist who exposed corruption in Tammany Hall
Journalist who reported on the Crimean War and the American Civil War

Tammany Hall in New York was the headquarters of the city's Democratic Party. During the mid nineteenth century, because of a series of scandals involving breathtaking political bribery and corruption, Tammany Hall to the American public came to be synonomous with immense urban political corruption.

Edwin Godkin established and edited the New York based weekly news magazine *Nation* in July 1865, just after the end of the American Civil War. Because it was politically independent, it was read by all shades of political opinion and social background, and as such, greatly influenced American public opinion.

In 1871 the *Nation*, together with the *New York Times* ran articles on the corruption in Tammany Hall. This campaign eventually led to William 'Boss' Tweed and Richard 'Slippery Dick' Connolly being exposed for outrageous corruption and milking of the New York City funds. For example, the City paid out from its funds ten times the estimate for building the County Courthouse, which, to cap it all, was never completed. And so much was paid out for floor covering at New York City Hall, it was said the entire building could have been carpeted three times over. By wielding unchecked political power and patronage, the 'Ring' as it was called, led by 'Boss' Tweed, grew immensely rich. And when he was rumbled, 'Boss' Tweed fled the country and escaped to Cuba.

In 1881, Godkin sold the *Nation* to the *New York Evening Post*, and merged the two, becoming the editor of both papers, and only gave up in 1899 on account of ill health.

An Irishman by birth, Godkin went to Queen's College, Belfast and then studied law at Lincoln's Inn, but was not called to the bar. Instead he became a reporter, being sent by the *Daily News* to the Crimea to report on the war there. He returned to England totally anti-war.

He worked on the *Northern Whig* newspaper in Belfast for a time before going to America in 1856. He continually sent back articles to the Daily News, and whilst in America, was admitted to the New York bar.

Although returning to England briefly, he was back in America by 1862 to report on the American Civil War. He covered the war for four newspapers: the English *Daily News*; and the American *New York Times, North American Review* and *Atlantic Monthly*. When the war ended, Godkin decided to become an American citizen, and it was then that he then established the *Nation*.

He was, not unnaturally, interested in the American political system and wrote three very influential books: *Reflections and Comments* (New York 1895), *Problems of Modern Democracy* (New York 1896) and *Unforeseen Tendencies of Democracy* (Boston 1898).

Whilst on a visit to England in 1902, Godkin died in Devonshire. Why he is buried in Hazelbech churchyard is unclear, as there is no obvious connection either with the village or the county. Nevertheless, here he lies with his American second wife Katherine.

Godkin was highly influential political reporter of his time, and it was said of him that the British establishment looked upon him as the "sane voice of American politics". The Godkin Lectures at Harvard University were established in his honour.

The tomb of Edwin Godkin, *for forty years a citizen of the United States.*

Albert Pell (1820-1907)

Agriculturist
Poor Law reformer
Introduced Rugby Football into Cambridge University

Having been to Rugby School, under the great Doctor Thomas Arnold, Albert Pell learnt the wonderful game that is named after the school. He only missed by a few years, being the contemporary of William Webb-Ellis, who in 1823, had picked up the football and run with it. Whilst at Trinity College, Cambridge, it was Albert Pell who introduced the game to the university.

Although the son of a judge, Albert abandoned the law as a career, and took up farming. In 1842 he bought a farm at Harrow. In 1846 he married his cousin Elizabeth Halford, and moved to a farm at Ely, but two years later, the couple moved to a farm at Hazelbech where they would remain for the rest of their lives.

The Pell memorial inside Hazelbech church.

And the actual grave, by the south door.

Albert built up his farm, and began agitating for reform in agricultural policy, especially in controls over cattle disease. Albert Pell was the first Chairman, and co-founder, of the Central Chamber of Agriculture in 1866.

Entering politics, in 1868, he was the Member for South Leicestershire, a seat he held for 17 years, and therefore in the right place to keep agitating for agricultural reform. He was a member on the Royal Commission on Agriculture in 1879, and went to the USA and Canada to study farming methods there. He was a member of the council of the Royal Agricultural Society, and he persuaded Cambridge University to pioneer new ways of teaching agriculture. For this he was created an honorary LLD. He wrote numerous books and articles on farming.

But he was also interested in the poor laws, and he was Chairman of the Central Conference on the Poor Laws from 1877-1898.

Albert Pell died in April 1907 and was buried in Hazelbech church, next to Edwin Godkin.

HIGHAM FERRERS

IN THE CHURCH OF SAINT MARY

Thomas and Agnes Chicheley (c1400)

Parents of Henry Chicheley, Archbishop of Canterbury

Henry Chicheley, Archbishop of Canterbury, was born in Higham Ferrers about the year 1362. His parents were Thomas, a merchant and trader, and Agnes (nee Pynchon) of Writtle in Essex. Thomas and Agnes were wealthy, there can be no doubt, as they owned two houses in the borough, and in 1381 Thomas was elected as Mayor of Higham.

The Chicheley brasses in front of Higham's 'Royal' tomb.

Of their three sons, William and Robert became leading City of London Merchants (of the Grocers' Company) with Robert becoming Lord Mayor of London in 1411 and William becoming Sheriff of London in 1409. Their third son Henry, after New College, Oxford, entered the Church and eventually became Bishop of St David's in 1408. Six years later he was made Archbishop of Canterbury and remained in office for 29 years. He is buried in Canterbury Cathedral.

Thomas died in 1400, and together with Agnes, lies in Higham Ferrers church under a brass plate. William and his wife Beatrice, are also buried nearby, under their own brass memorial plate.

?

The tomb in the Lady Chapel has always puzzled ecclesiologists. Although the brass on the tomb is of Lawrence Saint Maur, Vicar of Higham Ferrers, and dated 1337, it is not him inside the tomb, and it was never intended for him.

By the rich and ornate carving, with the Shields of the Royal Arms of England, the tomb was obviously made for a member of the royal family. Higham Ferrers was, and still is, in the Duchy of Lancaster, a royal estate, so a royal tomb is feasible. But for whom?

The theory now accepted is that the tomb was built for Thomas, Earl of Lancaster, Leicester, Derby, Lincoln and Salisbury (1277-1322). He was a nephew to Edward I but blotted his copybook somewhat, and was beheaded at Boroughbridge in 1322. He was buried at Pontefract, but by some quirk, he came to be regarded as a martyr and saint. His cousin, Edward III, tried three times to get the Pope to canonise Thomas, but failed. The theory is that the tomb was built to receive the body of Thomas after the Pope had made him a saint. But that never happened, and Thomas remained at Pontefract. Thomas in all probability had been born in the royal manor of Higham Ferrers, and to bring him home would have been logical, thus making Higham Ferrers the home of a venerated saint.

But the tomb *does* contain a body. In 1909, the tomb was opened. It contained the skeleton of a man and the dust of his decayed clothing, and nothing else. As there were no ecclesiastical relics in the tomb, as was usual with priest burials, the body was not that of Lawrence Saint Maur. So, who is it? The simple answer is, we do not know.

HORTON

IN THE CHURCH OF SAINT MARY

William, Lord Parr of Horton (?- 1546)

Present at the 'Field of the Cloth of Gold'
Uncle to Catherine Parr, Queen of England

What an *annus mirabilis* the year 1543 must have been for Sir William Parr and family. In July, he had seen his niece Catherine become Queen of England by marrying Henry VIII. Consequently, he had become the Royal Chamberlain; and on Christmas Day, the King and Queen created him Lord Parr of Horton.

He remained as Lord Chamberlain until his death in September 1546. And when Mary, his wife died nine years later, a magnificent table tomb was erected over their graves in Horton church.

The figure of Lord Parr on the tomb shows him in full armour. This is supposed to be a copy of the armour he wore on the 'Field of the Cloth of Gold', which means that he had been a member of the royal court probably before his niece was even born, which was in 1512.

The 'Field of the Cloth of Gold', in June 1520, just outside Calais, was an attempt by Henry VIII and Francis I of France to settle their differences. It consisted of several weeks of jousts and pageantry, but which was so enormously expensive and extravagant, that it fully deserved its nickname. As a diplomatic measure, though, not much came of it. But Sir William Parr, as he then was, was there, and the armour he wore on those heady midsummer days 470 years ago, can still be seen today on his tomb.

Unfortunately at the time of writing, Horton church is unsafe and visitors are not allowed entry. No photograph of the tomb therefore can be obtained.

ISLIP

IN THE CHURCH OF SAINT NICHOLAS

Mary Washington (1600?-1625)

Great great great aunt to George Washington

The Washington memorial, on the southern side of the chancel.

Mary Curtis was born at Islip about the year 1600, and in June 1621, married John Washington of Sulgrave. She died just four years later, having given birth to four sons, Mordaunt, John, Thomas (who died young in 1625 and was buried at Lowick), and Philip (buried in St Martin's-in-the-Fields, London in 1643). In all probability, Mary died either in childbirth, or as a result of complications resulting from producing a child a year for four years.

She never lived to become Lady Washington, as at that time, her husband's rank was given as 'armiger' and not knight or baronet as he later became. She was buried in her native parish, only a mile distant across the River Nene from where her husband is buried at Thrapston.

For a Washington family tree, *see* Sulgrave.

KETTERING

IN THE GRAVEYARD AT THE REAR OF THE FULLER BAPTIST CHURCH, GOLD STREET

Andrew Fuller (1754-1815)

Co-founder and first Secretary of the Baptist Missionary Society

Strangely enough, Andrew Fuller was never ordained, but it is as a church Minister that he is remembered. Born in Wicken in Cambridgeshire of humble stock, Andrew Fuller attended the Baptist church at Soham just a couple of miles away. He must have had extraordinary spirituality, because, in 1775, at the age of 21, and with no ministerial training, he was asked by the Baptist congregation at Soham to be their minister. Fuller accepted and spent the next seven years there.

In 1782, the Kettering Baptist congregation desperately needed a new Minister. Fuller was approached, and he agreed to come. He stayed for the rest of his life.

It is strange to believe, but up until that time, no established church paid much attention to any overseas missionary work. But stirrings of this sort were coming from the Baptist Ministers in and around Northampton, especially a young Minister called William Carey from Moulton.

The Baptist Missionary Society was formed at a meeting in Mrs Wallis' house in Lower Street, Kettering in October 1792,and the collection at the meeting to start a missionary fund raised £13 2s 6d. Fuller became Secretary, and a year later, William Carey sailed to India as the first Baptist missionary. Carey was to die in India and is buried there. Also influenced by the Baptist Missionary Society was a young Kettering printer called William Knibb. He eventually went to the West Indies where he found his vocation in anti-slavery work.

The table tomb of Andrew Fuller, to the rear of the present day Fuller Baptist Church.

Andrew Fuller continued as Secretary to the Baptist Missionary Society for the rest of his life, and continued making vast contributions – in spirituality as well as in money raised – to his cause of 'a Baptist society for propagating the Gospel among the heathen'. He wrote many articles (well over 150) in magazines on religious issues, and in 1838 a book of his collected works was published which went into four editions.

Two American universities honoured him. He received the Doctor of Divinity degree from both Princeton and Yale.

Andrew Fuller died in May 1815, and was buried in the tiny cemetery behind the Baptist Chapel in Gold Street. The present chapel, being built in 1860, is not the one that Fuller knew, but the site is the same.

IN THE LONDON ROAD MUNICIPAL CEMETERY

James Edwin Dray? (?1832-1894)
Rode in The Charge of the Light Brigade?

The mystery surrounding this grave will now never be cleared up. Is he, or isn't he? Did he or didn't he?

In the spring of 1894, a tramp appeared at Kettering Workhouse. He was dying of consumption, and within a month he would be dead. He said his name

Did he, or didn't he?

was John Davis, and was an ex-soldier of the 4th Dragoons. Somehow the rumour got about that he had rode in the famous Charge of the Light Brigade, but whether or not he himself had said that he had, remains unclear. Anyhow, he was buried in London Road Cemetery with full honours as befits a war hero, under the name of John Davis.

But a couple of weeks later, via a Mr Jenkinson of Tunbridge Wells who wrote to the *Kettering Guardian*, two Tunbridge sisters had claimed that John Davis was not John Davis, but their brother James Edwin Dray. And so the mystery started.

After much research by interested parties, the accepted wisdom is now that in this grave lies James Dray, and that he *could* have rode in the Charge. But why did he call himself John Davis? He never called himself Dray, and the two Tunbridge sisters never saw the man who lies in the grave, so it is only their assumption that the man is their brother. And in any case, although two soldiers by the names of John Davis and James Dray were in the 4th Dragoons in the Crimea, and the 4th Dragoons was one of the regiments that rode in the Charge, there is no direct evidence whatsoever that either man, Davis or Dray, actually rode in the Charge. Both men received Crimea medals with the *Balaclava* clasp, but the *Balaclava* clasp was given to everybody at Balaclava, not just the Light Brigade.

So there the matter rests. In the grave may or may not be James Edwin Dray, who may or may not have ridden in the Charge of the Light Brigade.

Sir Alfred East (1849-1913)

World renowned painter
Royal Academician

The bust of Sir Alfred East outside the Kettering Art Gallery which bears his name.

Although born in Kettering, Alfred East studied at the Glasgow School of Art, and inevitably in Paris at the Ecole des Beaux-Arts and the Academie Julian. First living in Glasgow, East soon settled in London, with studios in Spencer Street near to Westminster Cathedral.

His first exhibition at the Royal Academy was in 1883, and he became a regular exhibitor at Burlington House. He favoured landscapes, and in 1889 visited Japan, where his landscapes of that country are seen as some of his best work. He was elected ARA, and then a full Academician in 1913, just three years after he had been knighted.

The Art Gallery named after him in his home town was built in 1919 and houses some of his works. Go along and see them.

He had married Annie Heath in 1874, and they had one son and four daughters. Sir Alfred East died in September 1913, and is buried with his wife in the London Road Cemetery of his home town.

The tomb of Sir Alfred and Lady East in the London Road cemetery.

The newly restored East family memorial, at the entrance to the London Road cemetery.

Charles Wicksteed (1847-1931)

Engineer

Philanthropist donor of Kettering's Wicksteed Park

The story is told of the Kettering man who went on holiday to Great Yarmouth. Fancying a day trip whilst there, he signed up for a day's Mystery Tour - and finished up in Wicksteed Park. Which goes to show the nationwide fame of Charles Wicksteed's legacy to his adopted town. He was actually born in Leeds, the seventh child of the Reverend Charles and Mrs Jane Wicksteed. The Reverend Charles was the Minister of the Mill Hill Unitarian Chapel.

In 1854, because the health of the Reverend Charles needed it, the family moved to Upper Eyarth in north Wales. But the country air was so beneficial, and Charles was so taken with country life, that he gave up the church, and took a farm called Hafod-y-Coed near to Saint Asaph.

Charles junior was sent to school at Lancaster, which only confirmed his father's suspicions that Charles junior was no genius at book learning, and throughout his life would never write without spelling mistakes. But, he was practical, and made more in carpentry lessons than the rest of the boys put together.

Charles left school in 1863 and went to an engineering apprenticeship in Leeds, which he completed with relish. Next door to his place of work, stood John Fowler's Steam Plough Works. He borrowed money from one of his brothers, and set himself up in the steam ploughing business, in the early days when it was just staring to take over from horse drawn ploughs.

Concentrating on Norfolk, Charles ploughed for all the big landowners, including the Earl of Leicester at Holkham, and the Prince of Wales at Sandringham. An unfortunate accident at this time, when the steam engine rolled back on him, broke his thigh, which gave him a limp he was to have for the rest of his life.

After three or four years in Norfolk, he ventured farther afield, and in July 1871, finished up at Kettering. When he stopped to water his steam engine on the bridge over the Ise at Barton Seagrave, he was roughly told to go away by the local squire. Perhaps that is what persuaded him to stay in Kettering, which he did, for the next 60 years. He eventually owned Barton Seagrave Hall and estate. We remember Wicksteed's name; we do not remember the squire's name.

He continued his ploughing business in Northamptonshire, but needed a workshop for repairs. With financial help from his brothers again, he bought a small room, grandly known as the 'Stamford Road Works'. Although meant primarily for his own repairs, gradually work for other people started being done. This work prospered and eventually, he gave up the steam ploughing and concentrated on engineering. Many patents followed, but his biggest seller was bicycle stands, for the blossoming bicycle fashion of the times.

There were failures, notably a gear box invention in 1907, but he had brilliant successes too, such as the mechanical hacksaw, which made his fortune. So rich did he become that he wanted to give back some to the people of Kettering.

Land on the banks of the Ise brook, including the Barton Seagrave estate, was purchased under a trust in 1914, and this is now Wicksteed Park. And to go in the Park, he built playground equipment, for which today, his company is world renowned.

He had married Mary Jean Gibb in 1877, and eventually built a large house which he called Bryn-Hafod to remind him of his father's Welsh farm. Mary Wicksteed died in 1914, and Charles's constant companion after that was Jerry,

The inscription on the grave of Charles and Mary Wicksteed

his little dog. Jerry disappeared and was never found, and Charles Wicksteed, heartbroken, erected a small statue in the Park, which is still there to day.

Charles Wicksteed also involved himself in local politics, and was a Liberal, believing in Land Nationalisation. He was a Local Councillor and a County Councillor.

He died of influenza in March 1931, just 11 days before his 84th birthday. The Park named after him, has become a nationwide tourist attraction, ensuring the name of Charles Wicksteed, the man as well as the park, will never be forgotten.

Roger Lewin, GC (1915-1941)
George Cross winner

Only two George Cross winners are buried in Northamptonshire. Roger Lewin is one, and Dennis Copperwheat lies in Weekley churchyard.

Malta, because of its position, was of strategic importance during the Second World War. It was vital that the island was not captured. On the night of Sunday 3 November 1940, Flight Sergeant Raymond Lewin of 148 Squadron RAFVR, stationed in Malta, was the pilot of a bomber aircraft taking off on a mission. Shortly after take off, things went wrong. The plane began to lose height, and crashed into a hillside where it immediately burst into flames. Sergeant Lewin crawled out of his cockpit to see three of his crew climbing out of the escape hatch. That left his second in command who was still trapped inside the blazing plane, with its full fuel tanks and full complement of bombs.

The memorial to Roger Lewin, GC

Without fear for his safety, Sergeant Lewin, dived underneath a blazing wing, crawled into the fuselage of the aircraft, and dragged out his second in command. He managed this despite severe injuries to his face and legs. He dragged his wounded colleague 40 yards away from the aircraft to a hole in the ground where he shielded him with his body when the aircraft exploded just seconds later.

Flight Sergeant Raymond Mayhew Lewin, RAFVR, was awarded The George Cross, which was cited in the *London Gazette* of 11 March 1941. Raymond Lewin was promoted to Pilot Officer, but the wounds he received from his rescue were too severe for him to recover. He died on 21 November 1941 in Malta. He was 26. He was buried in the London Road Cemetery.

IN THE MUNICIPAL CREMATORIUM, ROTHWELL ROAD

George Harrison (1876-1950)

Painter, Poet and Local Historian

Although, of course, not buried in the strict sense, nevertheless, the final resting place of George Harrison (and of Frank Bellamy) is still tangible and is in their native town. Their ashes were scattered on the Gardens of Remembrance, where rose trees, still growing and blooming, are their memorials.

George Harrison, born in Kettering in 1876, was a hairdresser by trade, and this gave him his living. But in his spare time, his gift was to be a talented artist and poet.

Noticed by all three of the great Kettering born artists, Sir Alfred East, Thomas Gotch and John Nettleship, Harrison was especially encouraged by Sir Alfred East who tutored him regularly in his London studios during the 1890s. The kindness of Kettering friends, also enabled Harrison to go to Antwerp and Brussels for a summer to study.

His paintings, he favoured landscapes and country scenes, were exhibited widely and were well received by the art critics Travelling widely throughout his native county, sketching, painting, and penning poetry inspired by the scenes he saw, his articles on these forays appeared in the local press. He published six volumes of his *Poems and Sketches* between 1921 and 1946, but his magnum opus was his *Wanderer in Northamptonshire* published in 1947. Poems, drawings, local history notes and village descriptions, all appear as he saw them when he visited in the 1930s. We can look wistfully on this charming book and reflect. The world that George Harrison saw has slipped out of our consciousness, never to return, to be replaced by this selfish, uncaring, ill mannered and frightening world we have created today.

George Harrison died on the last day of 1950, and was cremated on Wednesday 3 January 1951.

Frank Bellamy (1917-1976)
Illustrator of 'Dan Dare', 'Doctor Who' and 'Garth'

What boy in the 1950s and 1960s did not read the *Eagle*? I did, but at that time I did not know, although I do now, that some of the pictures I saw were drawn by Frank Bellamy, who was a Kettering man.

Born in 1917, Frank Bellamy worked first in a shoe factory, but soon realised he wanted to be an artist, so he got a job in William Blamire's Art Studios in the High Street. After war service with the Royal Artillery, he returned to Kettering in 1945, where he stopped for a further three years.

By now married with a young family, Frank moved to live in Surrey because he started to work for the Norfolk Studios near to Fleet Street. During this time he freelanced for *Mickey Mouse Weekly*, but then to full time work with *Swift*, followed by the move to the famous *Eagle*.

The *Eagle* had been started in 1950 by the Reverend Marcus Morris and Frank Hampson, as a quality comic for boys. Hampson had created 'Dan Dare: Space Pilot' and drew the strip cartoons which appeared on the front page. Bellamy started work with the *Eagle* and his first strip cartoon 'The Happy Warrior', the story of Sir Winston Churchill, was the first strip cartoon to depict a man still living. Churchill himself congratulated Bellamy on the strip's accuracy. Other strip cartoons followed: 'The Shepherd King' the story of King David, and 'Marco Polo'.

Hampson left the *Eagle* in 1961. Another publisher had taken over, and he disagreed with the new direction they wanted for 'Dan Dare'. Frank Bellamy then took over, and the 'Dan Dare' strip cartoon became his.

Tempted away from the *Eagle*, he then went to *TV21* and drew 'The Thunderbirds' strip. Work on *The Sunday Times* and *Radio Times* followed, where he drew all the illustrations for the 'Doctor Who' cartoons.

Britain's answer to 'Superman' was 'Garth' in the *Daily Mirror*, and in 1971, Frank Bellamy was asked to take on this cartoon. He agreed, and drew the 'Garth' strip for five years until he died.

By now living in Geddington, Frank Bellamy died in July 1976. Like George Harrison, he was cremated, and his ashes scattered on the Gardens of Remembrance at the Kettering Crematorium.

KING'S CLIFFE

❀

IN THE CHURCHYARD OF ALL SAINTS

❀

William Law (1686-1761)

Religious author
Profoundly influenced John Wesley to establish the Methodist Church

The tomb of William Law, now almost indecipherable because of weathering.

William Law's tomb in King's Cliffe churchyard is in the form of a writing desk. Sadly however, the lettering is all but indistinguishable because of weathering. But here lies the man, who influenced Charles Wesley, and later his brother John, to set up the 'Holy Club' in Oxford when undergraduates there in the 1720s. Their 'Method' of a highly structured devotional life was directly influenced by Law's book *Christian Perfection* of 1723, and even more so by Law's next, and his greatest, book *A Serious Call to a Devout and Holy Life* of 1728.

William Law was born at King's Cliffe and went to Emmanuel College, Oxford. He graduated BA in 1708 and MA in 1712, and was ordained into the Church of England in 1711. So far so good, but in 1714 he was suspended from his degrees for failing to take the Oath of Allegiance to George I, and was ejected from his Fellowship at Emmanuel.

He became a curate in Cambridgeshire and possibly at Fotheringhay, and he opened a school for girls at King's Cliffe with an anonymous gift he had received. He was continually writing on religious matters, and his first great influential book was written during this time. In 1727, he went to live in Putney to become the tutor to the Gibbon family, especially to Edward Gibbon, who was to become the father of the great historian Edward Gibbon of *Decline and Fall of the Roman Empire* fame.

Law retired in 1740 and returned to King's Cliffe. There he set about living his life according to the rules he had set out in *A Serious Call.* In this, he was helped by Miss Hester Gibbon, who he had tutored at Putney, and Mrs Hutcheson, who donated their joint incomes to this venture.

When Law died in 1761, Miss Gibbon had the writing desk tomb erected, and when Mrs Hutcheson died, she was buried according to her instructions in the same tomb, at William Law's feet.

LAMPORT

IN THE CHURCH AND CHURCHYARD OF ALL SAINTS

The Isham family has been at Lamport for generations, and the majority are buried in the family vault. It would be impossible to mention all of them, so only Thomas, Charles and Gyles will be given in detail. However, other noteworthy Ishams also buried in the vault are:

Sir Justinian Isham, 2nd Baronet (1610-1674) MP for Northamptonshire
Sir Justinian Isham, 4th Baronet (1658-1730) MP for Northamptonshire
Sir Justinian Isham, 5th Baronet (1687-1736) MP for Northamptonshire
Sir Edmund Isham, 6th Baronet (1690-1772) MP for Northamptonshire
Euseby Isham, MA DD (1697-1755) Vice Chancellor of Oxford University

The wonderful family chapel at Lamport, where generations of the Isham family rest.

Sir Thomas Isham, 3rd Baronet (1658-1681)

Kept a Diary in Latin

Thomas Isham's Diary written in Latin is kept at Lamport. It covers the years 1671 to 1673, and a copy and translation of it was published in 1971. It is not concerned so much with national events, as Samuel Pepy's and John Evelyn's diaries are, but more with the local day to day living of the time.

The 1971 edition is well worth reading, not only for the text, but also for all the footnotes, which give so much genealogical and historical detail, that complete absorption by it is guaranteed.

Thomas Isham died young and never married. He is buried in the family vault at Lamport.

Sir Charles Isham, 10th Baronet (1819-1903)

Brought the garden gnomes to England.

What nicer way can there be of being forever remembered as the man who introduced the garden gnome into England? A passionate gardener, it was Sir Charles who laid out the shape of the Alpine Garden still to be seen at Lamport.

And to look after this garden, Sir Charles brought some gnomes over from Germany in the 1840s, and made them little homes in the garden so that they could raise their families. People say that they are not there anymore, but on quiet moonlight nights, if you look very, very carefully, and keep very, very still....

...this is who you might see

Sir Gyles Isham, 12th Baronet (1903-1976)

Professional actor
Local historian

Gyles Isham eventually became the 12th Baronet and had to settle down to manage the Lamport estate. But before that, he had decided that a life 'treading the boards' was for him.

Whilst at Oxford, he was in the OUDS, and acted often, receiving good notices. In 1926, he came down from Oxford, and turned professional. He acted at the Old Vic and at the Stratford Shakespeare Theatre, and went on many tours of Britain and America. Apparently he was quite good, and it was only the war that stopped him from going on to higher things.

During the war, he was commissioned into the 60th Regiment, the King's Royal Rifle Corps, and saw active service in France and Germany. He finished up at Lieutenant Colonel, being demobbed in 1946.

Gyles Isham was a local historian par excellence. After he returned to Lamport, a continuous stream of local history articles was published, especially in *Northamptonshire Past and Present*, which he edited for many years. It was during this time that Lamport Hall was used as the Northamptonshire County Record Office, before it moved to Delapre Abbey, and then to its present site in Wootton Park.

Gyles Isham never married and his successor to the baronetcy was a cousin. Gyles Isham died in January 1976, and his tastefully carved headstone is in All Saints churchyard, just a few feet away from John Graves.

John James Graves (1832-1903)

Founder and first president of the National Union of Teachers

John Graves was Headmaster of Lamport and Hanging Houghton Endowed School for the incredible length of 50 years, from 1851 until 1901. And also, equally incredibly, he started his teaching career in 1846, at the enormously experienced age of 14.

John Graves was born in London in January 1832. There is no record of what school he went to and what education he received, but it must have been a good one, for in 1846, he started teaching at Saint Anne's School, Soho. A year later, he moved to teach at Saint Paul's School, Cambridge. And another year later, in 1848, he became the Headmaster of the village school in Sileby in Lincolnshire.

By being married in 1851, this qualified Graves and his new wife, Ann, to follow the usual custom of the times, and take charge of a village endowed school. Such a school was Lamport and Hanging Houghton school (Hanging Houghton is a tiny hamlet inside Lamport parish) endowed with an income of £66 per year, by an Isham family charity.

At a combined salary of £45 per year, Ann Graves taught the infants' class and girls' needlework, and John Graves taught the older boys and girls. Their accommodation was provided free, and in their case, was in the same building

The simple headstone of Sir Gyles Isham in Lamport churchyard.

as the school, which was a newly built one at Hanging Houghton.

And there the John Graves stopped for 50 years. Ann died in 1882, and John married again, his new wife taking over the same arrangement of teaching duties.

Up to 1870, there was no national body to represent the teaching profession. Local ones existed, but they had no real power, and Graves was always mindful this. The details of the founding and history of the National Union of Teachers can be found elsewhere, but in September 1870, at King's College, London, the National Union of Elementary Teachers was formed with Graves as its first president. The title was changed to the National Union of Teachers a few years later.

In his first presidential address, Graves voiced some of the things that needing addressing, such as better pay and conditions, and a settled pension scheme. He stopped on the nation executive of the union until 1900, when he stepped down, at the age of 68.

One year later, he retired from teaching altogether, and in 1903, died at the age of 71.

John Graves and his second wife lie side-by-side in the tranquillity of Lamport churchyard.

LONG BUCKBY

IN THE CHURCH AND CHURCHYARD OF SAINT LAWRENCE

Eliza Gardner (?-1840)

Curate's wife who was 'frightened to death'

Was there ever such a strange case? Mrs Eliza Gardner, who was the wife of the Reverend Richard Gardner, Curate of Long Buckby, died whilst she was lying in bed, and having never set eyes upon her 'attackers'. The Coroner's Jury, having no physical injuries to go on, could only bring in the most amazing of verdicts, that of 'Death by fright'.

At 12.40am on Tuesday 11 March 1840, the Reverend Richard and his wife were asleep in bed. Suddenly they were rudely awakened by what sounded like their front door being smashed in. Fearing burglars, Richard opened the bedroom window and pointed a gun (unloaded) into the street, and heard footsteps running away. He went back to bed only to find his wife totally insensible and unconscious. A doctor was called, but Eliza Gardner was already dead - death by fright.

It seems that three of the local rag, tag and bobtail by the names of John Bree, John Holman and Thomas Vann, all in their late teens, had just been ejected from a local tavern, and in their intoxicated state decided to have some 'fun' on the way home. This consisted of kicking at people's front doors as they passed.

The Coroner's Jury at the Inquest on Mrs Gardner (who had probably died of a heart attack) committed the three men for trial. Thus they duly appeared at the Northamptonshire Assizes on Monday 20 July 1840 in front of Mr Justice Tindall.

However, at the trial, Tindall J disagreed with the Coroner:

"The deceased lady who was in a weak state of health" he said, "died almost while the noise and uproar were going on. But it would not be right to attribute her death to parties who neither knew of her existence nor had inflicted upon her any personal injury. If there had been terror by the pointing of a pistol at her, or if a blow had been inflicted, from which death might have ensued, the case would have had a very different aspect. But to make the working upon the fears and fancy of one individual the ground for a charge of manslaughter, would be too great and arbitrary a connection between cause and effect".

The manslaughter charge was therefore dismissed. But the judge bound over each of them for £40 to be on their good behaviour for the next three years. Eliza Gardner was buried in Long Buckby church, and a plaque placed in the church for all to read of the curious case of the Curate's wife who was 'frightened to death'.

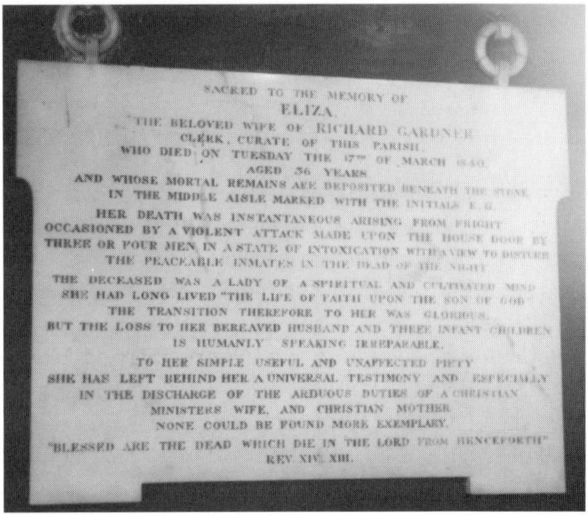

The memorial to Eliza Gardner inside Long Buckby church.

And ironically, the grave of John Bree, which lies a few yards away in Long Buckby churchyard.

LOWICK

IN THE CHURCH OF SAINT PETER

Edward, 2nd Earl of Wiltshire (?-1499)

Cousin to King Henry VII

Edward Stafford's mother was Constance Greene, daughter of Henry Greene of Lowick. His father was John, 1st Earl of Wiltshire, and his grandfather was Humphrey Stafford, 1st Duke of Buckingham. Humphrey was killed at the Battle of Northampton in 1460 and lies in Greyfriars (*see* Northampton, the Church of the Greyfriars).

Because Humphrey's son, Henry, married Margaret Tudor, he became the stepfather to Henry Tudor, later Henry VII. Edward, 2nd Earl of Wiltshire was thus the cousin (or 'step-cousin' if there is such a thing) of Henry VII.

The Greene and Stafford families owned Lowick before it was acquired by the Mordaunt family, later to become the Earls of Peterborough. For a family tree, *see* Great Addington.

The South Chapel at Lowick, with the tombs of Henry Greene; 5th Duke of Dorset and 2nd Earl of Wiltshire.

Sir John Germaine (1650-1718)
Lady Mary Germaine (?-1705)
Lady 'Betty' Germaine (1680-1769)
The 'Germaine Scandal'

Possibly not scandalous by today's measure of morality, nevertheless the antics of Sir John Germaine, Lady Mary Mordaunt and Lady 'Betty' Berkeley certainly provided Georgian England with common tittle-tattle at the turn of the 18th and 19th centuries. All three of the 'menage a trois' lie in the north chapel of Lowick church.

John Germaine, who was described as having 'defective morals…together with a total lack of education', was Dutch and it was rumoured that he was possibly the illegitimate son of William of Orange. Coming over to England with William and Mary when they became King and Queen of England, John Germaine arrived in England in the spring of 1688. Almost immediately it seems, unleashed upon the English aristocratic ladies, he began what used to be called 'carrying on' with the Duchess of Norfolk. The Duchess was formerly Lady Mary Mordaunt, daughter of the Earl of Peterborough, and heiress to Drayton House at Lowick.

The affair between the two became notorious, and the cuckolded Duke of Norfolk twice introduced divorce bills into the House of Lords, in 1691 and 1692, but failed both times. In those days, before it was all changed by the Divorce Act of 1857, divorces could only be obtained by Act of Parliament, which took a lot of money, and therefore only the prerogative of the rich.

Being thwarted in the divorce hearings, the duke then sued Germaine in the civil court for £50,000 damages for 'lascivious conversation' between Germaine and the duchess. In this, he eventually won, but was only awarded damages of 100 marks. A mark was 2/3 of a pound, or 13s 4d, so 100 marks was only £66, a far cry from the £50,000 asked for.

But this produced a lever, and in 1700 the Duke of Norfolk finally succeeded in obtaining his divorce. In the meantime, Lady Mary's father, the Earl of Peterborough had died, and she now owned Drayton House and estate. She and Germaine were still carrying on, and in September 1701, by a special licence from the Archbishop of Canterbury, Sir John Germaine, as he then was (he had been made a baronet in 1698) married Lady Mary Mordaunt.

Together the couple lived at Drayton House, but Mary died in 1705, being buried in the north chapel of Lowick church. Sir John's brother-in-law, the new Earl of Peterborough, not wishing this philandering fly-by-night Dutchman to get his hands on the family silver, promptly sued for the return of Drayton. Until the two Married Woman's Property Acts of 1870 and 1882, however, all the wife's property automatically became the husband's on marriage. The law was thus on Germaine's side. The Earl of Peterborough lost, and Germaine kept Drayton.

Thereupon, he promptly (within months) married Lady Elizabeth ('Betty') Berkeley, daughter of the Earl of Berkeley in 1706. Although coming from an old family, and also a personal friend of Dean Swift, tongues started wagging again, because at the age of 26, she was 30 years younger than her bridegroom. Sarah, the great Duchess of Marlborough was appalled, spreading rumours that Germaine was only an innkeeper's son. Nevertheless, John and Betty seemed contented enough, and three children resulted from their marriage.

Sir John Germaine died in December 1718 aged 68, leaving Drayton House and his first wife's fortune to his second wife. Lady Betty buried him near to

The North Chapel at Lowick, with the tombs of Sir Ralph and Lady Greene, and beyond, the Germaine monuments.

his first wife, and provided a handsome tomb for him. He was terrified of dying, and on his deathbed asked for the Last Sacrament, but was refused by Doctor Clarke, the Vicar of Saint James, Westminster.

Lady Betty Germaine lived on at Drayton, never remarried, and died there after 50 years of widowhood in 1769. She was buried with her husband and his first wife in the north chapel. She bequeathed the estate to her kinsman, Lord George Sackville, of the family of the Dukes of Dorset. Lord George's direct descendant, Charles Sackville, the 5th and last Duke of Dorset, also lies in a magnificent tomb in Lowick Church, having died in 1843.

MARSTON SAINT LAWRENCE

IN THE CHURCH OF SAINT LAWRENCE

Sir John Blencowe (1642-1726)

Member of Parliament
Baron of Exchequer
Judge of the Common Pleas

Marston Saint Lawrence had been in the hands of the Blencowe family for years, and John Blencowe was born there in 1642. He went to Christ Church College, Oxford and thence to the Inner Temple where he was called to the bar in 1673. He became a Sergeant at Law (equivalent to a QC) in 1689.

Brackley in those days was entitled to send a Member to Parliament, and Blencowe became the Member for Brackley between 1690 and 1695, and was fervently pro-government. He married well, having married a daughter of that great theologian, astronomer and mathematician of the 17th century, John Wallis (incidentally, from an old Finedon family, his grandfather having been born there) who at that time was Savilian Professor of Geometry at Oxford.

When Wallis refused the Bishopric of Hereford, he asked instead for favours for his son-in-law. Accordingly in 1696, Blencowe was made a Baron of the Exchequer Court (by some historical quirk, judges of the Exchequer Court were called Barons, rather than Judges) but one year later was transferred to the Court of Common Pleas with a knighthood.

Although not having a very distinguished career as a judge, he did court a bit of controversy in 1718. In that year, he concurred with his fellow judges when they supported the king, George I, who wanted to control his children's education and marriages himself, rather than having the House of Commons think it any of their business, as they had done before.

John Blencowe retired in 1722. Apparently he had to, because 'his faculties had decayed', but to compensate, he was allowed his full pay until he died. He spent his retirement trying to get his son to lay before Parliament his crackpot scheme he had invented to establish Longitude. Sir John, who was described as ' kindly, honest and blunt, but with no great qualifications', died in May 1726.

William Blencowe (1683-1712)

First salaried government code-breaker

Although William Blencowe was not the first government code-breaker there had been, he was the first to do it full-time and get paid for it. He had a good teacher. His maternal grandfather was no less than the Savilian Professor of Geometry at Oxford, Doctor John Wallis, who was already working on breaking the codes of letters and despatches from other countries intercepted by William III's government.

Wallis, on seeing his grandson's aptitude, taught him everything he knew, and in 1703, Blencowe succeeded Wallis as principal code-breaker for the government. And for this he received a salary of £200 per year.

The third son of Sir John Blencowe, William had been born in Marston Saint Lawrence and had gone to Magdalen College, Oxford, where his grandfather was Professor. He had graduated with a BA in 1701, and had been elected a Fellow of All Souls College. He started work for the government in 1703, a year before progressing to his MA (BA graduates of Oxford and Cambridge are automatically given the degree of MA, upon application, after an interval of a few terms).

In August 1712, Blencowe, still only 29 and with nine years valuable secret service work for the government under his belt, committed suicide by shooting himself. The inquest verdict was suicide during temporary insanity brought about by a fever. He was not buried in All Saints Church, Northampton as it says in the *Dictionary of National Biography*, but in the family vault at Marston Saint Lawrence parish church.

The Blencowe memorials in Marston Saint Lawrence parish church. That of Sir John Blencowe is the middle one of the group of three highest; and that of William Blencowe is to its left.

MORETON PINCKNEY

IN THE CHURCH OF SAINT MARY

Edward Bagshaw (?-1662)

Member of Charles I's Parliament besieged in Oxford
Religious and Political author

Bagshaw's tutor at Oxford was Robert Bolton (*see* Broughton). Whilst a student at the Middle Temple in 1639, Bagshaw preached an address condemning bishops who meddled in politics, thus showing where his political and religious views lay. In the following year, he entered the 'Long Parliament' as the Member for Southwark.

When King Charles I was forced to move to Oxford in 1644, Bagshaw went with him and sat in the king's 'anti-parliament' there. This consisted of those members of the 'Long Parliament' who had sided with the king.

But he was captured by parliamentary forces in 1644, and imprisoned in Southwark. In his prison cell he wrote many books on ecclesiastical (mainly anti-bishop) and political subjects, including his best known work *A Life of Robert Bolton*. He was released in 1646, dropped out of public life, retired to his country estate at Moreton Pinckney, and died there in 1662. He was buried in Moreton Pinckney church, but has no monument.

NORTHAMPTON
(including Abington, Dallington and Weston Favell)

❁

IN THE CHURCH OF ALL SAINTS

❁

Simon Wastell (?-1632)
Rewrote the Bible in poetry

Not only did Wastell put the Bible into poetry, but his verses begin with successive letters of the alphabet, for every chapter of the bible, Old and New Testaments. This wonderful feat was published in 1623 as *A True Christian's Daily Delight*. These are the opening verses of the first chapter of the Book of Genesis:

At first Jehovah with his word
Did make heaven, earth and light:
The firmament, the moone and starres,
The glistering sun so bright.

By him the earth was fruitful made
And every creature good:
He maketh man like to himselfe
And doth appoint his food.

Creation ended, god then rests,
And Sabbath day ordaines:
Plants Eden, and the fruit forbids,
For fear of endlesse paines

Dust of the ground was man made of:
Of rib out of his side
The woman: Adam nameth all:
Wedlocke is sanctified.

Eve by the serpent is deceived,
They fall most shamefully:
God them arraignes, doth serpent curse,
And putteth enmitie.

Although this book was reprinted (by Ferdinando Archer) in 1683, Wastell himself published a second, modified and enlarged, edition in 1629, called *Microbiblion or the Bible Epitome*.

After graduation from Queen's College, Oxford in 1585, Simon Wastell was headmaster of Northampton Free School from sometime in the 1590s until he died in 1632. He married Elizabeth Beckinoe in 1591 and they had eleven children. Elizabeth died in 1626, and Simon died in 1632, both being buried in All Saints church, but with no memorial.

Ferdinando Archer (1608-1705)

Poet

Did he witness the Great Fire of Northampton?

Ferdinando Archer was headmaster of Northampton Free School after Simon Wastell. And in 1683, he was so taken with Wastell's *Microbiblion* that he republished it.

He was not a bad poet himself, however. He transcribed into English a poem originally written in Latin by the vicar of All Saints, Simon Ford, describing the Great Fire of Northampton in 1675, of which Ford was an eyewitness. Archer's translation was called *The Fall and Funeral of Northampton*, and gives frightening detail of the behaviour of a large fire. The description is so graphic, perhaps Archer was also a witness, which is why he chose to translate the poem in the first place, adding his own observations to those of Ford. He was certainly in Northampton at the time, and it is inconceivable that he did not see at least some of the fire.

Here tumbles down a Chimney; there a Wall;
Then, the whole Fabric, Roof and all.
The spattering Stones, in flakes about the place,
and Slats, spit Wild-fire in the face.
Beams, Tracings, Rafters tumble in, and Floor;
Flames vomiting through every Door.
Each House of Stone a burning Oven, red
With its own Furniture is fed
Who with devouring Fire can longer dwell?
There to abide would be an Hell.

Archer was headmaster from 1646 until 1695, nigh on 50 years. He died aged 97 in 1705 and was buried, with no monument, in All Saints church.

IN THE CHURCHYARD OF SAINT GILES

Robert Browne (1550?-1633)
The first Nonconformist

People who do not conform to the teachings of the established Anglican Church are called Nonconformists. Among the groups that this term covers are Baptists, Methodists, Congregationalists, Presbyterians, Unitarians and Quakers. Their numbers now are very large, and they have organised churches themselves. But the man who started it all off, and is taken to be the very first Nonconformist is Robert Browne, who after a stormy life, now lies peacefully here in the churchyard of Saint Giles.

The memorial to Robert Browne in Saint Giles' churchyard - unfortunately not escaping the modern curse perpetuated by deeply inferior intellects which this society of ours now breeds.

Coming from a wealthy Stamford family, he could number amongst his relatives the famous William Cecil, Lord Burghley of Burghley House. This relationship was to prove very valuable on several occasions, as on the times that Browne was thrown into prison, he was always mysteriously released again soon after, a fact put down to Lord Burghley pulling strings behind the scenes.

Corpus Christi College, Cambridge was notoriously puritan, and whilst there Browne loudly denounced all things 'Popish'. After taking his degree in 1572, he started off by being a schoolmaster in London. But he started preaching his views in the open air. When the plague struck London in 1578, he moved to Cambridge where he met Richard Greenham, Vicar of Dry Drayton.

Greenham encouraged Browne to preach in the surrounding villages, but without a bishop's licence to do so. Because of his fame, however, this seemed to be overlooked, and the parish of Saint Benet's in Cambridge invited him to be a curate there. Which is strange, as Browne was not then ordained, conventionally at least. But whilst he was there, he formulated his theory that the existing church government was wrong, and he became vehemently anti-bishop. So when a friend obtained preaching licences for him from the Bishop of Ely, Browne tore them up and threw them into the fire.

His theory took root in his mind, and he concluded that the parish system was also wrong as well. He did not like 'leaders of religion' (such as bishops and even parish priests) and considered that people did not need a 'leader' to gain access to God.

He preached his views loudly, so much so, in fact, that the good parishioners of Saint Benet's could not agree with him any more. So he went to Norwich where he heard that there were people who shared his views.

His outdoor preaching soon gained him converts, and the 'Brownist' sect grew up – the first Nonconformist 'church'. But this gained enemies, and the Bishop of Norwich soon saw to it that Browne was clapped into prison. But Lord Burghley rode to the rescue, and Brown was released.

Sensing that things were getting hot, Browne and the Brownists escaped to Middelburg in Holland. There, in 1582, he published his two great books setting out his theories: *A book which sheweth the Life and Manner of all True Christians,* quickly followed by *A Treatise of Reformation without tarrying for any*.

Before long however, Browne's hot tempered quarrelsomeness caused him to fall out with the Middelburg Brownists, and so he was on the move again. This time he went to Scotland with about four or five families who still followed him.

But the same thing happened. Preaching in the open air, Browne violently stated his views. This of course led him to being brought before the Kirk elders, and because of his arrogance and self-importance, was promptly clapped into gaol again. And, yes, once again, he was released soon afterwards with no explanation.

Scotland did not want him, so he journeyed to London, where in 1584, he published another book *An answer to Mr Cartwright's Letter for joining with the English Churches*. Thomas Cartwright had been the Professor of Theology at Cambridge until he had been deprived, but who had criticised Browne. And yet again, he was thrown into prison – and yet again he was released.

His father was still living at Tolthorpe near to Stamford, and Browne sought to visit him, after which he felt the call to spread his views to the good people of Northampton. But his preaching upset the Bishop of Peterborough, who summoned the notorious Browne before him. And then promptly excommunicated him.

The effect was amazing. Browne was so shocked and taken aback that he meekly submitted to the Bishop. In return for pledges of good behaviour, he was made Master of Stamford Grammar School in November 1586. He remained at Stamford until 1591 when he was made Rector of Little Casterton in June, but then moved immediately to Achurch near to Oundle in September. The Bishop of Peterborough ordained him Deacon and Priest on the same day, Monday 30 September 1591, which, interesting to note, is some three months *after* he had been Rector of Little Casterton.

So Robert Browne was tamed. For 40 years he was to remain as Rector of Achurch, and cease his nonconformist agitation.

And that would have been that. But the old campaigner could not leave this life quietly. When, in 1630, the Parish Constable of Achurch asked for Browne's rate money, the old man, now just over 80, got so incensed that he hit the Constable.

The Constable, who in actuality was Browne's Godson, was loathed to do anything, but the local magistrate got to hear, and promptly had Browne carted off to gaol in Northampton Castle. Not surprisingly, Browne quickly succumbed to the unhealthy prison surroundings, and died in October 1633. He was buried in the churchyard of Saint Giles.

His followers were called Brownists, and Robert Browne's teachings over the years formed the foundations of the Congregational Church. In 1972, the Congregational and Presbyterian Church combined to form the United Reformed Church. Robert Browne, the first Nonconformist, is lying in Saint Giles' churchyard, and gently smiling.

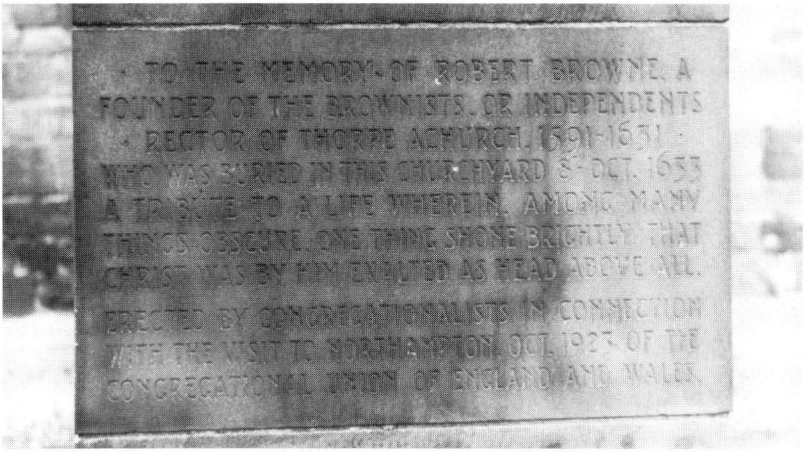

The inscription on Robert Browne's memorial.

IN THE CHURCH AND CHURCHYARD OF SAINT PETER

John Smith (1652-1742)

Engraver
Personal friend of Sir Godfrey Kneller and Sir Peter Lely

John Smith became famous for his portrait engravings, and thus met all the rich, famous and great of his day, including the Duke of Cumberland, ('Sweet William' or 'Stinking Billy' depending upon which side you are on) eventual victor at Culloden. Because he was considered the best, he became the favourite engraver of Sir Peter Lely, but more especially of Sir Godfrey Kneller who invited Smith to stop as a guest in his house for some time.

John Smith was born in Daventry, and articled to a printer in London. He studied under two of the great engravers of the time, Isaac Becket and Jan van der Vaart.

After 1700, Smith had his own shop in Covent Garden where he sold his own engravings, and there are still about 500 of his portraits in existence. Having made his money, he retired to Northampton where he died in 1742. He was buried in the churchyard of Saint Peter.

John Smith's plain and simple memorial in Saint Peter's church.

❀

William Smith (1769-1839)
'The Father of English Geology'

William Smith has no connection with Northampton, either borough or county, and the only reason he is buried in Saint Peters is because when he died, he was visiting George and Alice Baker. He is buried in the churchyard, under the west window.

He was born in Oxfordshire of humble origins, but he taught himself about fossils and geometry. Becoming an assistant surveyor, he gained great knowledge of the soil and rock stratigraphy for the whole of the country.

He became famous as an authority on drainage and irrigation and when his map of the stratigraphy of the British Isles was published in 1815, which was the first ever map of this sort, he laid the foundations of the science of stratigraphical geology. Not for nothing is William Smith known as 'The Father of English Geology'.

William Smith was honoured many times in later life, including the Wollaston Medal in 1831 and a government pension. His fossil collection is now in the British museum.

The impressive memorial to William Smith, as befitting 'The Father of English Geology'.

The actual grave of the 'Father of English Geology', under the west window of Saint Peter's church. The inscription William Smith LL.D can just be deciphered.

IN THE ABBEY CHURCH OF THE GREYFRIARS

Humphrey Stafford,

1st Duke of Buckingham (1402-1460)
Witness to the Trial and burning of Joan of Arc?
Killed at the Battle of Northampton
Step-Grandfather to Henry VII

This is a bit of a 'let-down' really, as the Abbey Church of the Greyfriars no longer exists, and the graveyard to the church was destroyed at the tail end of last century. However, if you want to see the site of Humphrey Stafford's grave, just take your life in your hands and stand in the middle of Greyfriars Bus Station, Northampton. And if you survive, that I am afraid, is the nearest you will ever get to it.

Where the grave of Humphrey, Duke of Buckingham *would* have been.

Humphrey Stafford was an advisor to Henry VI and accompanied him on his journey into France between 1430 and 1431. Perhaps Humphrey knew the king's nursemaid (*see* Cranford Saint Andrew), and perhaps he also saw the trial and burning of Joan of Arc in May 1431. Henry created him the 1st Duke of Buckingham in 1444, and Lord Warden of the Cinque Ports in 1450.

All in all, he was a politician of moderate views, and during the Wars of the Roses tried to mediate between York and Lancaster. Whilst fighting for Henry VI at the Battle of Northampton, Humphrey was killed. He was taken by the Grey Friars (the Friars Minor of the Franciscan order) and buried in their own church in Northampton.

His son, Henry married as his second wife, a certain Margaret Tudor, whose son by her first marriage, would become Henry VII. Humphrey's second son, John, would become the 1st Earl of Wiltshire, and his son, Edward, the 2nd Earl, lies in Lowick church. For a family tree, *see* Great Addington

IN THE ABBEY CHURCH OF SAINT JAMES

Sir John Catesby (?-1486)

Uncle of 'The Cat'
Judge of Common Pleas

As with the Abbey of the Greyfriars, the Abbey of Saint James no longer exists. It was dissolved by Henry VIII during his purge, and the buildings were gradually demolished. The only reminder we have of its existence now, is Abbey Street in Northampton, which stands on the site, and where in 1927, the last remaining wall of the old abbey was pulled down. As with the Greyfriars, the cemetery has long since been lost, but two important people were buried there.

John Catesby was uncle of the notorious and blood soaked William 'The Cat' Catesby, henchman to Richard III (*see* Ashby Saint Legers). When Henry Tudor defeated Richard III at Bosworth Field in 1485 and took the throne as Henry VII, he delayed reaffirming Catesby as a judge because of his nephew's shenanigans. But by the intercession of William Waynflete, Bishop of Winchester, Henry relented and reaffirmed John Catesby as a Judge of Common Pleas.

John Catesby had been called to the bar by the Inner Temple, made a Sergeant of Law in 1463, and in 1469, became the King's Sergeant of Edward IV (the king's own personal barrister). Edward made Catesby a Judge of Common Pleas in 1481 and knighted him a year later. John Catesby died in 1486, being buried in the church of Saint James.

Richard Woodville, 3rd Earl Rivers (?-1491)

Brother in law to Edward IV
Uncle to one of the Princes in The Tower
Uncle to Henry VII

Richard, 3rd Earl Rivers, is the only member of the Woodville family of Northamptonshire which so dominated fifteenth century England, to have been buried in his native county. His sister, Elizabeth, after becoming queen of England by marrying Edward IV, was buried in Saint George's Chapel, Windsor.

His father, the 1st Earl Rivers, and his brother John, being caught up in the imbroglio of the Wars of the Roses, were both executed at Kenilworth and buried there. Richard's brother, Anthony, 2nd Earl Rivers, came to a sticky end as well, when he was seized by the usurping Richard of Gloucester, who promptly had him executed, and then proclaimed himself Richard III the day after.

Richard Woodville thus became the 3rd Earl Rivers in 1483. But despite being attainted for treason by Richard, he managed to survive, and was restored in 1485 after Richard's defeat at Bosworth.

Richard had had the misfortune to see his sister's sons (Edward V, aged 13, and 10 year old Richard, Duke of York – 'The Princes in The Tower') disappear in mysterious circumstances, but had the 'last laugh' when his sister's daughter married Richard's deposer, to become Henry VII.

Richard died without heirs in 1491. Ironically, that same year saw the birth of his great nephew, who as Henry VIII would be destined to destroy the very Abbey where Richard willed that his body should be buried.

Abbey Street, Northampton, on the site of the Abbey of Saint James. The last parts of the actual abbey buildings were pulled down in 1927. The graves of William Catesby and the last of the Woodvilles have long since vanished.

IN THE UNITARIAN CHAPEL, KING STREET

George Baker (1781-1851)

County Historian

As is the case with the Greyfriars and Saint James' Abbeys, the burial place of George Baker no longer exists. King Street is still there, but all the buildings have long since gone, and in King Street today stands the *Moat House* Hotel. So if you want to be near the last resting place of George Baker, book a room and stay the night.

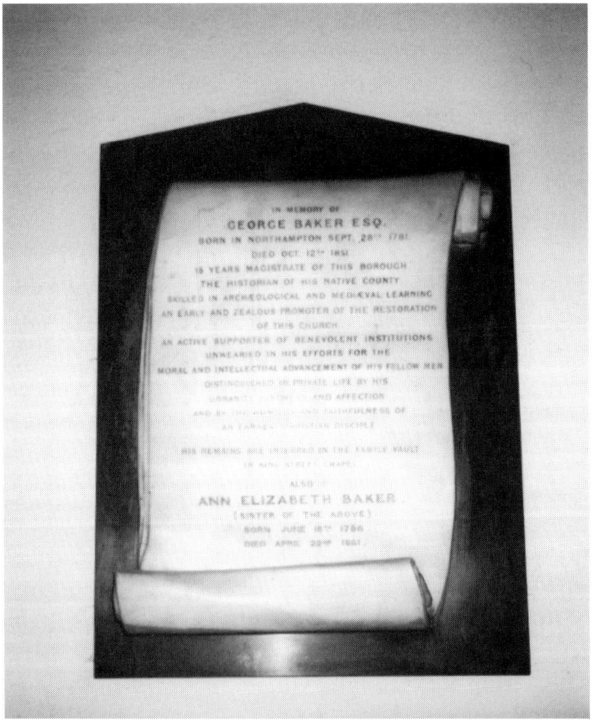

The tablet to George Baker in Saint Peter's church, Northampton. His actual grave in King Street Unitarian Chapel has long since disappeared.

Baker's *The History and Antiquities of the County of Northampton*, is one of the four great historical works of the county, along with Whellan's, Bridges' and Morton's. George Baker first proposed his great work in 1815, and he started collecting material straightaway. He did not have the money to publish it himself, and he had to rely on subscriptions. The first part appeared in 1822, the second in 1826, and the third in 1830, which completed the first volume. The fourth part was published in 1836, and some of the fifth part in 1841.

But at that point, some of his subscribers failed him, and he could not complete it. So in 1842, he was forced to sell all his manuscripts and library, and his work was never finished. This is one of the great shames of history, and is only partly mollified by having Bridges', Whellan's, and the work of John Cole (*see* Woodford) to fall back on.

George Baker never married, and lived with his sister on a small private income, in Haselrigg House, Marefair, which still stands, and was one of the few houses in Northampton town centre to survive the Great Fire of 1675. Although he and his sister were buried in the Unitarian Chapel, there is actually a monument to him in Saint Peter's Church, Northampton.

IN THE BILLING ROAD MUNICIPAL CEMETERY

Caroline Chisholm (1808-1877)

The 'Emigrants' Friend'

In Australia, Caroline Chisholm is regarded as one of the great founding pioneers of the country. So much so that her portrait is on the Australian $5 bank note. Yet in her native England she is virtually unknown.

Born Caroline Jones in Wootton, she married Archibald Chisholm, a soldier stationed at Weedon in 1830. Two years later the couple moved to Madras in India where, because of the vice and degradation she saw all around her, she opened schools to care for the young girls. These schools became known as the Female Schools of Industry. But in 1838 the couple had to leave India for health reasons, and they eventually finished up in Sydney in Australia.

Caroline Chisholm was struck by the helplessness of the female emigrants, and opened a home for the newly arrived colonists. This house provided a safe place for emigrant girls to stay, until they could find employment. On frequent

occasions, Caroline ventured into the outback to check upon suitable employment opportunities for her girls.

At first she was entirely self-funded, but later received contributions from interested authorities. Having set up the Australian end of the emigrant trail, Caroline and Archibald returned to London in 1846. There they established centres where prospective emigrants could receive help. And financial help too. Caroline established the Family Colonisation Loan Society which lent money for emigration to be repaid later.

So successful did she become that by giving evidence to the 1847 Select Committee on Emigration, she succeeded in changing government policy. Families of convicts transported earlier could now be sent out to join them when they had completed their sentence.

She wrote two books on her work. In 1850 her handbook *The ABC of Colonisation* was published, and soon afterwards, *Emigration and Transportation relatively considered.*

Once she had organised the London end of the emigration trail, Caroline Chisholm, with her husband, returned to Australia in 1854 and continued the work. The Chisholms stopped in Australia for a further 12 years, at the end of which, the emigration machinery

The inscription of Caroline Chisholm as 'The Emigrants' Friend'.

was well in place and working efficiently and smoothly. They returned to England in 1866 and retired.

Caroline Chisholm died in 1877. Archibald only survived a few months and was buried alongside Caroline in Billing Road Cemetery.

Caroline Chisholm's gift of compassion, coupled with her obvious administrative skills, was available at exactly the right time and place that it was needed. Her work eased the growing pains of an emerging country, and Caroline Chisholm will forever be remembered by her nickname of 'the emigrants' friend'. It is because of these very reasons, that there are now plans to apply for Caroline Chisholm's beatification, being the first step to full canonisation.

The grave of Caroline Chisholm.

James Kemp (1837-1868)

Murdered Police Officer

The gravestone to James Kemp, erected by public subscription.

James Kemp has two claims to fame. He was the very first Detective Constable of the Northampton Borough Police, appointed in 1864, and he was the first Borough policeman to die violently on duty.

Boxing Day in 1868 was a Saturday. Detective Constable Kemp had just finished his 'late turn' and at 10pm was heading home to his wife and children. At the bottom of Abington Street, he met two friends, and they went for a 'quick one' at a pub in Newland. Coming out of the pub at 10.30, the three men crossed Newland, walked by Holy Sepulchre church, and into Campbell Square.

Standing also on Campbell Square that night was William Bridgewater, who was drunk, and had a loaded shotgun. Bridgewater at that point was mentally unstable because of huge domestic problems he had encountered over Christmas. When he saw Kemp, coming towards him, he thought it was one of his brothers coming to get him. With no warning or compunction, Bridgewater fired at point blank range at Kemp. Kemp collapsed with fatal wounds to his left neck and shoulder, and would die in agony three days later, whilst doctors, unable to mend such a large wound looked helplessly on.

Bridgewater was arrested. Instead of being found guilty of murder, which it obviously was, the Jury (perhaps 'influenced') reduced the charge to manslaughter, and he received 20 years penal servitude. James Kemp was buried, and his headstone erected, by public subscription.

Joseph Ball (1783-1877)

First Chief Constable of the Northampton Borough Police

Already in charge of the old system of Northampton watchmen since 1828, Joseph Ball was the automatic choice to be the first Chief Constable of the newly formed Northampton Borough Police in 1836. The boroughs of the

country had been enabled to use the 'new police' system (i.e., professional, full-time police officers, instead of part-time amateurs) by the Municipal Corporations Act of 1835.

Northampton Borough Police was modelled along the lines of the Metropolitan Police of London, and would last right up until 1966. It was then (forcibly) amalgamated with the County Constabulary to form the Northampton and County Constabulary, which in 1974, was renamed to today's Northamptonshire Police.

Joseph Ball resigned in 1851 to make was for his successor, Henry Keenan. He lived on in retirement, and died at the grand old age of 94. Because of clearance of headstones in Billing Road Cemetery, the exact location of his grave is unknown.

Henry Keenan (1822-1901)
Second Chief Constable of Northampton Borough Police

Henry Keenan was born in Ireland, and was an Inspector of the Manchester City Police, when he was made Chief Constable of Northampton Borough Police in 1851. He was unmarried, but in 1859 married Jane Buswell, a local girl. They never had children of their own, but brought up Henry's niece and nephew, Henry, junior and Alice.

It was Henry Keenan, with his vast experience of a large city police force who introduced improvements and developments that Joseph Ball never could have done. Keenan was responsible for Northampton Borough Police being well managed and well thought of, with many of his ideas still being recognisable one hundred years later. He improved conditions in Fish Street Police Headquarters, where he also lived, and introduced working practices for the good of the officers of the force. It was Keenan who started the Detective Department and appointed poor James Kemp as the first Detective Constable.

He retired in 1887, and his wife died in 1889. Henry himself lived to see ten months of the new century and died in October 1901. As with Joseph Ball, his exact grave is unknown.

'Sir' Robert Fossett (1850-1922)

'The greatest bare-back rider of them all'

The only thing that could have gone on the tomb of Robert Fossett was a horse. "The horse is more reliable than any motor contraption" he once said "the motor is a stranger to me, and I to it". The beautiful and breathtaking tomb of Robert Fossett pays allegiance to the great tradition of the Fossett family for having the best riding acts ('jockey acts') in all the long history of the circus.

The Fossett family is one of the oldest families of the circus world, and over the years have intermarried with all the other great circus families. Robert Fossett was part of this tradition, and especially his family tradition of the jockey act.

At his height, he was generally reckoned to be the champion circus jockey. His favourite trick was to run across the ring with his feet encased in wicker baskets, and with a sack tied over his head, and then jump onto a galloping horse that had rosin sprinkled onto its back for greater grip for the feet – the 'rosinback'. He also liked to do the 'in character' horse acts, which acted out small plays involving spectacular horsemanship. His favourite of these was 'Shaw the Lifeguardsman' which acted out the 'Charge of the Light Brigade'.

He was not really knighted, but was known as 'Sir' Robert, after the fashion of the time -the 1890s. George Sanger, upon hearing that Buffalo Bill called himself 'The Honourable', not to be outdone, styled himself 'Lord' George Sanger. And thus, Bob Fossett duly became 'Sir' Robert Fossett.

During the latter nineteenth century, Robert Fossett's Circus remained a tented circus, rather than touring the music halls. Nobody knew exactly where the tradition of big tops came from, but Robert Fossett had a theory that the first circus tent was derived by a sailor, who alone had the expertise to handle large areas of canvas and rigging.

Robert Fossett died in 1922 aged 72. Why he is buried in Northampton remains unclear, as the local newspapers of the time neither mention his death nor his funeral. But be that as it may, here he lies, with his wife, Mary, and one of his sons. Go and see the tomb, it is well worth it to see the horse draped over with a mourning cloth, with its head downcast in sadness.

George Percy Abbott (1880-1923)
Pall bearer at Queen Victoria's Funeral
A member of Scott's last Antarctic expedition

George Percy Abbott sailed on the *Terra Nova* on 1 June 1910, as a member of Captain Scott's expedition to try to be the first to reach the South Pole. A Petty Officer in the Royal Navy, Abbott had been chosen for his physical fitness, and had actually been a pallbearer at Queen Victoria's funeral nine years earlier. Captain Scott did not sail with them, but remained in London for another six weeks to raise money, before joining the expedition at Cape Town in August 1910.

In his diaries, Captain Scott mentions Abbott as 'an exceedingly nice gentlemanly fellow', and at one point was trying to teach him taxidermy. Doctor Edward Wilson, the Chief Scientific officer, also mentions Abbott in his diaries, and remembered how adept he was at skinning penguins for dinner.

In Antarctica, Scott divided his expedition into two. His main party would be at McMurdo Sound, and from it would be chosen the men who would make the final assault upon the Pole. Another party, the 'Eastern Party', consisting of six men, would be landed in King Edward VII Land, 40 miles to the east under Lieutenant Victor Campbell of the Royal Navy.

Abbott was chosen to be in this party, but when they reached the Bay of Whales, they actually discovered that the ship *Fram* was already anchored there. On board was Roald Amundsen, who, by a remarkable coincidence, had also chosen the Bay of Whales as his jumping off point for the Pole. Because of this, Campbell's party went north, and became known as the 'Northern Party', being landed on Cape Adare. There they settled down to scientific research.

The story of Scott's expedition, and what happened to them, is well known. Because things went so horribly wrong, the 'Northern Party' was marooned for the whole of one Antarctic winter, with no supplies or contact.

In terrible conditions, the six men of this party managed to survive, but so bad did things become, that at one point Abbott actually lost his mind with the dreadfulness of his situation. However, they were eventually rescued, to the news that Scott was dead, and that Amundsen had beaten them to the South Pole anyway.

George Percy Abbott, by then in the Royal Air Force, died at the early age of 43. He was buried in Billing Road Cemetery of his home town, in what is now an unmarked grave.

IN THE TOWCESTER ROAD MUNICIPAL CEMETERY

After 1868, public executions were stopped, and all hangings thereafter were carried out privately inside gaols, with the bodies being buried inside the gaol perimeter. When the Northampton Borough Gaol on The Mounts in Northampton was closed and demolished in 1931, the bodies of the five murderers hung there were exhumed, and on the night of Wednesday/Thursday 22/23 April 1931, were reinterred in unconsecrated ground in the Towcester Road Cemetery.

Patrick Byrne (1841-1878)
Hung for the Murder of Samuel Griffiths and John Brooks

For the 'Militia Stores' double murder of Monday 2 September 1878, Militia Sergeant Patrick Byrne was hanged. Byrne, who was drunk, had been ordered out of his quarters at the Militia Stores in Great Russell Street, Northampton. In a fit of rage, he had used his rifle to shoot dead both Paymaster Sergeant Griffiths and Quartermaster Sergeant Brooks.

The north east corner of Towcester Road cemetery. The bodies of the seven murderers lie in unconsecrated ground under the far hedge, just to the right of the centre of the picture.

Andrew MacRae (1857-1893)
Hung for the Murder of Annie Pritchard

What is left of the body of Annie Pritchard is buried at East Haddon. For a description of MacRae's treatment of her, *see* East Haddon.

Richard Sabey (1843-1893)
Hung for the Murder of Louisa Sophia Johnson

Although the murder occurred in Finedon parish, the body of Louisa Johnson was taken to Burton Latimer village, which was nearer. She was buried in the new cemetery opposite Burton Latimer parish church, *see* Burton Latimer.

Joseph Parker (1875-1899)
Hung for the Murder of Mary Meadows

Joseph Parker and Mary Meadows had been courting for four years. When Joseph shot Mary in the head on the morning of Saturday 11 March 1899 in Kingsthorpe Hollow, Northampton, it was broad daylight, and in a public street. Nobody knows to this day why he did it. It never appeared to be of much consequence at the time, as the murderer had given himself up to a policeman minutes afterwards. Was it a suicide pact which went wrong? Was he going to shoot himself afterwards, but lost his nerve? The questions are many, and the answers few. Joseph Parker was hanged on Tuesday 11 July 1899.

Alex Claydon (1858-1901)
Hung for the Murder of Louisa Claydon

The murder and mutilation of the body of Louisa Claydon by her husband Alex is also unexplainable. Returning home drunk on the night of Saturday 6 July 1901, Alex had gone to bed besides his sleeping wife.

Waking up at 1am, he quite deliberately fetched a large metal rasp, and continually smashed it down on Louisa's head so many times, that the pathologist could not count the wounds. He then went downstairs, made himself some egg sandwiches, and then quite calmly returned to bed, and lay down to sleep alongside the battered corpse of his wife.

When he awoke three hours later, his shirt was soaked in Louisa's blood and brains. He then left the house, and walked off. He gave himself up to the police at Moulton three hours later.

Alex Claydon was hanged at Northampton Borough Gaol on Friday 13 December 1901.

Samuel Rowledge (1867-1904)
Hung for the Murder of Alice Foster

Samuel Rowledge and Alice Foster were engaged to be married, and were both in their 30s. It appears that Alice had a sharp tongue, and nagged Samuel continually because she thought him 'work shy', which he probably was.

In the early evening of Tuesday 15 March 1904, Samuel and Alice were together when they received a visit from Samuel's brother, Alfred. He told Samuel off about some work that he had not turned up for, and no doubt Alice chipped in her two penny worth as well.

Samuel stormed out, returning a few minutes later with a revolver. He fired three times, apparently all at Alice, but Alfred thinking the shots were for him, ran off through the door. At the later trial, the judge severely criticized Alfred for his 'cowardly actions'. Alice, however, died immediately.

No motive was ever forthcoming for this, and the defence barrister tried to plead insanity. He failed. Samuel Rowledge was hanged on Wednesday 13 July 1904.`

John Eayrs (1855-1914)
Hung for Murder of Sarah Eayrs

John Eayrs has the 'distinction' of being the last man hanged in Northamptonshire, in 1914. After that date, only one murderer (Alfred Arthur Rouse in 1931 *see* Hardingstone) in the county required the ultimate penalty, and that was carried out at Bedford.

John Eayrs was found guilty of the murder of his wife at Peterborough on Saturday 22 August 1914. The Eayrs' were notorious for being drunk and quarrelsome with each other, and John had continually threatened to 'do his wife in' for a long time because of her nagging.

On that Saturday evening, John and Sarah actually had a fight in the street. Sarah escaped and John chased her indoors. Just before ten o'clock, a neighbour hearing moans, discovered John in his backyard. He had made a half-hearted attempt at suicide with a knife by cutting his own throat. Upstairs, the body of Sarah was found with her throat completely cut.

John Eayrs was hanged at Northampton Borough Gaol on Monday 9 November 1914.

❁❁❁

ABINGTON

❁

IN THE CHURCH OF SAINTS PETER AND PAUL

❁

Sir Edmund Hampden (?-1629)

One of the 'Five Knights' of 1627

The tombs of Sir Edmund Hampden and his wife are the two table tombs on the right, in the north chapel of Abington church. The oblong tablet to the memory of Elizabeth Barnard compensating for the lack of acknowledgement of her grandfather on her actual tombstone, is above the table on the left of the picture.

The Stuart kings were always looking for easy money. Charles I thought he had found the perfect way, when he re-discovered 'forced loans'. Because he ruled by 'Divine Right' he thought he could force people to 'lend' him money. Sometime he got away with it.

But in 1627, five knights (John Corbet, Thomas Darnell, Walter Earle, Walter Heveningham and our Edmund Hampden) refused point blank to pay a 'forced loan' demanded by Charles I. He, not unnaturally, was unimpressed, and promptly threw them all into The Tower. And they, on their part, again, not unnaturally, objected.

In November 1627, they sued the king under the Writ of Habeus Corpus. Habeus Corpus (Latin: *you have the body*) was a writ in common law to deliver a person to court, or explain why they are being kept in prison without trial.

Charles won his case, and the Five Knights were returned to prison. But public outcry was so great that all five were released soon after. The Five Knights case effectively ended anymore 'forced loans' and caused the rights of the individual to be examined.

Edmund Hampden did not fare well. In a contemporary journal, the *Weekly Accompt* "he endured for a long time together close imprisonment in the Gatehouse about the loan money which endangered his life, and was a very great means so to impair his health that he never after did look the same man he was before"'

Sir Edmund Hampden died in 1629, and was buried in Abington church, his country estate.

Elizabeth, Lady Barnard (1607-1671)
Shakespeare's Grand daughter

Elizabeth Hall was born in Stratford upon Avon, the only child of John Hall and his wife Susannah, nee Shakespeare. She lived with her parents in Stratford and when the great man died in 1616 leaving her all his estate, she went to live at New Place, Stratford.

In 1626, as a young girl of 19, she married Thomas Nash, a Stratford barrister, but was left a childless widow in 1647. Two years later she married John Barnard and came to live at his estate in Abington.

The last of Shakespeare's direct descendants lies here, in the south aisle of Abington church, under the organ, and under the far grander monument to William Thursby. Only the merest desultory details of Elizabeth Barnard are engraved on the stone.

John Barnard was knighted by Charles II in 1661 and so Elizabeth became Lady Barnard. John Barnard died in 1667 and was buried in Abington church with a memorial. When Elizabeth died four years later, she was buried alongside her husband. But she was not considered important enough (remember, she was Shakespeare's grand daughter) to be added to the monument. However, this was rectified a few years ago, when a new tablet was placed in the north chapel acknowledging who she was.

DALLINGTON

IN THE CHURCH OF SAINT MICHAEL

Sir Richard Rainsford (1605-1680)

Lord Chief Justice of England
Member of the Commission for the rebuilding of London after the Great Fire of 1666

The aftermath of the Great Fire in London of September 1666 gave immense problems. The city needed rebuilding, but there were legal niceties to attend to. Who, for instance, owned what; and would they sell their plot if that was in the middle of a proposed new street? And what if they did not want to sell? And so on, and so on. A Commission was set up to look at these problems, and Richard Rainsford was chosen as a member, because at that time he was a Judge of the Exchequer Court.

Broadly speaking, the Commission failed, and Christopher Wren's grandiose new city plan was never adopted, because people just could not wait, and rebuilt their houses where they had been before, thus reinstating the original street plan. Nevertheless the Commission did influence Parliament in passing laws to make these new buildings better designed and therefore less of a fire hazard.

Born at Staverton, Richard Rainsford went to Exeter College, Oxford, but left with no degree. He entered the legal profession, being called to the bar by Lincoln's Inn in 1632. A Recorder is a barrister appointed as the sole judge for a borough's Quarter Sessions court, and Rainsford became the Recorder of Northampton in 1653.

On his restoration, Charles II called his first Parliament in 1661, and Rainsford sat as the Member for Northampton. He was made a Sergeant of Law (today we would call this a QC), and was so well though of that in 1663, he was knighted and made a judge.

In 1676, Richard Rainsford became the Lord Chief Justice of England. However, in 1678, he 'retired' aged 73. There was some talk that he was 'nudged' out of office because the powers that be wanted him replaced by Sir William Scroggs, who was seen as more staunchly Protestant, in an age when religious matters were taken far more seriously than they are today.

Rainsford had married Catherine Clark at Kingsthorpe in 1637, and they had five daughters and six sons. He died in 1680, and was buried in Dallington church, his country estate.

IN THE DALLINGTON MUNICIPAL CEMETERY

Susan Bostock (1862-1948)

Poetess

Three volumes of poetry *Spring Notes* of 1912, *The Call of the Uplands* 1913, and *The World of Heart's Delight* of 1930, mark out Susan Bostock as an accomplished poetess. Born in Northampton, she lived all her life in the town and died in 1948 at the age of 86.

From *Spring Notes*, come the first and last verses of 'A Yorkshire Mill Girl'.

You say she has a rugged face? Perhaps.
Too hard, scarce feminine enough? Ah, well,
Hers is a rugged life. Look at those hills,
A lurid darkening smoke for aye enwraps
Their barren sides, and may be (who can tell!)
Such cheerless gloom for aye her spirit fills.

What hidden tragedy within her eyes
Mikes silent protest! Death will draw someday,
His curtain o'er them. Will she wake at last
To welcome with a new and glad surprise
That other life, that greet eternal Day
Which fears no future, and which mourns no past

WESTON FAVELL

IN THE CHURCH OF SAINT PETER

James Hervey (1714-1758)

Personal friend of John and Charles Wesley
Religious author

The beautiful and impressive wall monument to James Hervey in Abington church.

Whilst at Lincoln College, Oxford, Hervey met John Wesley, who was a tutor there. He became great friends with the Wesley brothers and was in sympathy with their Methodism. But he never left the Church of England, and was ordained in 1736. After curacies at Oxford and Dummer in Hampshire, Hervey became Vicar of Stoke Abbey in Devonshire in 1738. It was here that he wrote his best known work *Meditations among the Tombs*. This is perhaps too sober sided for today's tastes, but when it was first published in 1746, it ran to 17 editions in one year, and by 1791, had notched up 25.

His father was Vicar of Weston Favell, and James returned there to be his father's curate in 1743. But his health was none too good and he went to London. His father died in 1752, and James returned to Weston Favell as Vicar.

Three years later he lost the friendship of John Wesley. In his book *Dialogues between Theron and Aspasio*, Hervey expounded views which upset Wesley, who published harsh criticism of the book. This stung Hervey, who responded with answers in none too friendly a vein, but never published them. They were only published eight years after Hervey's death, and then contrary to instructions in his Will.

James Hervey wrote prolifically on religious subjects, and a full edition of his works was published in 1769, which ran to six volumes. But he was far too dour a personality, which was reflected in his writings, to appeal to us today, and probably why he never married. He died in 1758 and was buried near to the high altar in Weston Favell church.

NORTON

IN THE CHURCH OF ALL SAINTS

Sir Richard Knightley (1533-1615)

Present at the Execution of Mary, Queen of Scots
Printer of 'The Marprelate Tracts'

Being the son of a wealthy landed gentry family, Richard Knightley in his youth had a happy, carefree and high-spirited youth. But in his maturity all that stopped, and he became known for his strict Puritanism.

He was a great friend of Robert Dudley, Earl of Leicester, who at that time was on intimate terms with Queen Elizabeth, and it was rumoured that he was trying to get the queen to marry him. Dudley had been created Earl of Leicester by her in 1564, and on behalf of the queen, he knighted Richard Knightley at Fotheringhay Castle in 1566.

Sir Richard Knightley was made Sheriff of Northamptonshire in 1568, 1581 and again in 1587. And it was in that year, in his capacity as Sheriff of Northamptonshire, that he attended the beheading of Mary Stuart, Queen of Scotland in the Great Hall of Fotheringhay Castle in February 1587.

At the same time as all this was going on, in Wales, a certain John Penry, an extreme Puritan, was being thrown into gaol for attacking the Welsh clergy and bishops when preaching in the open air. When he was released, he started writing pamphlets which outrageously and scurrilously attacked the pomposity of the bishops and their beliefs, in coarse sarcasm and bawdy wit. The pseudonym he chose to write under was 'Martin Marprelate'.

Being much in sympathy with the tenor of 'The MarprelateTracts', Knightley secretly started paying for more of the pamphlets to be printed and distributed. The press on which the tracts were printed was moved around the country so as to escape capture, and in the autumn of 1588, it was installed at Fawsley House, the manorial home of the Knightley family.

The next pamphlet in the series, *Epitome of Martin Marprelate*, was printed at Fawsley in the autumn of 1588. After Christmas, the press was moved to Norton, where Knightley had another house, and in the New Year, to Manchester, where it was eventually captured.

The government of the time was furious and outraged, and ruthlessly tracked down the perpetrators. Knightley was arrested and tried in the Star Chamber for Sedition and Treason. But on the intercession to the queen by John Whitgift, the Archbishop of Canterbury (who had himself been one of the objects of attack and ridicule), Knightley was released, but was deprived of his offices. John Penry was not so lucky (or had not the right connections - see below) and he was eventually hanged.

The only memorial to Sir Richard Knightley in Norton church, is this stained glass window in the south aisle.

Out of favour, Knightley wisely decided to lay low. He only surfaced again in 1605, when he petitioned Parliament on behalf of the Northamptonshire freeholders over an ecclesiastical matter. He was severely rebuked, and fined £10,000 for his pains.

He continued to stay on his country estates, away from the public eye, and he died in 1615. He was buried in Norton church besides his second wife, Elizabeth.

Lady Elizabeth Knightley (?-1602)
Daughter of the Lord Protector Somerset
Niece of Queen Jane Seymour
Cousin to Edward VI

Sir Richard Knightley's second wife was Lady Elizabeth Seymour. She was the second daughter of Edward Seymour, 1st Duke of Somerset, and Lord Protector of England from 1547 until 1550. Edward Seymour was a brother to Jane Seymour, third wife of Henry VIII, and mother to Edward VI (and the wife that Henry chose to be buried with him).

Lady Elizabeth Seymour was therefore niece of Queen Jane Seymour, and cousin to King Edward VI, and 'half-cousin' (if that is possible) to Queen Elizabeth I. This therefore would make Sir Richard Knightley related, in a roundabout sort of way, to Queen Elizabeth as well.

So do we have here a clue as to why Richard Knightley was released after 'The Marprelate Tracts' episode, whilst John Penry was hung? Perhaps John Whitgift, Archbishop of Canterbury, pointed out to Queen Elizabeth that perhaps it would be expedient to let Richard Knightley quietly back to his estates rather than risk possible embarrassment by imprisoning - or worse?

Lady Elizabeth Knightley died in 1602, and was buried at Norton.

Lady Elizabeth Seymour, as befits her rank, has this breathtaking monument.

OUNDLE

IN THE CHAPEL OF OUNDLE SCHOOL

Frederick William Sanderson (1857-1922)
Headmaster of Oundle School for 30 years

Behind the High Altar in the Chapel of Oundle School, there is a superbly carved memorial tablet:

Here lie the ashes of
Frederick William Sanderson
Headmaster 1892-1922
To whom God granted grace to
revive this ancient school which
is itself his memorial. By his
vision and enthusiasm he
transform'd the life of the school
promoted its vigorous growth
and enhanced its reputation.
Here rest also the ashes of
Jane Hodgson
his wife and helper.

Regarded as one of the great Oundle Headmasters, Sanderson built up the numbers and reputation of his school. When he started as Headmaster, there were 92 pupils. At his death, there were 500. New subjects were added, and the buildings extended, especially science and engineering blocks.

Frederick Sanderson went to Durham University and Christ Church College, Cambridge before teaching at Girton College and Dulwich College. He came to Oundle in 1892. In 1885 he had married Jane Hodgson, and they had two sons and one daughter.

Whilst lecturing in London in 1922, Sanderson died suddenly from a heart attack. His ashes, and those of his wife, rest in the chapel, and to his memorial tablet, nothing more need be added.

IN THE CHURCHYARD OF SAINT PETER

Robert Wild (1609-1679)

Presbyterian, but later Royalist, Poet

Robert Wild was once described as a fat, jolly and good Presbyterian. But when the Restoration of the Monarchy came in 1660, he seems to have done a complete about turn. After Oxford and Cambridge he was ordained by the Bishop of Peterborough and became curate of Aynho in 1639. Seven years later he 'intruded' to the living at Aynho.

In those religiously troubled times, parliamentary politicians, nicknamed Presbyterians because of their support of Presbyterianism (i.e. church government by a committee of clergy rather than a single bishop), forced ('intruded') their own Presbyterian clergymen into unwilling villages. Robert Wild was intruded into Aynho in 1646, and whilst there wrote a lot of poetry and articles supporting Parliament, Puritanism and Presbyterianism.

Come the Restoration however, and all the intruding ministers were ejected, and Wild moved to Oundle. But by this time, he seems to have been converted away from his former ideas. So much so, that in the Restoration year of 1660, he wrote his best known poem *Iter Boreale*.

This was inspired by General Monck's march from Scotland to London in 1659-60. Seeing the general confusion after the death of Oliver Cromwell in 1658, the exasperated General George Monck (later 1st Duke of Albermarle) marched south, entered London, refused supreme power, took parliament by the scruff of the neck, and started the process which a few months later restored Charles II to the throne.

Wild's *Iter Boreale* inspired by this became immensely popular in the less restrained Restoration age. Pepys mentions it in his diary, liking it enormously.

Robert Wild died at Oundle in 1679, and was buried in Oundle churchyard, in a grave, the location of which is now unknown. The following 'Two Epitaphs' is from the 1668 reprint of *Iter Boreale*.

For a Godly Man's Tomb

> Here lies a piece of Christ; a star in dust;
> A vein off gold; a china dish that must
> Be used in Heaven, when God shall feast the just.

For a wicked Man's Tomb

> Here lies the carcase of a cursed sinner,
> Doomed to be roasted for the Devil's dinner.

PAULERSPURY

IN THE CHURCH AND CHURCHYARD OF
SAINT JAMES THE GREAT

Sir Arthur Throckmorton (?-1626)

Friend and Brother in Law to Sir Walter Raleigh
Went with Raleigh to Cadiz

Sir Arthur's father was the famous Sir Nicholas Throckmorton, who amongst his many jobs in Queen Elizabeth's reign, was to act as her go between to Mary Stuart, Queen of Scotland. Sir Nicholas died in 1561 leaving six sons and one daughter.

This daughter, Elizabeth, or 'Bess' Throckmorton was a Maid of Honour to Queen Elizabeth. And it was at court that she caught the eye of the dashing Sir Walter Raleigh, old 'Muddycloak' himself. There must be more to it, perhaps jealousy on the part of the queen, but as soon as she found out that Sir Walter Raleigh and Bess Throckmorton were 'carrying on', Sir Walter was thrown into The Tower. He was released, but as he insisted on marrying Bess, which he did, he was banished from Elizabeth's court.

The lovely table tomb of Sir Arthur and Lady Throckmorton.

To get back into favour, Raleigh tried daring expeditions against the king of Spain, to bring back some Spanish gold. One such expedition was to Cadiz in 1596. And Raleigh took with him his brother in law, Arthur Throckmorton. The expedition was a success, Raleigh was accepted again at court, and Arthur Throckmorton was knighted.

Sir Arthur returned to Paulerspury to manage his estate. He was Sheriff of Northamptonshire in 1605.

Sir Arthur died in 1626. His tomb shows him and Lady Throckmorton reclining and gazing lovingly at each other – apparently 40 years married and never a cross word.

Edmund Carey
Father of William Carey

William Carey was born in Paulerspury in August 1761, son of Edmund Carey, the Parish Clerk and Schoolmaster. William Carey eventually became a Baptist Minister at Moulton, was one of the founders of the Baptist Missionary Society (*see* Kettering, Andrew Fuller) and its first missionary to India.

That William Carey did what he did, must be a reflection on the upbringing that his parents gave him. His father, Edmund, is buried at Paulerspury by the south porch of the church.

PIPEWELL

IN THE CEMETERY OF THE CISTERCIAN MONASTERY

Simon of Pattishall (?-1217?)

Chief Justice of the Common Pleas
Personal friend of King John
Present at the signing of Magna Carta?

Could Simon of Pattishall have witnessed that defining moment in English history, when King John was forced to accept Magna Carta? There is no reason why not, for at that time, Simon was a friend of King John and was his Chief Judge, travelling with the king on his wanderings about the country.

Simon was born in the Northamptonshire village of Pattishall sometime during the 1150s. Nothing is known of his family, but for him to be able to read and write, they must have been wealthy enough to afford his education.

Simon entered the administrative service some time in Henry II's reign (1154-1189), but it is in the reign of Richard I (1189-1199) that he makes his first documentary appearance. Escheats in medieval times were the property forfeited or confiscated by the crown when there was no apparent heir, and Simon of Pattishall was in charge of the Northamptonshire escheats. He was also in charge of Northampton castle.

But in 1190, his name appears as a junior Judge who tried the Kent and Surrey Assizes. A year later, he appeared as a Judge in a Northampton court, and was on the list of Judges that went to the Leicester, Lincoln and Norfolk Assizes. This obviously makes him a trained lawyer. He was also the chief Judge at the Northamptonshire Assizes of 1202 and 1203, the records of which were published in 1930 in Volume V of the books of the Northamptonshire Record Society.

In the spring of 1193, Richard I returned from his Austrian captivity, and he wanted money for another Crusade. Having said quite openly that everything was for sale in the country, Richard sold everything to the highest bidder. Simon of Pattishall paid 40 marks to become the Sheriff of Northamptonshire, which he remained for several years.

When Richard died in 1199, and his brother John became king, it was a disaster. Law and order broke down, and eventually judges no longer toured round the country to the Assizes. But though the Judges did not tour, the king did. He wandered all over the country taking some Judges with him, and we know that, after the year 1213, Simon was Chief of these Judges.

Two years later, King John fell out with Simon. Did Simon feel sympathy with the barons who he had witnessed forcing John to agree to Magna Carta? Who knows? Simon's lands were confiscated, but he was soon back in favour, as John needed all the friends he could get.

King John died in October 1216 from his gastronomic excesses, and it is believed that Simon died soon afterwards as well, probably in the early months of 1217. Simon was married, and one of his sons followed him into the law, and another, Hugh, became the Bishop of Coventry and Lichfield.

The Cistercian Abbey at Pipewell was founded in 1143, and the Abbott when Simon died was Robert of Pattishall, probably a relative. Simon of Pattishall was buried in the cemetery of the Abbey in a grave which is unfortunately now lost.

The burial ground of the Cistercian Monastery is believed to lie somewhere in the field beyond the fence.

QUINTON

IN THE CHURCHYARD OF
SAINT JOHN THE BAPTIST

James Dalgliesh Kellie-MacCallum
(1845-1932)

Chief Constable of Northamptonshire
The oldest and longest serving Chief Constable ever

Undisputedly the longest serving Chief Constable of any single county or borough police force ever, James Kellie-MacCallum was the only Chief Constable of Northamptonshire not to have had a police background. His previous career and experience had all been with the army, where for 16 years he had served with distinction when the British Empire was at its height.

James Dalgliesh Kellie-MacCallum was born in Edinburgh into the comfortably off upper classes. His land-owning father was a Deputy Lord Lieutenant and Justice of the Peace for Perthshire. James as befitting a young gentleman was educated at public schools before being bought an army commission.

So in May 1865, just two weeks before his 20th birthday, James became a Subaltern in the 79th Regiment of Foot, the Queen's Own Cameron Highlanders. Scarcely 13 months later, he went with his regiment to India, the 'Jewel of the Empire', where he was promoted Lieutenant in May 1868. He returned to England two years later.

In 1873, the wonderfully named King Coffee of the Ashantee people of West Africa (roughly corresponding to the modern country of Ghana) strongly objected to the transfer of his port, Elmina, from Dutch to British interest. He objected even more when the British refused to pay him any money to use the port as the Dutch had done, so he promptly revolted.

Consequently, to stop the king's tiresome petulance, and to impress upon him the might of the British Empire, an army was sent against him, under the command of Sir Garnet Wolseley (later Lord Wolseley, VC). The so called Ashantee revolt took nine months to suppress, during which time, four VCs were won, and the sickness rate of the troops was over 98 per cent.

Although the 79th Regiment did not take part in this campaign, Lieutenant Kellie-MacCallum was attached to The Black Watch, which was in the thickest fighting, receiving 104 casualties from 450 men. For his part in the campaign, Kellie-MacCallum received the Ashantee War Medal with the clasp *Coomassie*, which signified he was a member of the force that had crossed the Pra River and fought two battles of January and February 1874, which resulted in the capture of Coomassie, the Ashantee capital.

Returning to his regiment, Kellie-MacCallum remained with them until he went on the reserve list in 1880.

On Wednesday 19 October 1881, at the age of 36, he was elected the Chief Constable of Northamptonshire (taking over from Thomas Lees, *see* Guilsborough) which in those days also included the Soke of Peterborough, a position he was to hold for the next 50 years. This is the longest term of office for any Chief Constable anywhere, and not only that, at the age of 86 when he retired, he was the oldest as well.

In 1876, he had married Eleanor Frazer-Tytler of Inverness-shire and they had three daughters. After renting houses in Northampton, they built a house at Quinton in 1891, where Mrs Kellie-MacCallum died in 1909.

James Kellie-MacCallum received the King's Police Medal for Meritorious Service in 1914, and the OBE in 1920, being promoted to CBE four years later. He was also Deputy Lord Lieutenant for the county.

In today's police service, a Chief Constable would not be allowed to continue in office for 50 years, but would be compulsorily retired. But nevertheless, he was a real 'gentleman' if ever there was one. He could remember the name of every single one of his police officers on sight, always making a point of enquiring after their families - and always getting the details correct.

He retired on Monday 1 June 1931, although his last few months were soured by criticism of his force over the handling of the 'Blazing Car Murder' case (by Arthur Rouse, of an unknown man, *see* Hardingstone). Not surprisingly, he only lived a few months more. He died at Quinton on Wednesday 7 September 1932 and was buried next to his wife. A large number of police officers and family were at the graveside to hear a lone piper play *Flowers of the Forest* over his grave.

The grave of James Kellie-MacCallum, to the right. The cross marks the grave of one of his daughters.

ROCKINGHAM

IN THE CHURCH AND CHURCHYARD OF SAINT LEONARD

Lewis, 1st Baron Rockingham (1584-1653)

Had his knuckles rapped for losing Rockingham Castle to the Roundheads, but sweet talked his way out

By the time Sir Lewis Watson inherited Rockingham Castle in 1619, he had followed very much the well-worn path of the sons of the landed gentry. He had been to Oxford, called to the bar, and had been a Member of Parliament (for Lincoln). And on top of all that, he had been knighted as well.

He was a constant attender at the court of James I, where he was a close friend and confidante of the unfortunate George Villiers, Duke of Buckingham. Buckingham was the favourite of the month with King James, and he soon amassed a vast fortune by corruption. This only ended when he was assassinated in 1626. But by then, Lewis Watson had been made a baronet, and managed no doubt to distance himself from all the nastiness surrounding the demise of his former friend.

During the Great Civil War, Watson was on the king's side. But not too much, it seems, as on the eve of the outbreak of hostilities, he was summoned before the king to explain why he had 'failed to show a muster', in other words, failed to raise troops for the king.

Rockingham Castle, because of its commanding position, was a garrison that both sides in the war wanted as its own, and Watson was supposed to make it a Royalist stronghold. But on the sudden arrival of Roundhead troops under Lord Grey, Sir Lewis gave in without a struggle. He was expelled from Rockingham and went to his brother's house.

A few days later, he was arrested by Royalist troops under Colonel Hastings on a charge of treason for allowing Rockingham Castle to be captured. He was held at Belvoir Castle, and then taken before the king at Oxford. Lewis Watson was a barrister – he was a professional talker, used to using words for his own good. So well did he manage to sweet talk the king, that Charles forgave him, and actually ennobled him as the 1st Baron Rockingham.

When parliamentary forces captured Oxford after besieging it, Lord Rockingham was fined £5000. He returned to Rockingham Castle and died there in 1653. He had married twice, Catherine Bertie, who died young, and Eleanor Manners of the family of the Earls (later Dukes) of Rutland.

The Watson chapel in Rockingham church. Lewis, Baron Rockingham is buried here, but with no memorial.

Sir Michael Culme-Seymour, 3rd Baronet (1836-1920)

Admiral

Michael Culme-Seymour certainly saw some action in his 51 years in the navy. He was present at the major naval engagements of the mid-nineteenth century.

Joining the navy as a Midshipman in 1850, at the age of 14, he went straight into the Burma War of 1852, where the port of Rangoon was captured, and the British hold on Burma strengthened. The Baltic Campaign started in March 1854, when the British fleet sailed into the Baltic Sea, subdued the Russian fleet, and destroyed Helsinki.

The Crimean War of 1854-1856, was mainly an army campaign, but the navy provided valuable support in the Black Sea at the siege of Balaclava, and in the Sea of Azoff. The Second China War of 1858-1860 was waged because of maltreatment of European settlers in China. Eventually, Pekin was captured and the Chinese forced to sign a treaty. Michael Culme-Seymour was present at all that lot, when the British Empire was at its zenith.

He then entered his administrative period. In 1869, he was ADC to Queen Victoria, and between 1874 and 1876 was private Secretary to the First Lord of the Admiralty, who, as it happens, was another Northamptonshire man, George Ward-Hunt of Wadenhoe. By this time a Commodore, Culme-Seymour was further promoted to Rear Admiral in 1882.

He then went back to active service, but this time in command. He was in command of the Pacific Squadron from 1885 until 1887, and the Channel Squadron from 1890 to 1892, and then the Mediterranean Squadron between 1893 and 1897. On promotion to full Admiral, he was Commander-in-Chief, Portsmouth between 1897 and 1900.

He retired in 1901, after 51 years of naval service. Along the way, he had been awarded the GCB and GCVO, as well as succeeding as the 3rd Baronet in 1880. He lived in retirement at Wadenhoe. He had married Mary, daughter of Richard Watson of Rockingham in 1866. Mary died in 1912 and Michael died in 1920. Both were buried in Rockingham churchyard with views over the wonderful Welland valley.

Sir Michael Culme-Seymour, 4th Baronet (1867-1925)

Vice Admiral
Second Sea Lord

Following his father into the navy, Michael, junior was a Lieutenant in 1889, a Captain in 1905, and a Rear Admiral by 1916. He had married Florence Nugent in 1896, and they had a son and a daughter.

He was present at the great Battle of Jutland in 1916, for which both sides claimed victory, but in which the German Imperial Fleet was so badly mauled, that it was ineffective for the rest of the Great War. For the Battle of Jutland, Michael Culme-Seymour was Mentioned in Despatches and awarded the Commander of the Order of the Bath (CB).

After the war, he was the Commander of the Black Sea and Caspian Sea Squadron, and was Second-in-Command of the Mediterranean Squadron in 1920, the year he was awarded the KCB. That year also saw him promoted to Vice Admiral, and succeed to the Baronetcy when his father died. He was Commander-in-Chief of the North American and West Indies Station between 1923 and 1924, before becoming the Chief of Naval Personnel and Second Sea Lord.

Sir Michael Culme-Seymour died 'in harness' at the age of 58 in 1925. He was buried in Rockingham churchyard alongside his parents.

The Culme-Seymour graves in Rockingham churchyard.

RUSHTON

IN THE CHURCH OF ALL SAINTS
OR THE DEMOLISHED CHURCH OF SAINT PETER

Sir Thomas Tresham (?-1559)

Member of Parliament
Commissioner enquiring into the wealth of Cardinal Wolsey
Friend of Mary I
Grand Prior of the English Langue of the Order of St John

The Northamptonshire family of Tresham was Catholic and vehemently remained so despite the Reformation. This would lead to problems, and fines for Recusancy (*see* Bugbrooke) would financially cripple the family as well as give it some thorny times as it became involved against the king in the famous Gunpowder Plot.

Thomas Tresham was born at Rushton into a land owning family. His father had died by 1521, and Thomas inherited the estate. He was Sheriff of Northamptonshire in 1524–26 (and again in 1539-40 and 1555-56), and obviously noticed, because he sat on the Commission that enquired into the wealth of Cardinal Wolsey after he had fallen from power in 1529. Possibly as a result of all this good work, in other words, grabbing Wolsey's money and giving it to Henry VIII, he was knighted.

But Henry was a difficult king to serve. When he broke with Rome between 1532 and 1534 and made the country Protestant, Tresham had to retire to his estate because he refused to convert. The king could not control electors however, and Tresham sat for Northamptonshire in the Parliament of 1541-42.

When her brother, the Protestant Edward VI died in 1553, and despite his clumsy attempts to make the Protestant Lady Jane Grey his successor as monarch, Mary quickly saw off Lady Jane (in the 'nine days') and ascended the throne as Mary I. Immediately she tried to return the country to Catholicism. Tresham was now back in favour, and it was him who proclaimed her queen at Northampton in July 1553, and then became her personal bodyguard as she marched into London to take the throne.

Henry VIII and Edward VI had suppressed the English Langue of the

Knights Hospitaller of the Order of St John (*see* Stanford, Sir Ambrose Cave) but Mary revived it. She made her faithful servant, Sir Thomas Tresham the Grand Prior, and as such, this entitled him to sit in the House of Lords, which he did.

Mary died in November 1558, and before he would be affected by Elizabeth I's return to Protestantism, Thomas Tresham died just a few months later in March 1559. His tomb, in All Saints church Rushton, shows him in his full robes as the Grand Prior, the only tomb in the country so to do. However, there was another church in Rushton, Saint Peter, nearer to the Hall, and it is there that Sir Thomas was buried. Saint Peter's was demolished in 1785, and the tomb (and presumably the remains as well) were moved to All Saints.

The magnificent tomb of Thomas Tresham, wearing the robes of the Grand Prior of the Order of Saint John.

Sir Thomas Tresham (1543?-1605)

Imprisoned for Recusancy
Friend of Saint Edmund Campion
Builder of the Triangular Lodge
Father of Francis Tresham of the Gunpowder Plot

Because Thomas' father had died when he was only three, and his grandfather, Sir Thomas the Grand Prior, had died when he was about 13, young Thomas was bought up as a Protestant. It was seen as expedient by his guardians in those religiously troubled times. As such, he was able to enter the political life of the country and was Sheriff of Northamptonshire in 1573-74, and was knighted in 1577.

But in 1580, he reconverted to Roman Catholicism, and as such was able to give shelter to Edmund Campion (later beatified) in 1581. Campion, a Jesuit, had arrived in England in June 1580 to begin a new Jesuit Mission. This so alarmed the government that he was ruthlessly hunted down and had to go into hiding, being passed from house to house by sympathisers intent on keeping him out of harm. They failed. He was arrested in July 1581, and beheaded that December. In the retribution which followed, Tresham was arrested, tried, and spent seven years in the Fleet prison. Released in 1588, he retired to Rushton, but he was imprisoned again in 1597 and 1599 for Recusancy (*see* Bugbrooke) and annually fined huge sums of money.

It was in between these bouts of prison, that Tresham built his three surviving buildings (Triangular Lodge, Lyveden New Bield, and Rothwell Market Hall) and earned him the nickname of 'Thomas the Builder'.

Sir Thomas died on Sunday 11 September 1605, and this date is critical. Had his death occurred just two months later, English history would have been decidedly altered. Because of his father's death, Francis Tresham was perceived by the English Catholics to be a rich man, recently come into a large inheritance. He was approached by the Gunpowder Plotters for financial support. In all probability he was not that rich, as the family had been bled dry by the Recusancy fines, but the Plotters were not to know this. No need to tell the rest of the story, it is so well known, but Francis Tresham was arrested after the discovery of the Plot (did he write the revealing letter to his brother in law Lord Monteagle?) and placed in The Tower. He died a month later in December, and his body was mutilated. His head was stuck on a pole in Northampton and his headless corpse was unceremoniously dumped into a hole in the grounds of The Tower. Thankfully his father was unaware of all this. He had been buried in Saint Peter's church just three months previously.

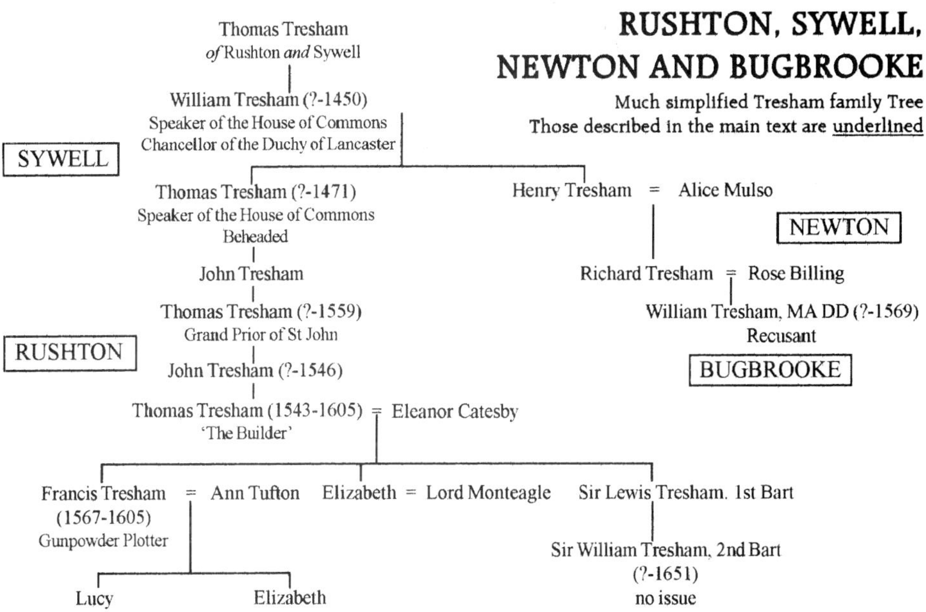

SIBBERTOFT

IN THE CHURCHYARD OF SAINT HELEN

Reverend Miles Joseph Berkeley (1803-1889)

Botanist

The greatest advances always seem to come from the ranks of the 'dedicated amateurs'. This is not a derogatory term, but means a person whose main livelihood lies elsewhere, and who therefore follows his 'hobby' with far greater passion than a paid professional normally does. Miles Berkeley must head this list - alongside Lord Lilford (*see* Achurch).

For it is not as a priest that Miles Berkeley is remembered, but as a world renowned botanist. His hundred of articles, books, and publications cover every aspect of botany, from the Irish potato disease of the 1840s, to gardening articles in the *Gardeners' Chronicle*.

Born at Oundle in 1803, Miles Berkeley went to Rugby School, and then to Christ's College, Cambridge, where he graduated BA in 1825, progressing to MA in 1828. He was ordained at Peterborough Cathedral in 1826, and his first Curacy was at Saint John's, Margate. In 1833, he became Curate of Apethorpe and Woodnewton, although he lived at King's Cliffe. He was made Rural Dean of Rothwell, but in 1868, was instituted to the living of Sibbertoft, where he remained for the rest of his days.

His contribution to the knowledge of botany, and more especially mosses and fungi, is inestimable. He was chosen to describe and catalogue, the fungi collected by Charles Darwin during his voyage on HMS *Beagle*; also to catalogue the collections from the expeditions of Hugh Cuming to the Philippines, George Thwaites to Ceylon, and the German botanist, Berthold Seeman, to Fiji.

Of his many books, *Introduction to Cryptogramic Botany* (1857), *Outlines of British Fungi* (1863) and *Handbook of British Mosses* (1867) are pioneering works, and remained standard references for years afterwards. He also wrote the volume on Fungi in Sir James Smith's *English Flora* of 1836.

He was a member and Botanical Director of the Royal Horticultural Society, and its Journal editor for 11 years. He was made a Fellow of the Linnaen Society in 1876, a Fellow of the Royal Society in 1879, and had the supreme accolade of a genus of algae, *Berkeleyea*, being named after him.

Increasing deafness caused his retirement from scientific work in 1879, though he continued his parochial work. He therefore presented his fungi collection of over 10,000 specimens, plus all his books and notes, to the Royal Gardens at Kew. When he died in 1889, his algae collection was presented to his old university, Cambridge, and thence to the British Museum.

Miles Berkeley was buried in Sibbertoft churchyard just by the south door of the church he had ministered in for over 30 years. Two years later, his beloved wife, Cecilia, was laid to rest besides him.

SOUTHWICK

IN THE CHURCH OF SAINT MARY

John Knyvet (?-1381)

Member of Parliament
Judge of the Common Pleas
Only the second secular
Lord Chancellor of England in 300 years
Executor of the will of Edward III

Born on an unknown date in Southwick, John Knyvet is known to have been practising law by 1347. He became a Sergeant at Law (what we would now call a QC) in 1357, and a Judge of the Court of Common Pleas in 1361. From 1362, he was also the Member of Parliament for Northamptonshire.

Ten years later he was made Lord High Chancellor of England by Edward III, which is the highest law officer in the country. His appointment was only the second non-clergyman ever to have been Lord Chancellor since the Norman Conquest 300 years earlier.

But in January 1377, he was dismissed. Edward III was on his deathbed with only five months to live, and he was well and truly under the influence of his son, John of Gaunt. Knyvet was dismissed, and the Chancellorship was returned to the clergy in the shape of Adam Houghton, the Bishop of Saint David's, and obviously one of John of Gaunt's 'yes men'.

Knyvet never held office again, but was not completely out of favour. He was consulted on a few legal matters, and was made executor of the will of Edward III in 1377.

He had married Eleanor, the daughter of Lord Bassett of Weldon, and they had two sons. John Knyvet died in 1381 and was buried in the nave of Southwick church. The gravestone is still visible, although the brass inlay that should have been there has long since been stolen.

The grave of John Knyvet is believed to be on the right.

STANFORD

IN THE CHURCH OF SAINT NICHOLAS

Sir Ambrose Cave (?-1568)

Knight Hospitaller of Saint John of Jerusalem
Member of Parliament
Chancellor of the Duchy of Lancaster
Friend of Elizabeth I who wore her garter on his arm

The year is 1099. The Second Crusade under Godfrey de Bouillon, Duke of Lorraine, lays siege to Jerusalem. The city falls in August; the Crusaders enter, and find a small band of Christian monks running a hospital. This small band under Gerrard of Provence start caring for the sick Crusader knights, who, in gratitude, build a bigger and better hospital for them. They take as their patron, Saint John of Jerusalem, who the Christians also call Saint John the Baptist. Thus was born the great Order of Knights Hospitaller of Saint John of Jerusalem.

Over the centuries, Priories of the Order (otherwise called Langues, which is the French word for tongue or different language) sprang up in many lands, England included, and sons of noble families were proud to enter the semi monastic life of the Knights Hospitaller. Sir Ambrose Cave was a Knight Hospitaller, as was Sir William Tresham who became Grand Prior of the English Langue (*see* Rushton where he is buried).

Sir Ambrose was attached to the Priory at Shingay in Cambridgeshire. He tried to become the governor there, but failed, but obviously stopped there, as in 1549, when the Priory was dissolved in Henry VIII's great monastic dissolution, Cave received a pension of £66 per year for past services. The *Dictionary of National Biography* states that as a Knight Hospitaller he had visited Rhodes, the Headquarters of the Order before it settled in Malta. But the year given is 1525. This cannot be as Suleiman the Magnificent ejected the Order from Rhodes on 1 January 1523. But as the Order had been in Rhodes since 1310, then Sir Ambrose could have visited, which he obviously did, the *DNB* just having got the date wrong.

After the Knights Hospitallers were dissolved (they did not really, they just went dormant, and were revived by Mary Tudor), Cave turned to politics. He was Member of Parliament for Leicestershire in the Parliaments of 1543, 1547 and 1543, and for Warwickshire in 1550, 1559 and 1562. Elizabeth I, who also promoted him to be her Chancellor of the Duchy of Lancaster, made him a Privy Councillor. He was chosen to be on the Commission to administer the Oath of Supremacy, and sat on many more governmental Commissions.

Cave was often at Court, and on one occasion, a garter slipped off Queen Elizabeth's leg. Cave picked it up and offered it back to the Queen who declined to take it. Cave straightaway slipped it on his left arm and swore that he would always wear it. And he did. There is a portrait of him where the garter is clearly shown.

Sir Ambrose cave died in 1568, and is buried in Stanford church, where he had his family home.

The lovely memorial in Stanford church to Sir Ambrose Cave, Knight Hospitaller and Chancellor of the Duchy of Lancaster. A visit to Stanford is recommended purely for the Cave memorials.

STEANE

IN THE CHURCH OF SAINT PETER

Sir Thomas Crewe (1565-1634)

Speaker of the House of Commons

The lovely table tomb of Sir Thomas and Lady Crewe.

Two things are of importance in the life of Thomas Crewe. Up to 1621 he had lived the standard life of a professional talker, by being a barrister and politician. In the parliament of 1620, he was the Member for Northampton Borough.

Queen Anne (of Denmark, wife of James I) had died in 1619 after 30 years of marriage. The king was 53 and wanted to marry again. It was Thomas Crewe, Member of Parliament for Northampton who stood up in the House of Commons and opposed the king's re-marriage. This, naturally, did not impress the king, and as a 'punishment', he sent Crewe away to Ireland on a Commission to look at aspects of Irish politics. For nine months of 1622, Crewe was away in Ireland and when returning across the Irish Sea, was actually shipwrecked on the Isle of Man.

James must have thought that Crewe had suffered enough. The following year, at a newly elected parliament, Thomas Crewe was knighted, and then became the Speaker of the House from 1623 until 1625, when he retired from politics to concentrate on the law.

James Touchet, eldest son of the 2nd Earl of Castlehaven, took his father to court in 1631 for unnatural offences. It was Sir Thomas Crewe who was the prosecuting counsel against the earl, who was found guilty and in 1633 forfeited his titles to his son.

Sir Thomas Crewe died in 1634 and was buried in the family vault of the chapel he had built at his country estate at Steane

John, 1st Baron Crewe (1598-1679)

Member of both the Short and Long Parliaments
One of the 'Secluded Members' in 'Pride's Purge'
On the Council that restored the monarchy
Escorted Charles II back from exile
Friend of Samuel Pepys

By being a member of the Council that asked Charles II to return to England as king, and being amongst the deputation that met him at The Hague and escorted him back to London, John Crewe was elevated to the peerage. He became the 1st Baron Crewe of Steane.

But it had not been easy. He had been imprisoned twice by Parliament. The first time, in 1640, when Member of Parliament for Northamptonshire in the Long Parliament, he was imprisoned for a year for failing to hand over papers of a Committee of Religion of which he had been the Chairman. And the second time was after the famous (or indeed, infamous) 'Pride's Purge'.

On Sunday 6 December 1648, Colonel Thomas Pride of the Parliamentarian Army had brazenly marched into the House of Commons with a troop of soldiers, and arrested 45 Members who favoured negotiating with the king rather than putting him on trial as the army wanted. The army wanted the king disposed of, and, indeed, would get their way two months later. John Crewe was one of the 'Secluded Members' arrested by Pride and he was thrown in gaol. Crewe had always had royalist sympathies, and in 1646, because he was the local Member of Parliament, had negotiated with the king when he was held prisoner at Holdenby House.

So by 'Pride's Purge' in 1648, Parliament rid itself of any opposition. Only when the king was on trial, was it thought safe to free the 'Secluded Members', and Crewe was released on 29 December.

In the Parliament of 1654, Crewe was again returned for Northamptonshire, and it was in this session that he moved a Resolution of the House deploring the execution of the king in 1649. And in the first parliament after the death of Cromwell (in 1658), Crewe again sat for the county. By then, it was clear that Richard Cromwell ('Tumbledown Dick') did not want to carry on like his father. It was this Parliament that proposed the restoration of the monarchy. And John Crewe as we know, became a leading member of the Council for the Restoration.

Lord Crewe of Steane then retired from active politics. He was a great friend of Samuel Pepys, the diarist, and is mention in the diary several times. Crewe had married Jemimah Waldegrave and they had six sons and two daughters.

Lord Crewe died in December 1679 and was buried in the family vault at Steane.

The Crewe monuments in Steane parish church, with the one to John, 1st Lord Crewe on the right.

Nathaniel, 3rd Lord Crewe (1633-1721)
Discredited personal friend and sycophant of James II
Bishop of Oxford and Durham

'There have been fewer meaner men in the annals of bishops' is the opinion of Arthur Mee's *Northamptonshire* of Nathaniel Crewe. And it is hard to disagree when confronted by his sycophancy and venality.

When he was a Fellow of Lincoln College, Oxford, Nathaniel Crewe so toadied to James, Duke of York, King Charles' brother, that in 1669, he was made Dean and Precentor of Chichester. And this was only five years after being ordained, with no parochial and pastoral experience. This was obviously James' influence, and it is hard to escape the feeling that James was using Crewe.

James, a Catholic, gambled that one day he would inherit the throne, as Charles II had produced no legitimate children (although plenty of the other sort), so to have a high ranking Protestant clergyman on his side would be highly beneficial. Which is why, in 1671, he persuaded his brother to make Nathaniel Crewe the Bishop of Oxford. And thus began what the *Dictionary of National Biography* calls his 'discreditable career as the favoured ecclesiastic of the Duke of York'.

It is inconceivable that a Protestant bishop could perform a wedding ceremony between two practising Catholics. But that is what Nathaniel Crewe did when he married James to Maria d'Este at Dover in 1673. A year later he was translated to the much richer and more powerful diocese of Durham, and became James' domestic chaplain. He also baptised Catherine Laura, James' and Maria's daughter in 1675.

So he continued. In 1685, James did indeed become king, and then started to turn the country Catholic. The Bishop of London, Henry Compton (of the same family as the Marquis of Northampton) objected, and was deposed. The administration of the London diocese was given to Crewe and to Bishop Sprat of Rochester, another of James' lackeys. As a result, Crewe was offered, and snapped up, the post of Dean of the Chapels Royal. Nathaniel Crewe is reported to have said "that he could not live without the king's gracious smiles". At one time, Crewe was only prevented from going to meet the Papal Nuncio on a visit to England, by his coachman who, knowing where he was going, refused point-blank to take him.

But James II failed to turn the country Catholic and in 1688 was forced to abdicate, in what historians call the 'Glorious Revolution'. Nathaniel Crewe also went into hiding, as well he might. He tried to toady to Parliament to excuse his actions, so although he was not included in a general pardon of 1690, he was allowed to remain as Bishop of Durham, although his powers of electing canons to the cathedral were taken from him. Severely chastened, he remained as Bishop of Durham for the rest of his life. Perhaps he had the last laugh, though, as with 47 years tenure, he was the longest serving Bishop of Durham ever.

He became the 3rd Lord Crewe in 1697 on the death of his brother Thomas, who was childless. In 1699 his first wife died, and she was buried at Steane. A few months later he married Dorothy Forster. This was a 'political' marriage, as the Forsters were an old and powerful north-eastern family, and he wanted to ingratiate himself with his diocese to make amends for his past naughtiness. However, even this was bizarre, as he was by then 67, and his bride was 24. But even with 43 years age difference, Lord Crewe still outlived his wife by six years. She died childless in 1715, and was buried in Steane chapel. It is said that Lord Crewe was heartbroken and would sit for hours gazing at her tombstone. So perhaps he deserves some shred of sympathy. He died in 1721 and was buried next to Dorothy.

The simple black marble slabs over the graves of Lord and Lady Crewe.

STOKE ALBANY

IN THE CHURCHYARD OF SAINT BOTOLPH

Thomas, 1st Lord Denman (1779-1854)

Defended Queen Caroline against her Divorce Bill
As Attorney General, drafted the great Reform Act of 1832
Lord Chief Justice
Anti slavery campaigner
Friend of Charles Dickens

George, the Prince Regent, was forced to marry Caroline of Brunswick in 1795. And they loathed each other. In 1820 the Prince Regent became George IV and tried to divorce Caroline for adultery. Lord Liverpool introduced a Divorce Bill into parliament, but when it came to the House of Lords, it came up against Thomas Denman.

Denman was an experienced barrister and defended Queen Caroline at the bar of the House of Lords. So good was his speech (it lasted for ten hours) that he succeeded in getting the divorce rejected, and Queen Caroline remained Queen Caroline. She died a year later, after suffering the embarrassing and scandalous refusal to be admitted to Westminster Abbey for her husband's coronation. Denman's actions naturally did not impress George IV and it was only by personal intervention of the great Duke of Wellington himself that stopped the king venting his wrath on him.

When George IV died in 1830, things became easier. Denman was knighted and made Attorney General. And it was Denman who drafted the Bill that finally became the great Reform Act of 1832. Students of British history need no reminding of what an immense landmark and breakthrough this was. If you do not know, shame on you, go and look it up.

Sir Thomas Denman was made Lord Chief Justice in 1832, elevated to the peerage as Lord Denman of Dovedale in 1834, and elected speaker of the House of Lords in 1835. Lord Denman sat in judgement on many famous trials and legal milestones of Victoria's reign: he abolished the death penalty for forgery; and passed a law which enabled people in court to affirm, if they objected to taking a sacred oath.

However, what he himself considered his greatest achievement, was to reduce the backlog of court cases by getting the courts to sit more often, rather that only during the very short legal terms. He was so proud of this, that in his Will, he directed that this fact should be engraved upon his tombstone.

But his later years were concerned with the abolition of slavery. From 1843 onwards, he published numerous pamphlets deploring slavery, and in 1848 came his finest hour on this point, when he forced the government to keep and upgrade the squadron of Royal Navy ships which patrolled the west coast of Africa looking for, intercepting, and arresting, slaving vessels.

He was a personal friend of Charles Dickens, but fell out with him over his crusade against slavery. Dickens made his character of Mrs Jellaby in *Bleak House* express views of Africans with which Denman did not agree, and he fell out with Dickens over this score.

Thomas, 1st Lord Denman died in 1854. Not perhaps the greatest Lord Chief Justice of all time, but certainly amongst the best. He was buried in Stoke Albany churchyard. Why he should be buried in Stoke Albany is unclear. He had no connection with the county, and the *Dictionary of National Biography* can shed no light. All I can guess is that one of his daughters married and lived locally, and nursed him during his last months, as he had suffered from several major strokes. But nevertheless, in Stoke Albany he lies, and his tombstone, when the moss is scraped away, proudly reveals what he considered his finest achievement. It reads:

BY THE AID OF HIS BROTHER
JUDGES GAVE TWO EXTRA
YEARS OF SITTINGS BETWEEN
1838 AND 1850 BY WHICH
MEASURE, EXTENDED TO OTHER
COURTS, DELAYS WERE
MADE ALMOST IMPOSSIBLE
IN ALL OUR COURTS
OF COMMON LAW

The stone tombstone over the grave of Lord Denman.

STOKE DOYLE

IN THE CHURCH OF SAINT RUMBOLD

Sir Edward Ward (1638-1714)

Attorney General
Lord Chief Baron
Tried, and sentenced to death Robert Charnock
Tried, and sentenced to death Captain Kidd, the pirate

Called to the bar by the Inner Temple in 1664, Edward Ward practised in the Exchequer Court, where he stayed for the majority of his career. In 1689 he declined to become a judge of the Common Pleas, but in 1693, did decide to become the Attorney General and was knighted. For some obscure historical reason, the judges of the Exchequer Court were given the title 'Baron' rather than 'Justice' and in 1695, Sir Edward became Lord Chief Baron, in other words, the chief judge of the Exchequer Court.

Although the Exchequer Court, as its name suggests dealt mainly in financial legal cases, its judges were competent to try criminal cases as well. And it is for being the judge in two famous criminal cases that Sir Edward Ward is remembered.

Robert Charnock was a Jacobite conspirator. He converted to Roman Catholicism when James II came to the throne, and was James' agent in the oppression of the Oxford colleges to convert to Catholicism. Come the Glorious Revolution of 1688, James was forced to abdicate, and Robert Charnock went as well. But in 1692 he returned and started plotting the assassination of William III. He was discovered and arrested in 1696. He was tried before Lord Chief Baron Ward, found guilty, and was hanged.

The other trial is far more famous. Probably the best known pirate of all time, William Kidd, known as Captain Kidd, was tried for piracy and treason in 1701. He was Scottish having been born in Greenock about 1645. After going to sea, he finished up in America, which then, of course, was still British.

Apparently he was a captain of a law-abiding trading vessel, but in 1696, the Governor of Massachusetts gave him the command of a ship, called

Adventure, and a roving commission to seize any pirates he found around the coasts of America. This was an attempt by the British to harass French shipping, as France was then at war with Britain.

But Captain Kidd, as soon as he hit the high seas and the Spanish Main, plundered everybody he could find – French, British, Spanish – it was all the same to him, it was easy pickings. His large treasure of gold, jewellery, doubloons and 'pieces of eight' which he amassed were rumoured to have been hidden (no doubt with a Treasure Map) on the island of Hispaniola. This treasure has never been found, so if it did exist, it could still be there. Eventually he was captured in Boston in 1699, and brought to England for trial.

At his trial, before Lord Chief Baron Ward in 1701, he pleaded that his actions had been forced upon him by a mutinous crew. The jury would have none of this, and found him guilty of piracy and treason. Sir Edward sentenced him to death, and he was hanged.

Sir Edward Ward died in 1714 and was buried in the church of Stoke Doyle, his country estate. His son rebuilt the church in contemporary style, and provided the magnificent tomb, which has a carving by John Rysbrack of Sir Edward's reclining full length figure.

The wonderful memorial to the Judge who passed the death sentence on Captain Kidd, the notorious pirate.

John Shillibeer (1786-1841)
Headmaster of Oundle School

In 1829, two men bearing the unusual surname of Shillibeer came to the fore. Both were from the same family. In London, a certain George Shillibeer started off the capital's very first 'bus service when his horse drawn coaches carrying over 20 passengers started to run from the City to Paddington. And in Oundle, John Shillibeer became Headmaster of Oundle School.

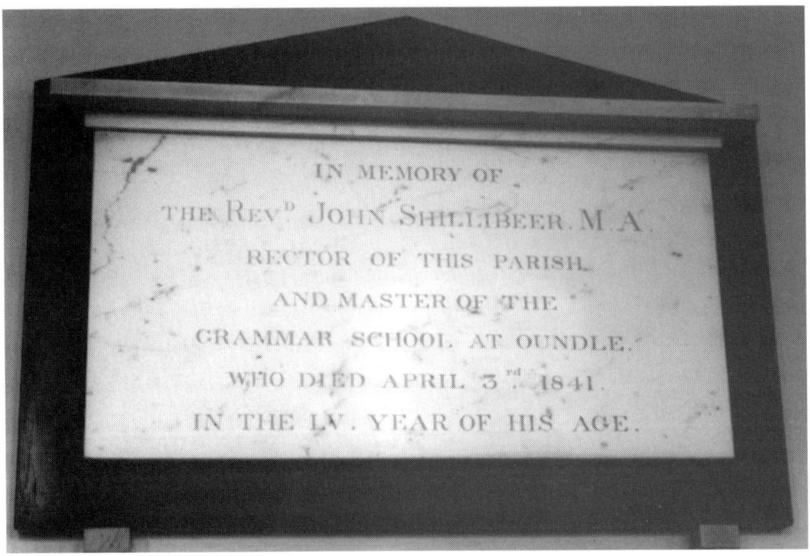

And the memorial to a much quieter spent life.

John Shillibeer had gone to Jesus College, Cambridge, had been ordained, and in 1823 became a curate at Oundle. In those days, the majority of schoolmasters were clergymen, and Shillibeer taught at Oundle School. Oundle School was a private school maintained by the Grocers' Company, one of the City of London Guilds.

In 1829 he was elected Headmaster, and as was the custom, took a local church living. He became Rector of Wadenhoe. He resigned Wadenhoe in

1831, and in 1833 became Rector of Stoke Doyle, where he remained for the rest of his short life.

Oundle School in those days had only 27 pupils, and Shillibeer started to build up the numbers. When he died suddenly in 1841, he had admitted 175 boys in those 12 years. He had also attempted to build the reputation of the school, and together with the Grocers' Company, had instituted two Exhibitions (Scholarships) to Cambridge University. He was a popular figure in Oundle, and his early death in 1841 came as a great shock.

He was buried in his parish church at Stoke Doyle, where there is a memorial. Another memorial was placed in Oundle church by public subscription.

SULGRAVE

IN THE CHURCH OF SAINT JAMES

Lawrence Washington (c1500-1584)

Mayor of Northampton

Great great great great great grandfather of George Washington

Born at Warton in Lancashire, Lawrence Washington served as bailiff to Lord Parr of Horton, who owned Warton manor. So that is how Lawrence Washington came to Northamptonshire - he moved to the county because his employer lived here, at Horton.

Beneath these brasses lies the great-great-great-great-great grandfather of the first president of the United States of America.

But in 1530, Lawrence Washington married Elizabeth Gough, who must have been quite a catch – she was a wealthy widow. Her first husband had been a prosperous merchant and burgess of Northampton Borough, who owned houses and property in the town. Washington appears to have taken over the widow's business, because he then left the employment of Lord Parr. He became a member of the Borough Council, and Mayor of Northampton in 1532 (and would be again in 1545).

Elizabeth must have died soon afterwards, because in 1538, Lawrence married yet another wealthy widow. Amy Pargiter of Greatworth owned the manors of Sulgrave and Stuchbury.

So Lawrence Washington came into the possession of Sulgrave Manor, and all his children were born there. He lived the life of a prosperous country squire and died in 1584.

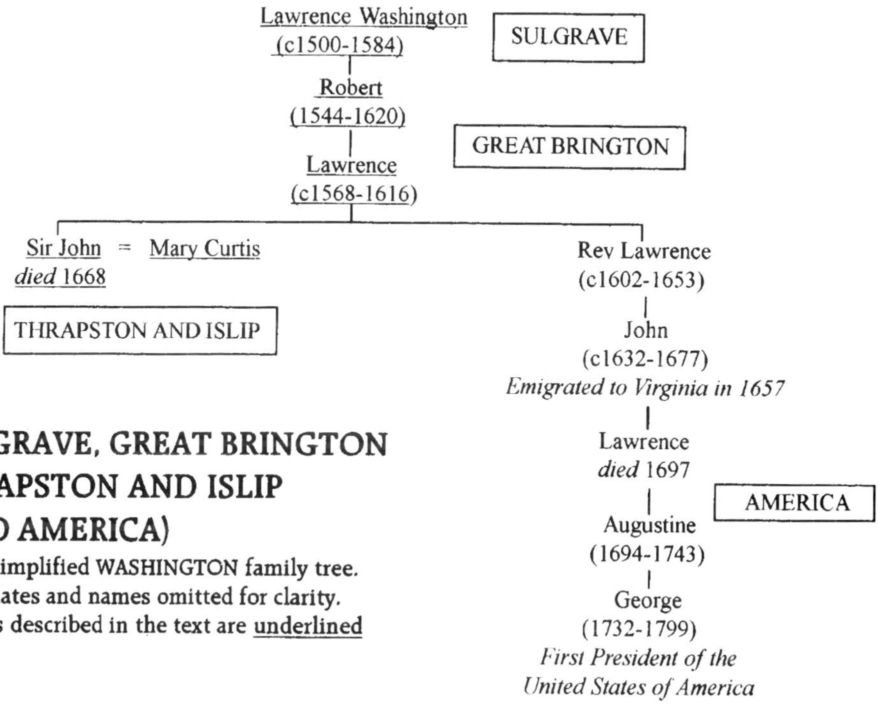

SULGRAVE, GREAT BRINGTON THRAPSTON AND ISLIP (AND AMERICA)

Much simplified WASHINGTON family tree.
Some dates and names omitted for clarity.
Persons described in the text are underlined

? SYWELL ?

? IN THE CHURCH OF SAINTS PETER AND PAUL ?

William Tresham (?-1450)

Attorney General to Henry V
Lancastrian Speaker of the House of Commons
Chancellor of the Duchy of Lancaster
Politically murdered by Lancastrians on suspicion of collaboration

This is pure speculation, it may or may not be right, but common sense suggests that Sywell should be the burial place of William Tresham. William Tresham was Attorney General to Henry V, had been the Speaker of the House of Commons four times, and in 1449 was created Chancellor of the Duchy of Lancaster. William Tresham was therefore an influential man in the Lancastrian hierarchy. To be suspected of collaborating with the Duke of York, then, was to say the least, not very clever of him. The two intended meeting at Northampton, but Lord Grey of Ruthyn, a staunch Lancastrian, got to hear.

Setting out from his Sywell home one September morning in 1450 on his way to Northampton, William Tresham was murdered in the vicinity of Thorplands in Moulton. Surely his body would have been brought back to his house at Sywell? And the next logical thing was to have him buried in Sywell church. There was simply nowhere else for him to go.

There are no brasses or memorials inside Sywell church, and the Registers do not go back that far. But until someone proves otherwise, Sywell has to be regarded as the burial place of William Tresham, Speaker of the House of Commons, and Chancellor of the Duchy of Lancaster.

For a Tresham Family Tree, *see* Rushton.

THENFORD

IN THE CHURCHYARD OF SAINT MARY

Michael Wodhull (1740-1816)

Bibliophile
Translator of Greek Classics

Michael Wodhull was one of those fortunates who could indulge his passion irregardless of what it cost. Michael Wodhull's passion was books. Collecting books.

Left a large fortune, Wodhull had a town house in Berkeley Square, London, and in 1765, rebuilt Thenford Manor, which is the present day building. He frequented all the nationwide book sales, and eventually his library at Thenford included rare first editions, as well as those specimens of printing in its infancy (between 1450 and 1500), which are called 'incunabula'.

To give an indication of how large his Thenford library was, in 1801 he arranged a sale of his *duplicate* books which took five days to complete. Two years later, another sales of his duplicates took eight days. When the library was eventually sold in 1886, 70 years after his death, the sale took ten days for the books, and another two days for the manuscripts.

Although leaving Brasenose College, Oxford with no degree, Wodhull was a formidable Greek scholar. He was the first to translate into English the complete works of Euripides, which was published in four volumes in 1782, and a second edition in three volumes in 1809.

After the Treaty of Amiens in 1802, which for a time gave peace between France and England, Wodhull tried his luck in the French book sales. But Englishmen were still treated with suspicion, and Wodhull was detained. He was only repatriated after falling ill.

Wodhull never fully recovered from this, and when Thomas Dibdin (renowned bibliographer, and cataloguer of Earl Spencer's library at Althorp) and Richard Heber (renowned bibliographer and brother to Bishop Reginald Heber, the hymn writer) visited him, they found him blind and dumb.

Michael Wodhull died in November 1816, and was buried in the churchyard at Thenford, in a grave which is now impossible to locate.

Thenford parish church. The grave of Michael Wodhull is here somewhere, although the actual spot is unknown.

THRAPSTON

IN THE CHURCH OF SAINT JAMES

Sir John Washington, 1st Baronet (?-1668)

Great great great Uncle of George Washington

John Washington was the son of Lawrence Washington *(see* Great Brington). He came to live in Thrapston after he had married Mary Curtis (*see* Islip). It was his nephew, John, his brother's son, who emigrated to Virginia in 1657, and who was the great grandfather of George Washington.

Sir John lived in a house which is still standing in Chancery Lane. He died in 1668 and was buried in a grave the location of which is now lost. There is, however, in the church, a tablet that carries the Washington coat of arms – a shield containing the stars and stripes.

The Washington coat of arms in Thrapston church.

IN THE CEMETERY OF THE BAPTIST CHAPEL, HUNTINGDON ROAD

Edwin Cottingham (1869-1940)

Clockmaker who made the Greenwich Mean Time clock

What better thing to be remembered for, than to be the craftsman who made the one clock that every other clock in the entire world is set by. Edwin Cottingham of Thrapston could have made such a claim, and his grave can still be seen in the grounds of the Thrapston Baptist Chapel.

Born in Ringstead, Edwin Turner Cottingham was apprenticed to Augustus Allen, a clockmaker of Thrapston, but his later skills were far above those of a small town clockmaker. He was also interested in astronomy, and studied it so proficiently, that in 1905 he was elected a Fellow of the Royal Astronomical Society.

His services as an astronomer and clockmaker were nationally called upon. He had the distinction of assisting Professor (afterwards Sir) Arthur Eddington, the Assistant Astronomer Royal and Director of Cambridge University Observatory, in his expedition to Principe to witness the total eclipse of the sun and to measure the deflection of light rays predicted by Einstein's Theory of Relativity. Cottingham was responsible for the calculations, and for making the clockwork mechanism on the especially designed camera.

Perhaps he was chosen for this work because a few years earlier he had restored a Harrison (*the* John Harrison of 'Longitude' fame) clock which the Royal Astronomical Society had in their chambers.

But perhaps his finest achievement is the building of the Greenwich Mean Time clock in Greenwich Observatory. He had tended for this in October 1919, and he delivered the clock in February 1921. This clock was set up and given extensive testing before actually being brought into use in October 1922, as *the* Greenwich Mean Time clock. It was accurate to within .01 and .03 seconds per day.

Because of this, Cottingham, in partnership with the Mercer brothers of Saint Albans, supplied a clock for Hong Kong Observatory. Cottingham made a duplicate clock, which is now on show in the Science Museum in London.

Up to a few years ago, an example of Cottingham's work was actually to be seen in Thrapston. It was the clock that regulated the chiming mechanism of the church clock. But one day, it was stolen. It had hung on the belfry wall, and was entirely unprotected. It was obviously so valuable, it was stolen to order, and is possibly now in some private collection abroad. I hope the new 'owner' is pleased with it.

Edwin Cottingham retired in 1928. He had married Elizabeth Smith, and their son Leslie entered the family business. Edwin Cottingham died in March 1940.

Edwin and Elizabeth Cottingham's extremely weathered headstone in Thrapston Baptist Church.

IN THE OUNDLE ROAD MUNICIPAL CEMETERY

Henry John Thurston (1904-1988)
Showman

From the Thurston's Fair family, Henry John was the grandson of Henry, senior, the founder of the family business. His father, Henry, junior, lies buried at Wellingborough (*see* Wellingborough, Doddington Road), and Henry John carried on with the family's traditional occupation.

Born at Leamington Spa in 1904, Henry John was educated at Norwich and Cambridge before joining his father (and indeed, uncles and cousins) in the family business. During the Second World War, he saw service with the RNVR, serving in the gunboats along the east coast of England.

The name of Thurston is well known in the eastern counties for its travelling fairs, which operated at various times dodgems, hydraulic rockets and roundabouts. Henry John continued until retirement, but as stated on his headstone, he was 'a showman to the end'.

Henry John Thurston and Ivy his wife, are buried side by side at Thrapston.

'A Showman to the End'

TITCHMARSH

IN THE CHURCH OF SAINT MARY

Erasmus (?-1654) and Mary Dryden (?-1676)

Parents of John Dryden, Poet Laureate

Erasmus Dryden was the second son of Sir Erasmus Dryden of Canons Ashby in the south of the county, and in 1630, he had married Mary, of the great Titchmarsh family of Pickering. All together, they had 14 children, but the oldest, John, born 1631, is the most famous.

It was John Dryden who became the most celebrated playwright, poet, essayist and critic of his time, and Poet Laureate from 1668 until 1688. So well regarded was he, that at his death, he was buried in Poets' Corner in Westminster Abbey, in the same grave as Geoffrey Chaucer. But his parents lie here, in Titchmarsh, their family home.

John (?-1701) and Elizabeth Creed (1644-1728)

Cousins to John Dryden and Samuel Pepys

Elizabeth Creed can be termed justly noteworthy for being closely related to two of the most famous literary figures of the seventeenth century. On her father's side, her cousin was John Dryden, the Poet Laureate; and on her mother's side, her cousin was Samuel Pepys, writer of the most famous diary of all time. And it was through Pepys, that she met her husband, John Creed.

Elizabeth Pickering was born in Titchmarsh in 1644. She was the daughter of Sir Gilbert Pickering, and her mother, Elizabeth, was the daughter of Sir Sydney Montagu. Her uncle was therefore Edward Montagu, 1st Earl of Sandwich, and the most famous Admiral of his day, whom Samuel Pepys (Secretary at the Admiralty) mentions several times in his diary.

John Creed was a civil servant. His origins are obscure, but in 1660, he was made Deputy Treasurer of the Fleet by Admiral Edward Montagu who had just been created 1st Earl of Sandwich. Thus John Creed became involved in the same circle as Elizabeth Pickering and Samuel Pepys. The inevitable happened, and in September 1668 Elizabeth Pickering and John Creed were married.

Samuel Pepys disliked John Creed, which is evident in his diary, and he made disparaging remarks about a man of his humble origins marrying into the landed gentry and aristocratic family of the Pickerings and Montagus. Nevertheless, John Creed was now his cousin by marriage, and he had to like it or lump it.

John Creed left the Admiralty in 1670, when he and Elizabeth came to live in Oundle. They bought Cobthorne House, which is still there, and is now the home of the Headmaster of Oundle School. John Creed died in 1701, and was buried in Titchmarsh, his wife's family estate.

This left Elizabeth a widow, and she went to live at Barnwell with her relations the Montagus, Earls of Sandwich. Her time was taken up with works of beneficence. She started a school for girls where she taught needlework and art. Herself a talented artist, many of her paintings are still in existence, as are needlework altar pieces and soft furnishings made for local churches. Elizabeth Creed died in 1728 and was buried alongside her husband in the family vault at Titchmarsh.

The monument to the parents of John Dryden in the south transept. Note the bust above the monument with the words THE POET.

The Creed monuments in the south aisle. That of John Creed is beneath the window, and the monument to his wife, is the Grecian Urn. The tablet on the left is to their son, Major John Creed, killed at the Battle of Blenheim, whose body was buried near to the actual battlefield.

TOWCESTER

❁

IN THE CHURCH OF SAINT LAURENCE

❁

William Sponne (?-1448)
Archdeacon of Norfolk

If you are able, go and see the tomb of William Sponne. It is a two tier table tomb, with the good archdeacon's effigy on the top tier, and 'the lively picture of death' on the bottom tier.

Archdeacon William Sponne was Rector of Towcester from 1422 until his death in 1448, when he died. He was also the Archdeacon of Norfolk.

The macabre tomb of Archdeacon Sponne.

WARKTON

❁

IN THE CHURCH OF SAINT EDMUND

❁

Ralph, 1st Duke of Montagu (1638?-1709)
Ambassador to the Court of Louis XIV

Ralph Montagu's rapid rise was apparently because of female influence at court. Make of that as you will. The death of his elder brother Edward, a Captain in the Royal Navy, killed at Bergen in 1665, enabled Ralph to take over his brother's job – Master of the Horse to the Duchess of York. Then straight on to the post of Master of the Horse to the queen (Catherine of Braganza, queen to Charles II). The Master of the Horse, a most responsible job, was in charge of the royal stables, and thus responsible for the transport for the royal household.

He became ambassador to France, to the Sun King himself, Louis XIV in 1669. Charles II was so pleased with his conduct, that when Montagu returned three years later, he was made a Privy Councillor. But relationships between the two men were to cool somewhat.

Never known for his marital fidelity, Charles II eventually produced 16 illegitimate children from eight different women. No doubt he attempted to increase this number, by chasing more women, one of whom was Elizabeth Wriothesly, daughter of the Earl of Southampton, and widow of the Earl of Northumberland.

To escape from the king's advances, Elizabeth fled to France. But it was Ralph Montagu who followed her, and in August 1673, the couple were married, much to the envy of the king. The marriage lasted, but according to contemporary accounts, they had started quarrelling almost immediately. But they did produce one son, 'Planter John'.

In 1676, Montagu returned to France as ambassador again, but this time blotted his copybook. He tried to purchase for £10,000 the office of Secretary of State, which strictly speaking, was slightly illegal. Whilst in Paris he had quarrelled with the Duke of Cleveland. This was a mistake. The Duchess of Cleveland was none other than Barbara Villiers, one of Charles' eight, and although she was not now his current favourite, nevertheless she still held some sway with him. It was on her direct involvement, that Montagu was sacked as ambassador. He promptly returned to England without permission, and for that, was struck off the Privy Council as well.

Having fallen from grace, Ralph got himself elected as Member of Parliament for Northampton, an easy enough thing to do in those days of patronage and pocket boroughs. Remember, he was still only Mr Montagu, as his father, Lord Montagu was still alive.

Thomas Osborne, 1st Earl of Danby, was the leading figure in the government. Openly, he was a Protestant, but in the Popish Plots of Titus Oates, he was named as a Catholic spy, who had secretly intrigued with France. Ralph Montagu was one of Danby's fiercest opponents. He entered into a secret pact with the French ambassador to reveal letters and documents that would prove Danby's guilt.

The king and Danby got to hear of this, and sent soldiers to surround his house to try and confiscate the documents. Too late, Montagu had hidden them.

In the House of Commons, Montagu stood up and told of the documents and the king's attempts to get them. The result was electrifying. The documents were produced and calls were made for Danby's impeachment. Charles then had no choice but to dissolve Parliament in December 1678. Sensing danger, and fearing for his life from the king, Montagu attempted to escape to France, and only just made it, narrowly escaping capture at Dover.

Whilst exiled in France, his father died, and he became Lord Montagu in 1684. A year later, Charles died and James II came to the throne. Ralph felt it safe to return. He managed to keep out of politics until the Glorious Revolution of 1688 which caused William and Mary to come to the throne. Because he became a supporter of William, he was restored to the Privy Council and created Viscount Monthermer and Earl of Montagu in 1689.

A year later his wife died. In 1692 he married Elizabeth Cavendish, daughter of the Duke of Newcastle who was very, very rich, and very, very mad. She said that she would only marry a crowned head. Montagu dressed up as 'The Emperor of China' and the couple married in 1692.

Ralph Montagu thought himself good enough to be a duke, and was disappointed when William III only made him an Earl. Ralph allied himself with the great Duke of Marlborough, and subtly started agitating for a dukedom. He hit the jackpot twice. Not only did Ralph's son, John, marry the Duke's daughter, Mary, but Ralph got his dukedom. In 1705 he was created Duke of Montagu.

Ralph, 1st Duke of Montagu died in 1709 and was buried in the family vault at Warkton. There is no monument to him in the church, and the vault has been sealed up, although the doorway to it is still visible in the north aisle.

John, 2nd Duke of Montagu (1688?-1749)
Notorious Practical Joker
'Planter John'

Perhaps John Montagu never grew up, because he remained a little scallywag all his life. His humour is best described as juvenile. Today, he would be the sort that starts throwing bread rolls about over the dinner table. It was his idea of fun to spray his guests with water, and to put itching powder into their beds.

Perhaps his most famous effort came in the year he died. In London's New Theatre, he advertised that a conjuror would squeeze himself into a quart (2 pint) bottle, and whilst inside, sing a song. Of course, nothing of the sort happened, and when the vast audience who had turned up, realised, the resulting riot burned the theatre down. John denied any involvement, and never made any recompense to the theatre owners for their financial loss.

But as in these cases, John had a serious side. Entering the army, he eventually became a General and Master-General of the Ordnance. In 1745, he raised his own cavalry regiment ('Montagu's Carabineers') which fought in the Jacobite Rebellion, but was disbanded after Culloden in 1746.

His father died in 1709, and he succeeded as 2nd Duke, and was awarded the KG in 1719, and GCB in 1725. George I in 1722 made him governor of Saint Lucia and Saint Vincent in the West Indies. Despite attempts at colonisation with a flotilla of ships, he failed, and returned home.

In 1705 at the age of approximately 17, he was married to Mary Churchill, daughter of the great Duke of Marlborough. This was a political marriage, as John's father, Ralph, Earl of Montagu was hankering after a dukedom, and by marrying his son to the greatest and most powerful family in the land at that time, thought he would enhance his cause.

The beautiful memorial to 'Planter John', the 2nd Duke of Montagu, in the chancel of Warkton church, directly opposite to that of his wife.

It worked, Ralph became a duke, and John became son-in-law to Sarah, Duchess of Marlborough, who was continually exasperated by John's behaviour. She actually had him banned from Blenheim for his behaviour at the reading of the Duke of Marlborough's will.

John and Mary Montagu's marriage seemed happy enough though, and they had two daughters. The elder, Elizabeth, married Henry, Duke of Buccleuch and started the Buccleuch connection with Boughton. The younger, Mary, married George, Earl of Cardigan to become the ancestor of Cardigan of Balaclava (*see* Deene).

Ralph Montagu had built and developed Boughton House and its gardens, to be the equivalent of Versailles. John carried on the work. To celebrate the coronation of George II in 1728, he wanted to plant an avenue of elm trees from Boughton to London. He only failed because the Duke of Bedford refused permission for the avenue to go over his land. So instead, he planted the equivalent mileage (72) all over his estate, and thus linked Boughton with the neighbouring villages by avenues of trees. Some of these trees still survive, despite the recent ravages of Dutch Elm Disease. For this feat, he was nicknamed 'Planter John'.

'Planter John' died from pneumonia in 1749. He was buried in Warkton underneath a magnificent tomb.

Mary, 2nd Duchess of Montagu (1690-1751)
Daughter of John, 1st Duke of Marlborough

Lady Mary Churchill was the youngest of the three daughters of the great Duke of Marlborough and his wife Sarah. At the early age of 15 she had been married to John Montagu, which was obviously for dynastic reasons. However, her marriage must have been reasonably happy, as it lasted for 44 years, and produced two daughters.

Although she must have lived the cosseted life of eighteenth century aristocratic luxury, she did see some life. In 1709, she actually visited her father at his headquarters in Flanders, whilst he was campaigning in the War of the Spanish Succession. She may even have witnessed his two great victories of that year, Oudenarde and Malplaquet.

But in that year as well, her father-in-law died, and she became the Duchess of Montagu, at the tender age of 19. She returned to Boughton House, and remained there for the rest of her life.

Widowed for just two years, Mary Montagu died in 1751, aged 61, and was buried in the Montagu vault at Warkton. Her magnificent memorial is in the chancel of Warkton church, exactly opposite to that of her husband.

The magnificent tomb of the Duchess of Montagu, daughter to the great Duke of Marlborough.

WEEDON LOIS

IN THE CHURCHYARD EXTENSION TO THE SOUTH OF THE PARISH CHURCH

Dame Edith Sitwell (1887-1964)

Author, Poet and Critic

Edith Sitwell devoted her life to literature, which is hardly surprising. Her two brothers Sachaverell and Osbert were equally famous for their literary talents. Born in Scarborough, Edith Louisa Sitwell was the daughter of Sir George Sitwell, Bart, and grand daughter of the Earl of Londesborough.

She was educated privately, but in 1903, a new governess, Helen Rootham opened up to her the spheres of music and literature. Edith had found her métier. In 1913, some of her poems were published in the *Daily Mirror*, and in 1914, she moved to a London flat taking Helen Rootham with her. They were to stay there for 18 years until 1932.

Then to Paris with Helen. Whilst there, Edith struck up a friendship with the white Russian émigré painter Pavel Tchelitchew. But in 1938, Helen died and Edith returned alone to London, where she stayed for the rest of her life.

During her lifetime she was awarded honorary LLD degrees from the Universities of Oxford, Leeds, Durham and Sheffield, and in 1954 became a Dame Commander of the Order of the British Empire. She died in London in December 1964, and was buried in Weedon Lois cemetery, a few yards away to the south of the parish church. At the far end of the cemetery, her grave has a wonderful view of green fields over a valley. Her poetic nature would have appreciated that.

The striking headstone of Dame Edith Sitwell.

For 50 years, Dame Edith Sitwell wrote poetry, prose and literary criticism. Her millions of words are much better described by more competent writers than I am, in the numerous biographies of her. I will, however, single out just one work, *Façade*, written in 1923. Not so much a violent new direction in music, as it has been described, but more of a tight swerve. Edith Sitwell's libretto to the music of an unknown and struggling composer, William Walton, was not well received on its debut. What a contrast today, when *Façade* is viewed as the masterpiece it is. Wonderful.

WEEKLEY

IN THE CHURCH AND CHURCHYARD OF SAINT MARY

Sir Edward Montagu (?-1557)

Commissioner into the wealth of Cardinal Wolsey
Commissioner at the trial of Catherine Howard
Lord Chief Justice of the King's Bench and Common Pleas
Member of the Regency Council for Edward VI
Drafted Edward VI's Will in favour of Lady Jane Grey
Imprisoned in The Tower as a result

The table tombs of Lord Chief Justice Sir Edward Montagu, to the right, and his son, another Sir Edward, to the left.

Being a friend of Henry VIII had its compensations as Edward Montagu found out. But it also had its drawbacks, and he found that out as well.

Cardinal Wolsey had fallen from grace in 1529 and Henry's Commission into Wolsey's wealth was far reaching. Montagu, as a leading Northamptonshire barrister, sat on the Commission to enquire into Wolsey's Northamptonshire possessions, and for this gained the friendship and gratitude of Henry. So pleased was he, that he made Montagu a Sergeant at Law (the equivalent of a QC) and Montagu entertained the king and queen for five days. This was 1532, so Henry was still married to Catherine of Aragon, his first wife, and it would be another year before Henry's marital shenanigans began.

Montagu obviously kept the friendship of the king, because at the Dissolution of the Monasteries, Montagu received nearly all the lands of Bury Saint Edmunds Abbey which lay in Northamptonshire. He was knighted in 1537, and became the Lord Chief Justice of the King's Bench in 1539.

After Henry's disappointment with Anne of Cleves, certain factions at the court pushed forward a flighty minx called Catherine Howard of the family of the Dukes of Norfolk. Henry and Catherine married in July 1540. But Catherine did not act like a queen of England should, and Henry, highly embarrassed, had her tried for High Treason in 1541, just to get rid of her. The examination and trial of Catherine was masterminded by Thomas Cranmer, and Sir Edward Montagu, as Lord Chief Justice, was a member of the Commission. They found Catherine guilty of unchastity before her marriage and she was beheaded in February 1542.

Montagu was transferred to be Lord Chief Justice of the Common Pleas in 1545. Still in favour with the king, he was chosen to sit on the Regency Council for Henry's son Edward.

Henry died in January 1547 and Edward VI took the throne at the age of 10. The Regency Council was headed by Edward Seymour, Duke of Somerset, but he was soon ousted by another self-seeker in the form of John Dudley, Earl of Warwick who quickly granted himself the title of Duke of Northumberland.

Northumberland wanted to continue in power, so he 'leant' on the king to change his Will, ostensibly to continue the Protestant religion. The successor chosen by Northumberland was Lady Jane Grey, who did have a claim to the throne, but not as strong as Mary Tudor's, Edward's half-sister. Coincidentally, Lady Jane Grey just happened to have married Northumberland's son, Guilford, just two months before, at the tender age of 16.

Sir Edward Montagu, as Lord Chief Justice, was instructed to draft Edward's Will in favour of Lady Jane. Apparently he refused, saying it was treason. But Northumberland obviously pressured him as well, and the Will was made. Edward died in July 1553; Lady Jane Grey took the throne for nine days, but was quickly deposed by Mary Tudor who took the throne as Mary I. Then the recriminations began. Sir Edward Montagu was thrown into The Tower. But two months later he was released on payment of a £1000 fine and forfeiture of a large part of his estates.

But as he had retained Boughton House at Weekley, he retired there and died just four years later. He was buried in Weekley church and his tomb has his recumbent effigy dressed in the robes of a Judge.

Edward, 1st Baron Montagu of Boughton (1562-1644)

Member of Parliament
Fervent Royalist and personal friend of both James I and Charles I
Imprisoned by Parliament during the Civil War

Edward Montagu was the grandson of Lord Chief Justice Montagu, and was born in 1562 at Boughton House. After Oxford, he became a student of the Middle Temple and was called to the bar. But he sought a political career, and became Member of Parliament for Brackley in 1601, and for Northamptonshire between 1603 and 1611, then again in 1614 and 1620-1622.

King James I was crowned in Westminster Abbey in July 1603, and Edward Montagu attended the coronation. He must have assisted or otherwise ingratiated himself, because James made him a Knight of the Bath at the coronation. Becoming a fervent Royalist he was created the 1st Baron Montagu of Boughton in 1621.

When James died in 1625, Montagu continued loyal service to Charles I. He undertook numerous tasks for the king, including the assessment for Ship Money in Northamptonshire in 1635. Ship Money was originally levied on ports, but Charles in his never ending grab for money, extended it to the whole of the country in 1634. This did not impress the populace, and was one of the many grievances which lead to the Great Civil War.

Obviously on the king's side during the Civil War, Montagu was arrested by Parliament in 1642, and clapped in The Tower. But because of his advanced age (he was 80) was released to 'house arrest' at his London home. He died in June 1644, being buried in Weekley. His memorial plaque faces the tombs of his parents and grandparents.

The memorial to Edward, 1st Baron Montagu.

Edward, 2nd Baron Montagu (1616-1684)
Member of the 'Long Parliament'
'Capturer' and 'Gaoler' of Charles I at Newark and Holdenby

Edward Montagu was Member for Huntingdon in the 'Long Parliament' which started in the summer of 1640, just after the 'Short Parliament' had been dissolved. It was destined to sit for nearly 20 years, but in 1644, Montagu's father died, and he took his place in the Lords as the 2nd Baron Montagu.

During the Civil War, a Scottish army was 'hired' to help against the king, and Lord Montagu was on the English Commission attached to this army. As such, in May 1646, when the king was besieged at Newark, Montagu treated for the surrender of the garrison, which it did, and thus the captured king became a prisoner of the Scottish. Only after the Scottish had received a big pay-off, was the king released into the care of Lord Montagu who took him to Holdenby House near Northampton, where he was held in custody.

In June 1647 came the famous incident when Cornet Joyce took charge of the king at Holdenby and took him to Hampton Court. Lord Montagu went with him and attended until the king 'escaped' to the Isle of Wight in November 1647. Lord Montagu then drops out of the picture, and to his credit never took part in the trial of the king, which led to his execution in January 1649.

Lord Montagu returned to Boughton House. He was unaffected by the Restoration of the Monarchy in 1660, and died in January 1684. He was buried in the family vault at Weekley.

Sir William Montagu (1619?-1706)
Member of the 'Short Parliament'
Attorney General to Queen Catherine
Lord Chief Baron
Personal friend of Titus Oates
Assisted Judge Jeffreys at the 'Bloody Assizes'

Son of the 1st Lord Montagu, and brother of the 2nd, William Montagu was called to the bar by the Middle Temple in 1641. He was the Member for Huntingdon in the 'Short Parliament'. The 'Short Parliament' was called in the spring of 1640, but was so critical of the king, that he dissolved it within a month. The 'Long Parliament' soon followed, and this would sit throughout the Commonwealth.

Montagu returned to his legal practice, but upon the Restoration of the Monarchy in 1660, was the Member of Parliament for Cambridge University. In 1662, he was the Attorney General to Charles II's queen, Catherine of Breganza, and in 1676 was created Lord Chief Baron. The judges of the Exchequer Court, normally involved in financial trials, were called 'Barons' rather than 'Justices', but were still competent to sit over criminal cases as well.

In the year 1685, as soon as he had come to the throne, the Catholic James II had brought to trial the anti-Catholic agitator, Titus Oates, the originator of the 'Popish Plot' scare. William Montagu was called as a character witness for Titus Oates, who was found not guilty. And in July of that year, the so-called Monmouth Rebellion was crushed at the Battle of Sedgemoor. The consequent trials of these 'rebels' in the towns of the Western Circuit during the Summer Assizes of 1685, came to be known as the 'Bloody Assizes' from the number of rebels who were hanged. The notorious Judge Jeffreys was the chief judge, but he was ably assisted by William Montagu (as well as Creswell Levinz, *see* Evenley).

But a year later, Montagu was sacked. James II was trying to return the country to Catholicism, and was going about it by blatantly dispensing with some laws that did not suit him (called 'dispensing powers'). Montagu was sacked because he was not in favour of the king's use of these powers.

He returned to his legal practice. He died in 1706, and is buried in the family vault at Weekley.

Charles Montagu-Douglas-Scott (1862-1936)

Poet

Grandson of the 5th Duke of Buccleuch, Charles contracted polio at the age of three. This left him crippled for life, and he always had to use crutches. His talents were channelled into poetry, and he published several volumes. His main work was an anthology *Northamptonshire Songs and Others* in three volumes published between 1904 and 1906. His *Tales of Northamptonshire* was published posthumously in 1936. Trevor Hold (in *A Northamptonshire Garland*) calls the poetry of Montagu-Douglas-Scott 'some of the most evocative of the county ever written'. Consider this one verse from his poem 'Fotheringhay in Winter' from his *Tales of Northamptonshire*.

The skies are grey o'er Fotheringhay
The loitering church, the tumbled mound;
The Nene meanders on its way
Without a sound.
The fields are flat on either bank;
The ploughlands rich, the meadow rank;
The climate's gloomy, cold and dank.
And this is all one notes today
Around.

Becoming very reclusive after the death of his father, Charles died in March 1936 and was buried in the Montagu-Douglas-Scott corner of Weekley churchyard.

Weekley churchyard. The grave of Charles Montagu-Douglas-Scott is the cross on the extreme left, whilst the headstone on the right is to John Alfred Gotch.

John Alfred Gotch (1852-1942)
Architect and Author

Of the well known Kettering family, John Gotch came from an artistic family; his brother, Thomas Cooper Gotch, becoming a famous artist. John was educated at Kettering Grammar School, King's College, London, and had periods of study in Zurich.

He was articled to a Melton Mowbray firm, which had an office in Kettering. On the death of his employer, Gotch took over the practice, and went in to partnership with Charles Saunders. This partnership lasted for well over 50 years, and the practice is still in existence in Kettering.

Gotch designed many local buildings, including the Alfred East Art Gallery and Cenotaph in Kettering, and it is clear that he was a traditionalist, not bothering too much with modern trends in design and materials. At one point, he collaborated with Sir Edwin Lutyens in the design of the Headquarters of the Midland Bank, which is in The Poultry in the heart of the City of London.

In 1923-1925, he was President of the Royal Institute of British Architects, and remained on its Council for over 30 years. Also becoming an authority on architectural history, Gotch wrote many books, the first in 1886, and the last in 1939, just three years before he died at the age of 90.

He had married Anne Perry of Nottingham, and they had a son and a daughter. The son was killed in action in the mincing machine of the Western Front in 1916. Anne Gotch died in 1924, and John Gotch was 18 years a widower. He died in 1942, and is buried alongside his wife on the south side of Weekley churchyard.

Dennis Copperwheat, GC (1914-1992)
George Cross winner

Only two George Cross winners are buried in Northamptonshire. Roger Lewin lies in Kettering's London Road Cemetery, and Dennis Copperwheat sleeps peacefully in Weekley.

In the desperate struggle to get supplies to relieve the Siege of Malta, in March 1942, a convoy left Alexandria bound for Grand Harbour, Valetta. The escorting ships were headed by Rear Admiral Vian in HMS *Cleopatra*, and on the 20th came the first attack when a 'Hunt' class destroyer was torpedoed.

From thereon the convoy came under constant heavy attack, from surface ships and dive-bombers, in what has come to be known as the Battle of Sirte. So heavy was the enemy attack that only 5,000 tons of fuel and supplies reached Malta from the 26,000 tons which had left Alexandria.

One merchant ship limped to within 40 yards of the entrance to Grand Harbour. She was fully loaded with ammunition – and was fiercely ablaze. If she blew up, Grand Harbour would be permanently damaged, allowing no other ship access.

Lieutenant Dennis Copperwheat of HMS *Penelope* was sent aboard with a small party of ratings with orders to scuttle her. This was a suicidal mission. Ammunition was exploding on all sides, and the whole ship could have erupted at any second. Eventually Lieutenant Copperwheat set the charges, and sending his party to safety fired the charges himself. They exploded with a terrific force, which lifted him bodily, and caused near fatal wounds. Lieutenant Copperwheat and his party then only just managed to reach safety.

Lieutenant Dennis Arthur Copperwheat, RN, was awarded The George Cross, which was cited in the *London Gazette* of 17 November 1942.

Dennis Copperwheat was promoted to Lieutenant Commander, and survived the war. He died in 1992, and is buried underneath the south transept window in Weekley churchyard.

WELDON

❁

IN THE CHURCH AND CHURCHYARD OF SAINT MARY

❁

George Jeffreys (1610?-1685)

Organist to King Charles I
Highly regarded and prolific composer

George Jeffreys would have been much more famous had he not closeted himself away in the countryside far removed from the focal point of the national musical life. That is the opinion of *Groves' Dictionary of Music.*

It is not known where George Jeffreys was born, or where he studied, although it is thought he may have been in Italy at some point. But in 1643 we meet him as the king's organist at Oxford where king Charles I made his headquarters during the Great Civil War. And probably that is where he met Christopher Hatton.

Christopher Hatton of Kirby Hall in Northamptonshire was an ardent Royalist and was attached to the king's court. Because he turned out to be on the losing side, in 1646, Hatton was exiled to France, and needed someone to look after his Northamptonshire estate at Kirby. George Jeffreys apparently filled the bill, because as there was no king's court any more, then a royal organist would be twiddling his thumbs

So George Jeffreys moved to Weldon and looked after the Hatton estates. He stopped in Northamptonshire until he died in 1685, being buried in Weldon church, but with no monumant. And it is this seclusion in the countryside away from the main stream of English music (represented in those years by Purcell, Blow and Gibbons) that is bewailed by *Groves' Dictionary*.

However, whilst at Weldon Jeffreys did compose prolifically. Many of his compositions are still preserved in Christ Church, Oxford, the Royal College of Music and the British Museum. Arguably his best known work is his 'Erit Gloria Domini' from his *Cantica Sacra* of 1672. 'This' according to Groves' 'provides a highly individual solution to the problem of combining English polyphony with Italian declamatory techniques'.

George Jeffreys (1678-1755)
Poet and Dramatist

George Jeffreys, apart from two or three attempts at work, seems to have spent his life in luxurious leisure sponging off his cousin the Duke of Chandos. In return, he occasionally penned a few poems and a couple of plays.

His father was Christopher Jeffreys, himself the renowned organist son of the composer George Jeffreys. George, junior was born at Weldon and was sent to Trinity College, Cambridge, where he graduated BA in 1698 and MA in 1702. He became a Fellow and lecturer in Latin, but he left in 1709.

He was called to the bar by Lincoln's Inn, but never seems to have practised. His next job was in Ireland. Doctor John Hartstonge had been Bishop of Ossory since 1693, but had been translated to Derry in 1714, where Jeffreys joined him as his Secretary. Hartstonge died in 1717 and Jeffreys returned to England. A job in the Custom House followed, but it is not known for how long he was there, possibly no more than four or five years.

His play *Edwin* was published in 1724, so it is likely he had already been living with the Duke of Chandos for a couple of years which had given him the time needed to write it. He died in 1755, so that could mean he remained living off his relatives for over 30 years.

A play *Merope* was published in 1731, and then nothing more for 23 years until *Miscellanies in Verse and Prose* appeared in 1754.

George Jeffreys died in 1755, believed unmarried, and was buried near to his grandfather in Weldon church, again, with no memorial.

Bless'd by those lips, whose touch divine
    Might wasting life repair;
To nectar it converts the wine
    To gladness ev'ry care.

Give me that balm to ease my pain,
    My cordial when I faint
And let the Relique still remain
    To witness for the Saint.

Two verses from *The Peach Stone* by George Jeffreys (1678-1755)

John Clark (1786-1863)

Fought at the Battle of Trafalgar in HMS *Royal Sovereign*
Doctor in Weldon for 45 years

Being born in 1786, John Clark was just 19 in 1805, yet he had already joined the Royal Navy as a Trainee Surgeon. Nothing is known of his life previous to his naval service. But we do know what he went through on Monday 21 October 1805, serving in HMS *Royal Sovereign*, at the Battle of Trafalgar, the best known of all the British naval victories and possibly the most famous sea battle ever.

John Clark's Christmas Gift .

HMS *Royal Sovereign* was the flagship of Admiral Cuthbert Collingwood, who was Nelson's second in command. It was a three-decker battleship of 100 guns. Nelson's plan was for the British fleet to sail in two parallel lines at right angles to the combined French and Spanish fleet (lined up in Indian file) in an attempt to cut the enemy line into three sections. HMS *Victory* would lead the northern line and HMS *Royal Sovereign* would lead the southern line. Because of light winds and the angle of the enemy line, *Royal Sovereign* was the first ship into action, at 11.45am, a good 15 minutes before *Victory*, which engaged at 12 midday. *Royal Sovereign* crossed to the rear of the Spanish flagship, the 112 gun *Santa Ana*, carrying the Spanish Admiral Ignacio Alava, and engaged her, together with the nearby French ship *Fougeux*.

The slaughter on both sides was terrible, later described as a 'butcher's shambles' (shambles being the old word for abattoir) and young John Clark, together with the other surgeons must have had no time to think of the battle above their heads, as they literally hacked off mangled limbs using no anaesthetic.

At one point in the battle, *Royal Sovereign* was under fire from no less than five enemy ships, which had completely surrounded her, and because of the ferocity of their crossfire, their cannon balls were actually colliding with each other in mid air. But by the timely intervention of HMS *Mars*, HMS *Tournant* and HMS *Belleisle* who chased off four of these attackers, *Royal Sovereign* was just left to contend with the *Santa Ana*.

Completely outclassed by the superior gunners of the *Royal Sovereign, Santa Ana* finally surrendered at 2.15pm (and incidentally, one and a quarter hours after the death of Nelson) with 340 casualties from a crew of about 700.

John Clark had lived through the most crushing blow the Royal Navy ever gave to an enemy. So much so that Napoleon gave up his idea of conquering Great Britain and turned instead to the land conquest of the rest of Europe. This of course continued for another ten years until Napoleon was disposed of once and for all, at Waterloo in 1815, and in which another Northamptonshire man was involved (*see* Aynho, William Cartwright).

John Clark stopped in the Navy until 1818, during which time he must have qualified as a medical practitioner. He came to be the country doctor at Weldon in that year, and stopped for 45 years until he died in 1863 aged 77. A plaque is in Weldon church, and a headstone is in the churchyard near to his actual grave.

The grave of Doctor John Clark, survivor of the Battle of Trafalgar.

Another reminder of the Battle of Trafalgar. The west window was given by Horatio Nelson himself to Sir William Hamilton, no doubt in compensation for taking his wife from him. The window came into the possession of the Rector of Weldon, William Finch-Hatton, who gave it to the church in 1897.

WELLINGBOROUGH

IN THE DODDINGTON ROAD MUNICIPAL CEMETERY

John Alexander (1845-1922)

Police Superintendent who had a legal stated case named after him

Because today we have all day opening of public houses, seven days a week, with a blasé attitude to the use of alcohol, it is easy to wonder what all the fuss was about in the case of *Penn versus Alexander*. But 100 years ago, the 'demon drink', and the obtaining of it by the working classes, was looked upon with a fear almost bordering on paranoia. The Licensing Act of 1874 had prohibited the opening of public houses on Sundays, except for the refreshment of 'bona fide travellers'.

William Penn, landlord of the *White Lion* at Little Houghton, was observed by the police to be opening on Sundays during the month of April 1892. Men were walking the four miles from Northampton to Little Houghton, drinking at the *White Lion*, and then walking home again.

The police pounced, and William Penn was summoned for illegally opening on Sundays. In the way of legal matters, the police summons was issued in the name of the chief officer of the district. In this case, it was the Wellingborough Divisional Superintendent, John Alexander. So the case of *Penn versus Alexander* went to court.

The police said that men walking from home, drinking, and then walking back home again, were not 'bona fide travellers'.

Penn said they were. The Northampton Magistrates believed the police and convicted Penn, and fined him £5. He appealed, and the case was referred upwards to the Northamptonshire Quarter Sessions.

The Quarter Session dismissed the appeal and upheld the conviction. Penn appealed again, to the next level, the Court of Appeal. Lord Coleridge, the Lord Chief Justice, sat with Judges Hawkins, Day and Collins. And they dismissed the appeal as well, ordering that the conviction should stand.

What's left of the tombstone of John Alexander.

Whilst today with our different licensing laws, it has no significance whatsoever, in the quarter century before the licensing laws were altered during the Great War, the case of *Penn versus Alexander* was one of the chief stated cases for the regulation of Sunday opening of public houses.

John Alexander, born in Lincolnshire, had joined the Northamptonshire County Constabulary in 1866, at the age of 21. He was the Superintendent in charge of the Wellingborough Division from 1890 until he retired in 1897.

Hector Daniel Macleod (1863-1942)

The first police officer in the entire world to capture a criminal using a motor car

Every 'cops and robbers' film worth its salt finishes up with a car chase. Today such things are commonplace. But where did it all start? In Northamptonshire in 1899, that's where, because the Northamptonshire County Constabulary was the first police force in the entire world to arrest a criminal after a car chase. And the police officer involved was Hector Macleod, who lies peacefully in Doddington Road Cemetery.

The arrival of Barnum and Bailey's circus in Northampton for the Easter Holiday in April 1899 caused excited ripples in the town. Naturally the

Hector Macleod when a young police constable stationed at Wellingborough, early 1890s.

advanced publicity had whipped up a frenzy of excitement, and it was to be expected that someone's criminal mind would take advantage.

True enough, an unemployed printed, Frederick Phillips printed some 'Free Tickets' and sallied forth to make his fortune. On Thursday 27 April 1899, just a few days before the circus was due, he visited three shops, all run by ladies, in then what were small villages on the outskirts of Northampton.

Posing as an advance publicity manager, he asked whether he could put a poster in the shop window, in return for which the lady would receive the 'Free Tickets' for the 3s seats. When the gullible ladies agreed, Phillips dished out his forged tickets saying that he would bring the poster in the next day, but it was customary "just to give a small sum to cover necessary expenses".

Amazingly, all three women fell for this. Harriet Scott of Far Cotton gave him 1s, Agnes Cotton of Duston gave him 6d, and Jane Botterill of Dallington gave him another 6d. With the money in his pocket, Phillips was soon on his way out of town.

It was the complaint of Jane Boterill, who realising that she had been duped, alerted Hector Macleod, then a Sergeant and stationed at the County Headquarters in Angel Lane, Northampton. Hearing that the criminal was seen leaving the town along the Weedon road, Sergeant Macleod then took the step that would put him in the history books.

Jack Harrison, who lived in Marefair, was the proud owner of a new fangled Benz motor car, and Macleod commandeered both vehicle and driver so that the criminal could be brought to justice. Driving out of town along the Weedon road, Macleod and Harrison soon caught up with Phillips between Harpole and Flore.

Despite his protestations of innocence, Phillips was arrested by Macleod and brought back in the car to Angel Lane. In reporting the case a week later, the *Autocar* magazine wondered whether at any time during the 'chase' the speed limit had been exceeded, which at that time was a highly exhilarating 12 miles per hour.

Phillips, after two remands, eventually pleaded guilty to obtaining money under false pretences, and was bound over for twelve months on forfeit of £10.

And so Frederick Phillips had his five minutes of fame which ensured his name would never be forgotten. His captor went on to greater things, eventually becoming Deputy Chief Constable (under James Kellie-MacCallum, *see* Quinton) and retired in 1931 to live at Wellingborough.

The grave of the first policeman in the whole world to catch a criminal using a motor car.

Henry Thurston, junior (1881-1964)
Showman

Who in the eastern counties of England has never heard of Thurston's? For over 130 years, the name has meant 'travelling fairs'. And every year, at the feast day of every village and town, the fair used to come, with dodgems, roundabouts and sideshows. I well remember Finedon Feast every September being one of the great focal points of the year. Finedon Feast was the start of autumn, so soon we would have Bonfire Night and then Christmas. And I am sure that every other village lad experienced the same tingle when seeing the fair arrive and start setting up.

Henry Thurston, senior, started in 1868 with a horse operated street roundabout. He built up the business around the eastern counties, and once appeared at a Royal Garden Party at Sandringham in 1910. He had four sons, Stanley, Charles, William and Henry, junior.

Henry Thurston, junior, was born at Chelmsford in 1881. Each of the four brothers entered the family business and when Henry, senior died in 1917, Henry, junior carried on his roundabouts, steam organs and scenic railways. In 1920, he added chairoplanes, and eventually dodgems.

In the Second World War, when all the carnivals were closed, he became a skilled aircraft fitter. But after the war finished, he was back on the road again, although now tending to stick mainly to Northamptonshire. He retired in 1954 and passed his business over to his son Henry John (*see* Thrapston, Oundle Road).

He had married Margaret Barker, and the couple lived in retirement in Wellingborough. Henry, junior, died in 1964, and Margaret in 1966, both being buried in the Doddington Road cemetery.

Henry Thurston's grave, quietly away from the hurly-burly of the fairground.

IN THE LONDON ROAD MUNICIPAL CEMETERY

John Askham

Poet

John Askham was born in Wellingborough, worked in Wellingborough, and died in Wellingborough, but his five volumes of poetry published between 1863 and 1893 show a far from parochial nature. He was a shoemaker, and first appeared in print in the *Wellingborough Independent* in the 1850s. George de Wildes of the *Northampton Mercury* was so impressed that he made

Askham his Wellingborough correspondent, which led to other newspapers taking him on as a 'stringer', as a freelance journalist is called.

In 1871 he gave up making shoes and became the School Board Attendance Officer and in 1875 the Wellingborough Sanitary Inspector. He was medically retired in 1887, but continued to publish poems until his death in 1894. He was twice married.

His poetry has been compared with John Clare, but he could write about industry as well as the countryside. Consider this extract from his poem *The Singers*, named not for their voices, but for the shoe sewing machines they worked.

> Round and round with monotonous sound,
> Till rattle the windows, and shakes the ground,
> Till the roof resounds, and the rafters ring
> With the noisy chorus the 'Singers' sing.
>
> With the opening day their songs begin-
> Clatter, and clamour, and toil, and din-
> Your can scarcely hear your fellow speak
> From day to day, from week to week.

The vandalised grave of John Askham.

Luke Knight

Police Superintendent injured in the 1852 Wellingborough Election Riot

A General Election took place in Wellingborough in July 1852. Polling in those days was a wild affair, unlike today. So much so, that a large body of men assembled at Wellingborough Town Hall in the hopes of being sworn in as Special Constables for the day in case of riots (plus the 3s 6d that went with it). When eventually they were all dismissed without their services being required, they promptly rioted.

The mob tore down the actual polling booth itself, then ripped up the cobblestones and started throwing them about. The Chief Constable of Northamptonshire, Mr Henry Bayly, and Superintendent Luke Knight in charge of the Wellingborough Division, were both attacked with stones, receiving injuries to the head. Luke Knight was actually knocked out cold, and so serious were his injuries that at one point it was considered to be nearly fatal. Although he recovered, he never returned to work, and was medically pensioned seven months later.

Eventually he recovered enough to work for the borough, when he became the rate collector and assistant overseer, and is described as such in Francis Whellan's *History, Topography and Directory of Northamptonshire* published in 1874. Luke Knight died in 1877. His headstone in London Road Cemetery has the inscription 'His end was Peace'.

WHITTLEBURY

SOMEWHERE IN WHITTLEBURY PARISH?

Boudicca (?-61)
Queen of the Iceni

The revolt against the Romans, by the Britons led by Boudicca, the widow of King Prasutagus, is one of the legends of English history. The roots of the revolt were deep, and resentment against Roman rule had been growing for years.

In AD60, Prasutagus, King of the Iceni, had died, and Boudicca, instead of being treated like a queen, as she thought she should, had suffered the indignation of having her possessions brutally confiscated, and her daughters violated. And that was just the spark needed to light the tinder.

The subsequent rampage by the Britons, with the complete destruction of Camlodunum (Colchester), Londinium and Verulamium (Saint Albans), shook the Romans to their marching boots. Only the superior generalship of Suetonius Paulinus, with parts of the IInd and XXth Legions, together with the whole of the XIVth Legion, brought the rebellion to a halt.

The site of the final battle is unknown, but it is believed to be somewhere in the midlands of England, north of Saint Albans. Being defeated, Boudicca took poison, and was buried by her followers. But here is the crunch, nobody knows for sure where this was.

In 1907, Doctor Edward Scott, Keeper of Manuscripts at the British Museum, discovered two deeds of Whittlebury parish of the 1280s. In one deed was a reference to 'ded queene more' and in the other 'le dedequene furlong'. Using this, he constructed a theory that Boudicca was buried somewhere in Whittlebury parish.

Pure speculation, maybe, but with the lack of any evidence to the contrary, who is to say that Doctor Scott is wrong? I know what I would like to believe.

IN THE CHURCHYARD OF SAINT MARY

George Linnell (?-1789)
Murdered Parish Constable

George Linnell was of the well known Whittlebury family, but had moved to Pattishall, where he became the Parish Constable in 1789. In the days before the regular police (which in Northamptonshire started in 1840), a village man was chosen to be the Parish Constable for the year, and into his hands was placed not only the responsibility for criminal law and order, but civil law as well. Thus he was responsible for maintenance of highways, short measures by local tradesmen, bastardy orders, and so forth. And for all this, he received no wages whatsoever.

Into the village of Pattishall moved Doctor Gordon and family from London. Doctor Gordon started practising medicine in the district, but being of a violent temperament, soon got into several affrays with the locals. A complaint was made to George Linnell about a physical assault by Doctor Gordon, and a warrant was procured for his arrest.

Linnell approached the house, to be met by Winifred Gordon, apparently as truculent as her husband. On being told her husband was not there, Linnell retreated, as obviously the situation was volatile, and it was equally obvious that Winifred Gordon was lying.

About an hour went by, and Linnell tried again, this time with reinforcements from the village. They were met by Winifred again, but this time her 19 year old son, armed with a shotgun, was also there.

The Gordons refused Linnell entry. This provoked the villagers to hurl sticks and stones at the Gordon house resulting in broken windows and broken tempers. Winifred screamed at her son to use the shotgun, which he did to great effect, by killing George Linnell instantly. Thomas Gordon was captured by the villagers, along with Winifred.

At the Northamptonshire Summer Assizes of 1789, WinifredGordon was found guilty of incitement to murder and was gaoled. Thomas Gordon was found guilty of murdering George Linnell, and was hanged on Northampton Racecourse on Tuesday 18 August 1789.

George Linnell was taken to his home village, and buried alongside his family in Whittlebury churchyard.

The grave of George Linnell, believed to be the middle tombstone, where the words 'Linnell' and 'murdered' can just be made out.

WICKEN

IN THE CHURCHYARD OF SAINT JOHN THE EVANGELIST

George, 2nd Baron Penrhyn (1836-1907)

Member of Parliament
Industrialist
Race Horse Owner

George's mother was the fabulously wealthy Julianna Dawkins-Pennant, a rich heiress of Penrhyn Castle. No doubt as a condition of marriage, in 1841 the family adopted the surname of Douglas-Pennant, and soon George's father was elevated to the peerage as Baron Penrhyn.

Young George was sent to Eton and Christ Church College, Oxford, and then wanted to join the army, but his father stopped him. He did, however, in later life become a Major in the part-time Caernarfonshire Rifles, and an honorary colonel of the Royal Welch Fusiliers.

Between 1866 and 1868, George was a Member of Parliament for Caernarfonshire under Benjamin Disraeli. These were the days of the see-saws between Disraeli and Gladstone, and when Gladstone took over in 1868 he lost his seat. He was back again in 1874 when Disraeli returned, only to be out again when Gladstone took over yet again in 1880.

But in 1886 his father died, and he became the 2nd Lord Penrhyn inheriting a 27,000 acre estate in Wales, plus the Bethesda Slate Quarry. The annual income of these two should have been £217,000 per year, but his father had left the management in the hands of a committee, so in 1886, the estate was almost bankrupt.

Lord Penrhyn set about to remedy this, and went about it in his own way. This seemed not to be popular, and the business was beset by strikes.

The showdown came in 1897, with the biggest strike up until then. Lord Penrhyn had been a champion of free labour, and he had refused to bow down before trades unions. No compromise could be reached, so Lord Penrhyn promptly closed the quarry. This led to uproar, and questions being asked in parliament, and Penrhyn was forced to re-open.

But exactly the same thing happened again, and in 1900, he closed the quarry for a second time, but straightaway re-opened it with 600 non-union men. Penrhyn refused to employ the strikers and refused to recognise the unions. The resulting rioting caused the frightened magistrates to call in the local cavalry to maintain order, as the local police were swamped.

Again questions were raised in the House and Lord Penrhyn suffered vicious attacks from journalists. In 1903 he brought a libel action against W.J. Parry who wrote in the left-wing *Clarion*. Penrhyn won the case, but only received £500 damages plus costs, which obviously reflected the jury's thoughts on it.

However, from then on, he did start employing union men alongside non-union men, and to his great credit treated both sets of workers equally. In 1907, for instance, because of bad weather disrupting work, he gave all his workers a 10% bonus.

Lord Penrhyn was a noted horse breeder. He was President of the Jockey Club in 1887, and in 1898, his horse *King's Messenger*, won the Goodwood Cup; and in 1894, his horse, *Quaesitum*, won the Chester Gold Cup and the Ascot Vase.

Lord Penrhyn was basically a good man, and because of his strict church views, wanted to treat all men as equal - union or non-union, churchman or non-conformist. However, because of this, he perhaps could not appreciate the changes going on in the world about him.

He married twice, in 1860 Blanche Rushout who died in 1869; and in 1875, Gertrude Glynn. In total he had 15 children. He died at his London home, but was buried at Wicken, his country house, in March 1907.

Wicken's beautiful churchyard, the last resting place of Lord and Lady Penrhyn.

WOODFORD

IN THE CHURCH AND CHURCHYARD OF SAINT MARY

John Cole (1792-1848)
Historian

John Cole was a self-publishing historian of matchless quality. All in all he wrote and published over 100 books on the history of the places in which he had lived – Lincoln, Hull, Scarborough, and, of course, Northampton. So good was he, that historians constantly used him as a source. George Baker, for instance, for his *History of Northamptonshire*, drew heavily upon Cole's work.

Over 70 of John Cole's books are preserved at the British Museum. They are wonderfully and tastefully printed, some on coloured paper, and all are scholarly researched, and deserve a far wider recognition than they have at the moment.

Born at Weston Favell, John Cole was apprenticed to a Mr Birdsall, a bookseller on Northampton Market Square. He wrote his first book *History of Northampton and Vicinity* in 1815. Two years later he married Susanna Marshall and they bought a bookshop in Lincoln. Then moving on, bought bookshops at Hull, then Scarborough, where he stopped for ten years, and finally back to Northampton in 1830.

But by 1835 he was almost bankrupt and had to move to Wellingborough. He kept a school there, and was considered eccentric. His downward spiral continued, and he was forced again to move to Ringtstead, and then to Woodford, where he died in 1848 in total poverty. He was buried in Woodford church. Unfortunately, the memorial which was erected to him, was moved in the 'restoration' of the church a few years later, and is now completely lost.

Kitty (?-1865)
Indian servant

The simple headstone in Woodford churchyard, just has the inscription "Kitty, after years of faithful and loving service in India and England, fell asleep in Christ 27 May 1865". That is all we know of her.

The story in the village is that she was servant to the Rector, who at that time was the Reverend Christopher Smyth (Rector 1856-1884), but there is nothing to suggest that he was ever in India. Kitty thus remains a mystery. Was she Indian? There is no surname, so in all probability she was. What story lies behind this simple headstone? We shall never know.

Kitty, *not now as a servant...*

WOODNEWTON

IN THE CHURCHYARD OF SAINT MARY

Nikolai Polakovs (1901-1974)

'Coco the Clown'

Coco's trademarks were his enormous boots and baggy checked trousers, and bright red hair, which quite inexplicably suddenly stood straight up on end. Coco's appearance in the circus ring was always greeted with delight by the children, for Coco the Clown was the most famous, most adored and most recognised clown of his generation.

He was Russian, born in October 1900 in a theatre in Besinowitz in Russian Siberia, where his father was the 'property master'. The circus in Russia is looked upon very differently than it is in this country. It is revered as an art form, and to be a circus artiste is a highly regarded profession. Young Nikolai was apprenticed to Rudolfo Truzzi, an Italian émigré who owned a circus. It was Rudolfo who gave Nickolai the name of his alter-ego, by taking the repeated syllable of his real name NicKOlai PolaKOvs. Originally it was spelt Koko, but it finally took the more pleasing form of Coco.

During the Great War, Coco served with the 11th Siberian Regiment. But during the confusion of the Russian Revolution and resulting civil war, he sometimes found himself fighting for the Bolsheviks ('The Reds'), and sometimes for the Mensheviks ('The Whites').

He married Valentina in Riga in 1919 and eventually they had two sons and four daughters. In the 1920s, he went to Germany and acted both in films and on the stage, but his real love was the circus, and he became a clown in the Circus Busch in Berlin.

But Bertram Mills had started a circus in London's Olympia in 1920, and impressed with Coco, offered him a contract to star, both at Olympia and in the touring circus he planned to start in 1929.

Nickolai and Valentina arrived in England in December 1929, and stayed for the rest of their lives. Every summer he toured the provinces with Bertram Mills' Circus, and every winter he was at Olympia for the Christmas season.

The second World War saw him touring with the legendary ENSA. After the war, he dedicated himself to road safety, and adopted a large walking stick shaped and painted like a Belisha Beacon. For this work he was awarded the OBE. His autobiography *Behind my Greasepaint* was published in 1950.

Coco retired to Woodnewton where he was surrounded by his family, which by now contained many grandchildren.

Nickolai Polakovs, Coco the Clown, died in Peterborough General Hospital in September 1974, and was given a very large circus funeral in Woodnewton churchyard. His beloved Valentina was laid to rest beside him nine years later.

Coco's grave, on the north side of Woodnewton church.

YARDLEY HASTINGS

IN THE CHURCH OF SAINT ANDREW

Reverend Edward Lye (1694-1767)

Lexicographer who influenced Samuel Johnson

Edward Lye, though perhaps not as well known as Samuel Johnson, was arguably, just as influential in the development of the English language. I wonder what he would think of it today, with its ungrammatical grammar, nouns used as verbs, sloppy pronunciation and wrongly stressed words?

Edward Lye's father was Vicar of Broadhampton in Devonshire, and young Edward was born in Totnes. He was educated at Crewkerne and then at Hart Hall, Oxford. He graduated BA in 1716, and progressed to MA in 1722.

He was ordained a priest by the Bishop of Peterborough in September 1719, and remained in the Diocese of Peterborough all his life. He was first a Curate at Orlingbury in 1719, and then Vicar of Little Houghton in 1720. In 1737 he also became Vicar of Yardley Hastings which he held in plurality with Houghton until 1749, when resigning from Houghton, he became solely Vicar of Yardley Hastings. He remained at Yardley for 30 years, and died in 1767, being buried in an unmarked grave in Yardley Hastings churchyard.

Those are the bare bones of his life. The detail is far more interesting.

At university he became interested in the Anglo Saxon language, and therefore in the history and etymology of the English language. In the Bodleian Library at Oxford, Lye came across a manuscript of a dictionary started by Francis Junius but which had remained unpublished at his death in 1677.

It was Lye who took this dictionary, made many additions, prefaced it with his own Anglo Saxon grammar/dictionary, and published it in 1743. It was this dictionary of Lye's which directly influenced the great Doctor Samuel Johnson, perhaps the best known of the English lexicographers, to start his own dictionary three years later in 1747, and which took eight years to complete. Johnson always acknowledged his debt to Junius and Lye.

Lye continued his work, and in 1750 published *Sacrorum Evangeliorum Versio Gothica* which was a Gothic version of the Gospels. In that year also, he published his *Anglo Saxon Grammar*, and because of his work, was elected a Fellow of the Society of Antiquaries.

For many years, Lye had been working on an Anglo Saxon/Gothic dictionary. Although he finished it, he could not get it published until he received financial help from Thomas Secker, then Archbishop of Canterbury. The dictionary had just started to be printed, when Lye died in August 1767. The work was completed and published posthumously in 1772.

The lexicographer who inspired Doctor Johnson. The memorial to Edward Lye in Yardley Hastings church. Note the dictionary, ink well and quill.

BIBLIOGRAPHY

BELGION, Helen *Titchmarsh Past and Present* Privately published 1979
BRADFORD, Ernle *Siege: Malta 1940-1943* Penguin 1982
COMPTON, Piers *Cardigan of Balaclava* Robert Hale 1972
COWLEY, Richard *Policing Northamptonshire* Brewin Books 1989
COWLEY, Richard *Guilty M'Lud! The criminal history of Northamptonshire* Peg and Whistle Books 1998
Dictionary of National Biography
EDGELL, H. A. R. *Champions of the Cross* Privately Published 1983
FEATHERSTONE, Donald *Colonial Small Wars 1837-1901* David and Charles 1973
FORMAN, Joan *Haunted East Anglia* Jarrold 1974
GARDINER, Juliet, WENBORN, Neil (editors) *The Companion to British History* Collins and Brown 1995
GORDON, Major L. L. *British Battles and Medals* Spink 1971
GORDON, Peter *The Wakes of Northamptonshire* NLIS 1992
GREEN, Jonathon *Chasing the Sun: Dictionary makers and the dictionaries they made* Pimlico 1997
HELLICAR, Eileen *Prime Ministers of Britain* David and Charles 1978
HOLD, Trevor *A Northamptonshire Garland* Northamptonshire Libraries 1989
HUXLEY, Elspeth *Scott of the Antarctic* Weidenfeld and Nicholson 1977
JACOB, E. F. *Archbishop Henry Chichele* Nelson 1967
LUMMIS and WYNN *Honour the Light Brigade* Hayward and Son 1973
MARLOW, Norman (editor) *The Diary of Thomas Isham* Gregg 1971
MEE, Arthur *The King's England: Northamptonshire*
MIDDLEBROOK, Martin *The First Day on the Somme* Penguin 1984
MOORE, R. *The History of Desborough* Gerald Coe, Desborough, 1982
PEVSNER, Nickolaus *The Buildings of England: Northamptonshire* Penguin 1961
Register of the George Cross This England 1985
ROSKILL, Stephen *Earl Beatty: The last naval hero* Collins 1980
SOBELL, Dava *Longitude* Fourth Estate 1996
STENTON, D. M. (editor) *The Northamptonshire Assize Rolls 1202, 1203* Northamptonshire Record Society, Volume 5 1930
STEVENSON, P. M. *William Carey* Oliphants 1953
STRAWSON, John *The Duke and the Emperor: Wellington and Napoleon* Constable 1994
WEBSTER, Graham *Boudicca* Batsford 1993
WICKSTEED, Hilda *Charles Wicksteed* Privately published 1933